Dedication

To Liberty's, where I first learned to look.

Phaidon Press Limited
Regent's Wharf
All Saints Street
London N1 9PA

First published 1996
© 1996 Phaidon Press Limited
ISBN 0 7148 3000 3

A CIP catalogue record for this book is available from the British Library.

Printed in Hong Kong

Captions

Endpapers:
Designed by Walter Crane and manufactured by Jeffrey & Co
The Sleeping Beauty, 1875
Machine-printed nursery wallpaper

Half-title page:
William Morris (1834–96)
From *A Note by William Morris on his aims in founding the Kelmscott Press*, 1898
This was the last publication of the Kelmscott Press, one of the major artistic achievements of the Aesthetic Movement.

Title page:
Thomas Dewing
Detail of *The Days*
[See page 147]

Contents page:
Helena De Kay Gilder
Cover for *The New Day*
[See page 59]

THE AESTHETIC MOVEMENT   LIONEL LAMBOURNE

Φ

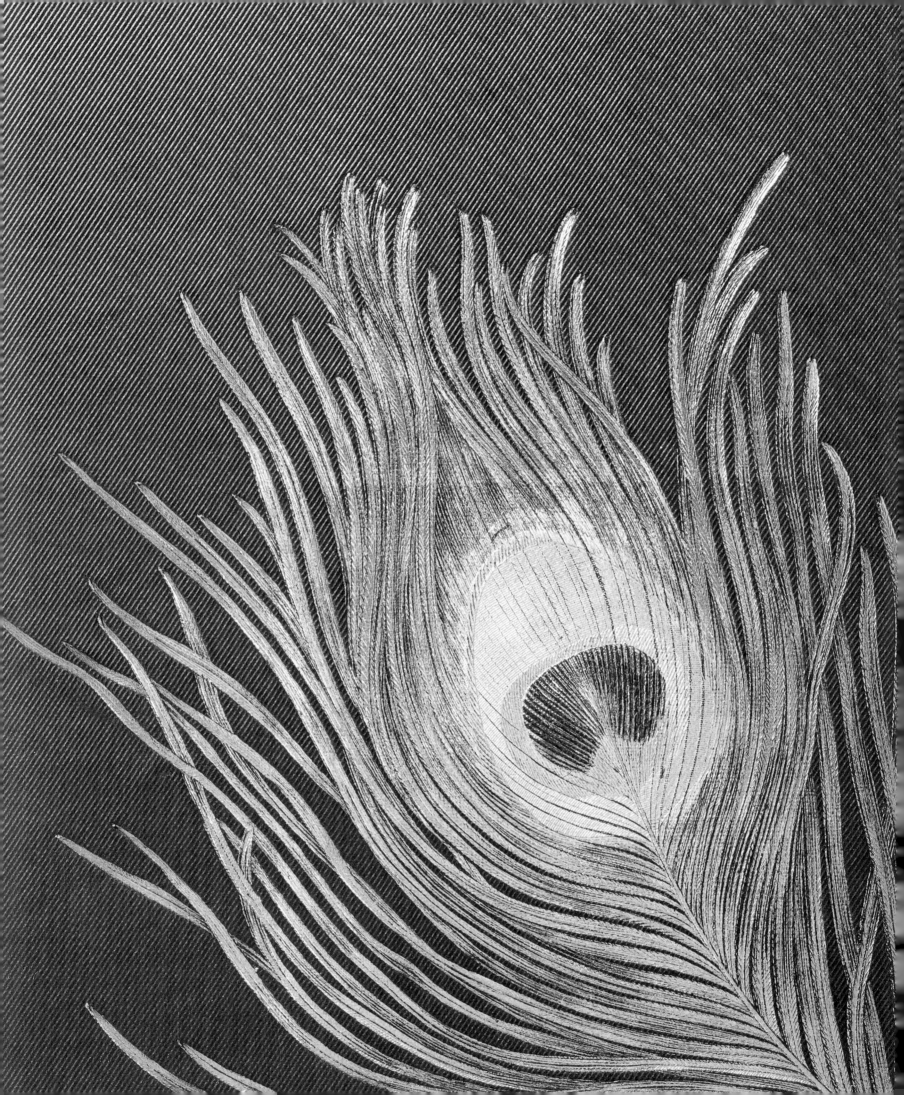

I don't regret for a single moment having lived
for pleasure. I did it to the full, as one should do
everything that one does to the full. There was
no pleasure I did not experience. I threw the
pearl of my soul into a cup of wine. I went down
the primrose path to the sound of flutes. I lived
on honeycomb.

So wrote Convict C/3/3 in a lonely cell at Reading Gaol a century ago when reviewing his life in a long letter to a friend. Severely restricted in the literature available to him in prison, Wilde re-read the New Testament with heightened awareness, and in *De Profundis* wrote of the centrality of Christ for the western artistic tradition, blending Christianity with Aestheticism:

… wherever there is a romantic movement in Art, there somehow, and under some form, is Christ … He is in *Romeo and Juliet*, in *The Winter's Tale*, in Provençal poetry, in *The Ancient Mariner*.

We owe to him the most diverse things and people. Hugo's *Les Misérables*, Baudelaire's *Fleurs du Mal*, the note of pity in Russian novels, the stained glass and tapestries and quattrocento work of Burne-Jones and Morris … Verlaine's poems, belong to him no less than the Tower of Giotto, Lancelot and Guinevere, Tannhäuser, the troubled romantic marbles of Michelangelo, pointed architecture, and the love of children and flowers …

Both the extraordinary range of Wilde's list and the dramatic vicissitudes of his life provide useful boundaries for a study of the Aesthetic Movement and its primarily literary heir, the Decadence. Like Wilde's own life, the Aesthetic Movement contained work of great beauty, high comedy, exquisite sensitivity, and gross sentimentality. It was a movement deeply concerned with the visual arts, valuing the frame as much as the picture, placing much emphasis on listing the individual components which make an attractive room setting – a 'Home Beautiful'. Its origins had their roots in the 1870s, the years when Wilde first came to public attention as an undergraduate with his famous encounter with the Oxford University hearties who had tried unsuccessfully to tip his collection of blue and white Chinese porcelain into the river. His flamboyant dress, devotion to 'culchah', and witty joke about the difficulty of 'living up to his blue china' were widely publicized. He always had a genius for self-publicity and a few years later was memorably satirized as Bunthorne, a character in *Patience*, the comic operetta by Gilbert and Sullivan first produced in 1881.

The opening lines of Bunthorne's first song possess a strange appositeness to Wilde's situation in his cell. Life, as so often happens, had imitated Art.

Am I alone and unobserved? – I am

Then let me own, I'm an aesthetic sham

This air severe is but a mere veneer

This cynic smile is but a wile of guile

This costume chaste is but good taste misplaced

Let me confess! A languid love for lilies does *not* blight me!

I do *not* care for dirty greens by any means! I do *not* long for all one sees

That's Japanese.

I am not fond of uttering platitudes in stained-glass attitudes.

In short, my medievalism's affectation,

Born of a morbid love of admiration!

Wilde's 'morbid love of admiration' ensured that his life was the most notorious demonstration of the ambiguous injunction to youth of the Oxford don, Walter Pater:

Not the fruit of experience, but experience itself, is the end … What we have to do is to be forever curiously testing new opinions and courting impressions, and never acquiescing in a facile orthodoxy … To burn always with this hard, gemlike flame, to maintain this ecstasy, is success in life – words once acclaimed by Wilde as 'the holy writ of beauty'.

Both Wilde, and the poets of the 1890s, described by W.B. Yeats as 'the tragic generation', flourished in the 'Decadence', which in the 1890s dominated the arts, finding its most potent visual expression in the drawings of Aubrey Beardsley. The decade possesses a perennial fascination which has led to many attempts to describe its special aura, from the simplistic adjectival descriptions of 'naughty' or 'yellow' to academic studies on its sexual anarchy. The Decadence relates to the Aesthetic Movement of the 1870s and 1880s in much the same way as in the eighteenth century the Rococo emerges from the Baroque.

Henri de Toulouse Lautrec (1864–1901)
Portrait of Oscar Wilde, **1895**
Watercolour, 60 x 49 cm
It is not recorded whether Wilde and Lautrec ever met, although Lautrec was present at Wilde's trial and seems to have drawn this portrait from memory. He has introduced into the background the shadowy tower of Big Ben looming through the fog.

To appreciate the cultivation of these exotic flowers we must first turn back to the earlier origins of Aestheticism and the study of the nature of the beautiful …

To define beauty, not in the most abstract, but in the most concrete terms possible. To find, not a universal formula for it, but the formula which expresses most adequately this or that special manifestation of it, is the aim of the true student of Aesthetics, who will ask ...

Opposite: Aubrey Beardsley (1872–98)
D'Albert in Search of his Ideals
From *Mademoiselle de Maupin*, 1898
Almost sixty years after its publication in 1835, virtually as an act of homage, Beardsley illustrated Gautier's strange philosophical romance, *Mademoiselle de Maupin*. It was to become virtually required reading for the Aesthetes of the 1890s.

...What is this song or picture, this engaging personality presented in life or in a book, to *me?* What effect does it really produce on me? Does it give me pleasure? And if so, what sort or degree of pleasure?

Right: Edward Burne-Jones (1833–98)
Pygmalion and the Image: The Heart Desires, 1868–70
Oil on canvas, 97.5 x 74.9 cm
This is one of a series of four paintings which epitomizes the conflict between the real and the ideal, between the classical tradition and the Pre-Raphaelite sensuality. The story, taken from Ovid, tells how a sculptor's beloved image comes to life.

The Aesthetic critic ... will remember always that beauty exists in many forms. To him all periods, types, schools of taste, are in themselves equal ... The question he asks is always: in whom did the stir, the genius, the sentiment of the period find itself?

WALTER PATER, *STUDIES IN THE HISTORY OF THE RENAISSANCE*, 1873

Aesthetics is the name given since classical times to the study of the nature of the beautiful, and the theories which have evolved defining what is meant by the word beauty. Aristotle's *Poetics* asserts that beauty is the mean between two extremes, while Plato's teachings are in keeping with his general belief in an absolute and perfect ideal behind all appearance. Thus beauty in finite things arises from their correspondence to their ideal archetype. The doctrine of Plato is expressed by the poet John Keats in his *Ode on a Grecian Urn* in the lines:

Beauty is truth, truth beauty.
That is all Ye know on earth, and all ye need
to know.

As a modern discipline Aesthetics began in the mid-eighteenth century with the publication by Baumgarten of his book *Aesthica*. A host of major German writers followed, notably Kant, Lessing, Schiller and Winckelmann. Winckelmann's writings on classical art were an important inspiration for the neo-classical movement and much admired by Walter Pater, the Oxford don who became the leading exponent of the discipline in late Victorian England. Aestheticism also had important literary beginnings. It was the flamboyant French poet, novelist and critic, Theophile Gautier (1811–72) who wore cherry red and green satin clothes, who first formulated the concept of '*L'Art pour L'Art*', 'Art for Art's sake'. He denied that art could, or should, be in any way useful, a theory he elaborated in the preface to his novel *Mademoiselle de Maupin*. This apologia for lesbian love reveals both Gautier's love of physical beauty (he haunted the Greek rooms of the Louvre, and took up weight lifting) and his interest in sexual alternatives. He wrote:

Nothing is really beautiful unless it is useless; everything useful is ugly, for it expresses a need and the needs of man are ignoble and disgusting, like his poor weak nature. The most useful place in a house is the lavatory.[1]

Gautier delighted in such unconventional remarks, believing that one of the artist's functions was to irritate or shock 'the philistines', a belief which became widely adopted by a generation of young followers. His views held a special significance both for the poet and art critic Charles Baudelaire (1821–67) and the brilliant young painter, the American James Abbott McNeill Whistler (1834–1903). In the 1850s Whistler read with interest Gautier's advocacy of '*transposition d'art*', by which, for example, poetry attempted to suggest the effects produced by the other arts. Sonnets were called pastels, and pastels sonnets.

Baudelaire, like Gautier earlier and Wilde later, possessed a charisma which made him a potent influence on a whole generation. Like them, his way of life flouted conventional morality. His controversial book of poems *Les Fleurs du Mal*, published in 1857, was prosecuted for impropriety, and became a legend, as did his advocacy of the pleasures of drugs and absinthe. His verse, simple in form but rich in vocabulary, sprang from a keen delight in the passionate and sensual aspects of life. But the musky potency of *Les Fleurs du Mal* with its musical language and evocative images was only one aspect of Baudelaire's genius. His *Curiosités Esthétiques* and *L'Art Romantique* (1868) are the works of one of the most important critical minds of the time. He was immensely influential on the emergent Symbolist Movement and one of the first to appreciate Edouard Manet.

Baudelaire was also an important formative influence on English Aestheticism, although in the passage between Paris and London his ideas frequently suffered a sea

Charles Baudelaire (1821–67)
Self Portrait, c. 1860
Pen and red chalk,
20 x 12.5 cm
This is one of a series of self-portrait drawings, which may have been intended, but were not actually used, for the second editions of *Les Fleurs du Mal*. According to Baudelaire's publisher, this was the best of the group.

Eliot's remark, 'had Swinburne known anything about vice or sin, he would not have had so much fun out of it', applies more justly to other feebler English poets, for like Baudelaire, Swinburne's critical writing possessed great originality. Swinburne believed passionately in the concept of the primacy of the artist and not the critic or patron as the controlling arbiter of taste and style. He first crystallized these feelings in his essay on William Blake published in 1866. 'Art', he said, in a remark which became something of a battle cry for the Aesthetes, 'can never be the handmaid of religion, exponent of duty, servant of fact, pioneer of morality', a theme which he echoed repeatedly. His *Poems and Ballads* of 1866 were savaged on moral grounds by middle-class critics to whom Swinburne retaliated by shaking his fist at 'public virtue ... a rank and rapid growth, barren of blossom and rotten at the root'.

Both Baudelaire and Swinburne believed that artistic aims could best be achieved by synaesthesia – the blending of differing senses and emotions using interrelationships described

William Bell Scott (1811–90)
Algernon Charles Swinburne,
1860
Oil on canvas, 47 x 31.7 cm
'The most extravagantly artistic person alive in the world today' was Guy de Maupassant's opinion of Swinburne. This portrait showing Swinburne standing before the wild seas off the Northumberland coast with which he so strongly identified, captures vividly the young poet's mercurial temperament.

change. His great admirer, the young English poet Algernon Charles Swinburne (1837-1909), put it as follows in a mood of severe self-criticism:

Some singers indulging in curses,
Though sinful, have splendidly sinned,
But my would-be maleficent verses
Are nothing but wind.

Swinburne's lyrics, although influenced by Baudelaire, carried their own rhetoric and a more strident masochistic sensuality. T.S.

Simeon Solomon (1840–1905)
Walter Pater, **1872**
Pencil, 30 x 21 cm
The subtle cadences of Pater's prose style have been antipathetic to the taste of the late twentieth century. His close friend Simeon Solomon has caught something of Pater's reticent, introspective personality in this portrait of a man who, once described as a 'Caliban of Letters', was rarely painted.

by Baudelaire as *'correspondances'*. Echoes of such beliefs were to surface later, both in Whistler's use of musical analogies to describe his work and Proust's evocative mingling of remembered pleasures with continuing artistic experiences. Of equal resonance were the critical teachings of Walter Pater who wrote of the tendency of one art to 'pass into the condition of some other art', and how 'music seems to be always approaching ... pictorial definition'. He claimed that poetic analogies 'between a Greek tragedy and a work of Greek sculpture, between a sonnet and a relief, of French poetry generally with the art of engraving' are 'more than mere figures of speech'. These considerations led to his famous conclusion that 'all art constantly aspires to the condition of music'. A Fellow of Brasenose College, Oxford, Pater led an uneventful life, although he had once been heard to say: 'I would give ten years of my life to be handsome'. He did, however, live a rich intellectual life,

reflected notably in the conclusion to his *Studies in the History of the Renaissance* (1873). This work contains essays on Botticelli, then a neglected artist, and his celebrated evocation of Leonardo's *Mona Lisa* ('She is older than the rocks among which she sits ...'). Pater writes in the conclusion of the book of 'the desire of beauty, the love of art for art's sake'. He also offered the famous advice to youth, so often repeated in different ways by his followers such as Oscar Wilde, to live for the enjoyment of life and new experiences and to strive always 'to burn with a hard, gemlike flame'. These theories were to be elaborated by Pater in such seminal works as *Marius the Epicurean* and his essay *Grace and the Greeks*.

In England, by the 1870s, these powerful intellectual concepts became associated with the esoteric cult of beauty. As the critic Grant Allen pointed out in 1877, British painters and poets were concerned 'with themes derived mainly from the storied or imagined past'. This devotion to mediaevalism ultimately derived from the Pre-Raphaelites and with it went a new emphasis on the decorative arts, and the value of ornament. Besides such lofty concerns, there also arose a cult for what might be described as the higher silliness – the worship of the lily, the sunflower and the peacock's feather. To understand why such themes so intrigued the figures who first grappled with Aesthetic concerns in the 1870s, it is necessary to turn back to the very different beliefs of the pre-Victorian era.

In 1832, after the passage of the Reform Bill, a horrified Duke of Wellington looked down at a House of Commons packed with newly emancipated middle-class industrialists and remarked that he had never seen so many bad hats in his life. By 'bad hats' he implied that the new MPs were nouveau riche arrivistes, who lacked the qualifications of gentlemen,

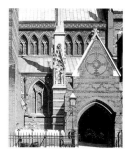

William Butterfield (1811–1900) Exterior and interior details of All Saints Church, Margaret Street, London, 1850–9 The widespread High Anglican interest in the Gothic style in the mid-Victorian era was sustained by concern for ritual. Churchgoers liked to see ceremonial rites conducted against a background of deep glowing colours. More than any other mid-Victorian architect, Butterfield used the Gothic style with determined originality, achieving startling effects with polychrome and applied decoration in brightly coloured materials. All Saints Church was highly influential and remains a bastion of the High Anglican tradition. It is interesting to reflect that it was as a choirboy here that Laurence Olivier first experienced the love of dramatic ritual that led to his distinguished career in the theatre.

notably by not owing their status to inherited land, but deriving their wealth from the new industrial heart of England in the Midlands and the North.

In the same spirit in our own day, the Tory political diarist Alan Clark expressed his disdain for his colleague Michael Heseltine (a wealthy man by anybody's standards), by quoting the remark of Chief Whip Michael Jopling: 'The trouble with Michael is that he had to buy his own furniture', implying 'new money' rather than inheritance. Both of these comments, although separated by a century and a half, reflect continuing patrician upper-class attitudes. They throw into sharp focus the different concerns of the essentially middle-class Aesthetic Movement which was peopled by figures who very definitely bought their own furniture, albeit made to the latest and most fashionable designs.

In the growing conurbations of Victorian England, linked by the rapid growth of the railways, the development of industries based on iron, steel and steam led to larger and more complicated machines producing more goods so that the old cottage industries were starved out. The more enterprising hand workers set up as manufacturers, the less enterprising became machine minders. The word 'master' ceased to mean a man who was master of his craft and came to mean a man who was the master of others.

Many expressions of distress over the effects of the onward march of industrial materialism were voiced. The dynamic architect A.W.N. Pugin (1812–52), who built some hundreds of churches and eight cathedrals for the newly emancipated Roman Catholic Church, believed fervently that Gothic architecture alone offered moral, spiritual and visual excellence.

His highly influential book *Contrasts*

(1836) related Gothic style to Christian principles. The activities of Pugin and his architectural followers, notably William Butterfield, G.E. Street and William Burges, mirrored the progress of the Oxford Movement and the religious controversies associated with the names of Keble, Pusey and Newman.

Many years later, the political leader W.E. Gladstone recalled the disgraceful state of the Church of England before the dawn of the Oxford Movement. He enlarged on the baldness of the services, the horrors of the so-called music, 'the coldness and indifference of the lounging or sleeping congregations although the much-vaunted religious sentiment of the English public ... in impenetrable somnolence endured it, and resented all interference with it.'[2]

The Oxford or Tractarian Movement radically changed this situation but not without causing great controversy. The initial aim of the Movement was to defend the Church of England as a divine institution with an independent

Simeon Solomon
Two Acolytes Censing, Pentecost, **1863**
Watercolour, 40.2 x 35 cm
Solomon's deep interest in ritualistic subjects led him to depict such differing themes as a rabbi carrying the Scrolls of the Law, a Roman Catholic priest elevating the host and a Greek Orthodox acolyte holding a censer and a sprig of myrtle blossom.

spiritual status. In the process, many church traditions of the seventeenth century were revived, including its liturgy and rituals. With this revival of sacramentalism there arose the desire for far more ornate High Church ceremonial, which often met with violent opposition. Yet many worshippers with Aesthetic tastes were deeply drawn to the cult of the Virgin, Saint Days, the narcissus and arum lilies banked before the altar, the candles, altar lights, the clouds of incense dispensed from censers and, above all, the elaborate ceremonies. When, for example, the Oxford don Walter Pater, or his intimate friend the young Jewish artist Simeon Solomon (1840-1905) attended Mass at a High Anglican Church such as St Alban's, Holborn, London, their appreciation of the splendid vestments worn by the celebrant, was heightened by their knowledge that the garments were derived from the costume of formal classical Roman dress.

The most impressive monument of the High Anglican Movement is William Butterfield's elaborate red brick church, All Saints, Margaret Street, London, in which stained glass, murals and ornate jewel-studded plate combine to produce one of the most remarkable of all High Victorian church interiors.

These religious developments were paralleled by the critic John Ruskin's potent critical advocacy for Gothic ornament as a national style, voiced in *The Seven Lamps of Architecture* (1849) and *The Stones of Venice* (1851–3).

In *The Two Paths: being lectures on art and its application to decoration and manufacture* published in 1859, the only book Ruskin devoted solely to decorative art, he charged his readers 'to get rid, then, at once of any idea of Decorative art being a degraded or a separate kind of art', and called for a re-evaluation and nurturing of arts produced in and for the

home. He reasoned that as the furnishing of the home was very largely a female prerogative their choice of decoration and ornament was endowed with moral purpose. Shopping itself was transformed, for when women returned with new examples of 'art', fine or decorative, they became aesthetic missionaries, sharing Ruskin's mission 'to teach that whatever was great in human art was the expression of man's delight in God's work'. In Ruskin's terms 'God's work' equated exactly with the patterns on textiles, carpets and wallpapers – then almost invariably images of flowers and foliage.

In establishing the central significance of ornament and pattern throughout the Aesthetic period, it is difficult to overestimate the importance of *The Grammar of Ornament* published in 1856 by Owen Jones (1809-74). In it Jones made permanent the immense range of his knowledge of ornament that hitherto had gained him such varied commissions as the decoration of the Khedive's Palace in Egypt,

Left: Owen Jones (1809–74) Plate 4 'Egyptian No. 1' From *The Grammar of Ornament*, 1856
Owen Jones claimed that the Egyptian style, though the oldest, was the most perfect. He said: 'the language in which it reveals itself to us may seem foreign, peculiar, formal and rigid, but the ideas and the teachings that it conveys to us are of the soundest'.

Opposite left: Owen Jones Plate 42 'Moresque No. 4' From *The Grammar of Ornament*, 1856

Opposite right: John Ruskin (1819–1900)
Part of the facade of San Michele at Lucca, 1845
Watercolour and body colour, 33 x 23.3 cm
Ruskin wrote to his father on 6 May, 1845: 'I sit in the open warm afternoon air drawing the rich ornaments on the facade of San Michele. It is white marble inlaid with figures cut an inch deep in green porphry and framed with carved, rich, hollow marble tracery.' Ruskin later wrote about this building in *The Seven Lamps of Architecture* and *The Stones of Venice*.

a major role in the arrangement of the Crystal Palace and the compilation of a standard work on the Alhambra.

One of the first books to be lavishly illustrated with 100 coloured plates by the chromolithograph process, it showed some 1,000 examples of ornamental art. It virtually introduced western artists to Islamic decorative themes, thus providing an alternative to naturalistic decoration by demonstrating the beauty of flat, abstract and geometric surface ornament. Jones's remarkable eye for decoration included the ability to analyze the primitive art of the Pacific with a welcome absence of the prejudiced condescension so common in the Victorian age.

For Jones, whose theories were not new but very influential:

the ornament of a savage tribe, being the result of a natural instinct, is necessarily always true to its purpose; whilst in much of the ornament of civilized nations, the first impulse which generated received forms being enfeebled by constant repetition, the ornament is oftentimes misapplied ... by superadding ornament to ill contrived form. If we would return to a more healthy condition, we must even be as little children or as savages; we must get rid of the acquired and artificial, and return to and develop natural instincts ... the secret of success in all ornament is the production of a broad general effect by the repetition of a few simple elements ... the essence of beauty is a feeling of repose ...

In 1887 Lewis F. Day, a designer and theoretician, gave a succinct and still valid assessment of Jones's importance in his *Art Journal*:

Indeed it was as a theorist rather than an

15

artist that he made his mark ... His influence was immense. His *Grammar of Ornament* marks a point, and a turning point, in the history of English ornament. The 'principles' he enunciated were not such as one can endorse 'en masse' ... they were

every cheap villa builder between this and Bromley, and there is scarcely a public-house near the Crystal Palace but sells its gin and bitters under pseudo-Venetian capitals copied from the church of the Madonna of Health or Miracles ... my present

Far left: Christopher Dresser (1834–1904) 'Leaves from Nature No. 10' From *The Grammar of Ornament*, 1856

Left: Christopher Dresser 'Leaves and Flowers from Nature No. 8' From *The Grammar of Ornament*, 1856 A pupil and apprentice of Owen Jones, as well as a trained botanist, Dresser contributed a few plates of 'nature's ornaments' to Jones's great compendium of designs.

many of them not principles at all ... it would be nearer the mark (however irreverent) to call them 'tips'; and as such they were of immense value to manufacturers, decorators and designers, who were floundering ... the influence of Ruskin, and of Pugin before him, counts also for something, but I attribute even more weight to the teachings of Owen Jones, because he appealed and touched the manufacturers ... much to the improvement in the taste of their productions.[3]

By the 1860s the Gothic Revival had triumphed overwhelmingly, to the embarrassment of even its greatest advocates. Years later even Ruskin, writing from his home in Denmark Hill, was to regret the sham Gothic buildings which his advocacy had inspired:

I have had indirect influence on nearly

house is surrounded everywhere by the accursed Frankenstein monsters, of, indirectly, my own making.

We sympathize with Ruskin just as we do with Mr Crumpet of Crump Lodge, Brixton, in Charles Dickens's *Household Words*. Mr Crumpet is used to symbolize an undiscriminating admirer of all lavish naturalistic ornament who visits the Chamber of Horrors of Bad Design set up by the purist Henry Cole in Marlborough House, the ancestor of the Victoria & Albert Museum. Mr Crumpet shudderingly recalls his deep embarrassment:

I could have cried Sir. I was ashamed of the pattern of my own trousers, for I saw a piece of them hung up there as a horror. I dared not pull out my pocket handkerchief while anyone was by ... when I went home I found that I had been living among horrors up to that hour. The paper in my parlour contains four birds of paradise, besides bridges and pagodas.

The young William Morris sulked outside the Great Exhibition of 1851. He was

arts. Morris's whole life was to become a crusade to improve design standards in an age of machine mass production. The foundation of Morris & Co in 1861 and the display of their art furniture in the Great

Simeon Solomon
Middleton Cheney Church, Banbury, mid-1860s
Stained-glass windows
One of the first churches to be filled with Morris & Co stained glass, Middleton Cheney remains a most rewarding site for all those interested in Morris. Virtually all the artists associated with the Firm are represented here, including Morris, Rossetti, Philip Webb, Madox Brown, Burne-Jones and Simeon Solomon. The Old Testament themes of Adam and Moses and David and Saul project a highly individual Hebraicism.

overwhelmed by the methods of mass production and the power of the machine to sew, knit, embroider, carve, paint and put to shame all human skills while letting eclectic ornament run riot in the decorative and applied

Exhibition of 1862, mark the beginning of Morris's long career in which he revived the crafts of stained glass and tapestry weaving, and created books, rugs, wallpapers and textiles. He said of his flat patterns: 'I must

Edward Burne-Jones and Morris & Co
Love and the Pilgrim,
c. 1872–1903
High-warp wool tapestry
This composition, originating in *The Romaunt of the Rose* by Chaucer, was used in turn for needlework, as an oil painting and finally (after the death of its designers) as a tapestry in 1903. Thus it symbolizes Morris's and Burne-Jones's lifelong design partnership and love of Chaucer.

have unmistakable suggestions of gardens and fields, and strange trees, boughs and tendrils ...'
In his preface to *The Earthly Paradise* of 1868 he enjoined the reader to turn from the harsh industrial present to a mediaeval Utopian London:

Forget six counties overhung with smoke,
Forget the snorting steam and piston stroke,
Forget the spreading of the hideous town;
Think rather of the pack horse on the down,
And dream of London, small and white and clean,
The clear Thames bordered by its gardens green ...

The foundation of Morris & Co was a key event at the dawn of the Aesthetic Movement. The aims of the firm were set forth in a prospectus, or rather a manifesto, which is worth quoting extensively:

The growth of Decorative Art in this country, owing to the efforts of English Architects, has now reached a point at which it seems desirable that artists of reputation should devote their time to it ... Up to this time, the want of that artistic supervision, which can alone bring about harmony between the various parts of a successful work, has been increased by the necessarily excessive outlay,

consequent on taking one individual artist from his pictorial labours ... the artists whose names appear ... here ... will undertake any species of decoration, mural or otherwise, from pictures, properly so called down to the consideration of the smallest work susceptible of art beauty ...

The 'Firm's' activities were soon to effect a revolution in interior decoration. Morris & Co secured its first major decorative scheme at St James's Palace where between 1866 and 1882 redecorations were undertaken in several of the state rooms. Lady Mount-Temple, whose husband was a member of the royal household and played an important part in this commission, once entertained the Pre-Raphaelite painter Dante Gabriel Rossetti to dinner with remarkable results. As she wrote in her *Memorials* (1890):

You remember our dear little house in Curzon Street; when we furnished it, nothing would please me but watered paper on the walls, garlands of roses tied with blue bows!, glazed chintzes with bunches of roses, so natural they looked, I thought, as if they had been just gathered

Philip Webb (1831–1915) and William Morris (1834–96)
St George's Cabinet, **1861**
Mahogany and pinewood on a painted and gilded oak stand
Designed by Philip Webb, the front of this cabinet has been painted by Morris with scenes from the life of St George. The newly established Morris & Co exhibited several pieces of painted furniture at the Great Exhibition of 1862. This medievally inspired cabinet was attacked for its poor craftsmanship and second-rate painting.

Above: Lewis Carroll (1832–98)
Photograph of Dante Gabriel Rossetti, 1863

Below: Morris & Co Armchair, 1885–90
Morris & Co sold this chair from about 1869, describing it as the 'Morris adjustable back chair'. The design was a copy of a vernacular version of a late Georgian armchair found near Hurstmonceaux in Sussex. It was widely copied on the continent and in the USA.

(between you and me, I still think it was very pretty), and most lovely ornaments we had in perfect harmony, gilt pelicans or swans as candlesticks, Minton's imitation of Sèvres, and gilt bows everywhere.

One day Mr Rossetti was dining alone with us, and instead of admiring my room and decorations, as I expected, he evidently could hardly sit in ease with them. I began to ask him if it were possible to suggest improvements!

'Well,' he said, frankly, 'I should begin by burning everything you have got!'

I think I may be pleased with our humility, that after this insult, when our staircase needed renovation, we asked his firm to do it up for us!

A Morris paper was hung on the walls, and a lovely little bit of glass by Burne-Jones filled the staircase window. Now our taste was attacked on the other side, and all our candid relations and friends intimated that they thought we had made our little house hideous! Somehow, we got to like it more and more, and

now I think nearly all people confess that they owe a deep debt to the Morris & Co firm, for having saved them from trampling roses under foot, and sitting on shepherdesses, or birds and butterflies, from vulgar ornaments and other atrocities in taste, and for having made their homes homely and beautiful.[4]

How clearly this passage reveals the new status of design which can be seen to claim equality with (if not superiority to) the painter. We also find in a quotation from Morris's lecture, *The Lesser Arts of Life*, something of his attitude to wallpapers:

I think the real way to deal successfully with designing for wallpapers is to accept their mechanical nature frankly to avoid falling into the trap of trying to make your paper look as if it were painted by hand.

Morris's credo 'Have nothing in your homes which you do not think to be beautiful or know to be useful' (intriguingly the exact reverse of Gautier's earlier precept), was only one of the planks in the Aesthetic platform.

Another was a growing sense of malaise at the Philistinism of mid-Victorian life, and a determination to ameliorate it. For Morris this led to his devotion to the socialist cause but there were other possibilities and as the century progressed some less advantaged workers became inspired by such books as Samuel Smiles's *Self Help* (1859). Immensely influential on both sides of the Atlantic, it preached the ethic of hard work by charting the lives of successful figures who reached the top by their own studies and endeavours. In translation it was to become influential in the emergent Japan of the Meiji era, helping to formulate the Japanese work ethic.

In England, from this new monied class sprang the Nonconformist or Evangelical speculative collectors whose patronage proved so important to the Pre-Raphaelites. One such figure was T.E. Plint of Leeds who commissioned Ford Madox Brown's *Work*. He insisted on modifications to the artist's original conception and the introduction of the figure of a fashionable lady distributing Biblical tracts, the figure of Thomas Carlyle the philosopher, and so on. Such a collaboration would have been anathema to the foremost painter of the Aesthetic cause, James Whistler, whose relations with his major patron the shipping and telephone magnate Frederick Leyland, dubbed the 'Liverpool Medici', were to end in disaster.

Many such collections passed into the public domain through gifts and bequests, to enhance the newly-founded local art galleries of the Midlands and the North of England. In the short term the flow of new money into contemporary art made these merchants' homes into 'Palaces of Art'.

This term comes from the Poet Laureate, Alfred Lord Tennyson's poem *The Palace of Art* which conveyed this ideological conflict by its allegory of a soul who resides for years in splendid isolation, 'a quiet King', before realizing the error of living exclusively for art and rejoining the natural world. But Tennyson was far from wholeheartedly approving of Aesthetic doctrines, because he shared the alarmed reaction so common in Britain to French innovations:
Art for Art's Sake! Hail, truest Lord of Hell!
Hail Genius, Master of the Moral Will!
The filthiest of paintings painted well
Is mightier than the purest painted ill!
Yes, mightier than the purest painted well
So prone are we toward the broad way to Hell.

Throughout the 1860s and 1870s the clash between Philistinism and artistic idealism grew more and more intense, and the reaction against the belief that art must serve other purposes whether moral or social became more profound. Matthew Arnold also wrote on this dilemma and attempted in 1863 a

definition of the role of the Philistine in society: 'Philistinism! We have not the expression in English. Perhaps we have not the word because we have so much of the thing', a thesis he elaborated in his *Culture and Anarchy* of 1869. In it he categorized the middle classes as Philistines, urging them to reform by cultivating the Hellenic virtues of 'Sweetness and Light' – 'Sweetness' being the enjoyment or creation of beauty, and 'Light' being the desire to see, to learn the truth.

Like 'Art for Art's Sake' and 'Beauty is in the Eye of the Beholder', 'Sweetness and Light' became one of the useful clichés with which to categorize Aesthetic attitudes. Another clichéd term was 'intensity', one of the requisite emotions of the true Aesthete. Such emotions were mocked by Du Maurier in an eight-year-long series of cartoons for the cheerfully Philistine *Punch* from 1874 to 1882.

As a young man Du Maurier had known Whistler as an art student in Paris and also was on friendly terms with other leading figures of the emergent Aesthetic Movement. A letter of his of 1864[5] vividly highlights why their work caused such concern in more orthodox circles:

The other night I went to a bachelor's party to meet Rossetti and Swinburne at Simeon Solomon's. Such a strange evening; Rossetti is at the head of the pre-raphaelites [*sic*], for Millais and Hunt have seceded; spoilt so to speak by their immense popularity; whereas Rossetti never exhibits and is comparatively unknown; this strange contempt for fame is rather grand. He is also a great poet, and his translations from the early Italian poets are the finest things in their way that have been done. As for Swinburne, he is without exception the most extraordinary man not that I have ever met only, but that I ever met or heard of; for three hours he spouted his poetry to us, and it was of a power, beauty and originality unequalled. Everything after

Dante Gabriel Rossetti
The Day Dream, **1880**
Oil on canvas, 157.5 x 92 cm
Originally entitled *Monna*
Primavera, **but soon renamed**
The Day Dream, **the painting**
shows Jane Morris sitting in
the fork of the sycamore tree
in Rossetti's garden at Cheyne
Walk, an open book on her
knee and a sprig of
honeysuckle in her hand. Of
all the many portraits Rossetti
made of Jane this was his
favourite. On its frame he
wrote a sonnet which
expresses his desire to escape
from life's hard realities. He
painted the work through the
winter of 1879–80, months
during which Jane Morris
once again became a regular
visitor at Cheyne Walk.
Rossetti sold the painting for
£735 to Constantine
Alexander Ionides, a Greek
businessman of rare artistic
discrimination whose
collection is one of the great
treasures of the Victoria &
Albert Museum.

seems tame, but the little beast will never I think be acknowledged for he has an utterly perverted moral sense, and ranks Lucrezia Borgia with Jesus Christ; indeed says she's far greater, and very little of his poetry is fit for publication.

By the 1870s the work of these poets and painters was far better known, or rather notorious, for as Du Maurier predicted in his letter they had become highly controversial on moral grounds. Simeon Solomon came in for particular censure. The most famous incident in what might be described as the unending battle between 'Mrs Grundy and the Aesthete' occurred in October 1871, with an anonymous attack entitled *The Fleshly School of Poetry* in the *Contemporary Review* on Rossetti's and Simeon Solomon's paintings and Rossetti's (unclaimed) pre-eminence as a poet, specifically citing Rossetti's *Jenny* and *Troy Town* as 'unhealthy', capable of 'stifling the senses with overpowering sickliness' and more excitingly as having 'spasmodic ramifications in the erotic direction'.

Rossetti, in a reply entitled *The Stealthy School of Criticism*, exposed the author as the jealous poet Robert Buchanan, who unabashed, responded yet again by accusing Swinburne with extensive plagiarism from Baudelaire's *Les Fleurs du Mal* (1857). Buchanan was to some extent justified in these remarks, for certainly Baudelaire was revered by the Aesthetes for his pose of morbid sensitivity, and later by the Decadents for his opium- and hashish-induced explorations of strange and exquisite sensations. Indeed these aspects of Baudelaire's work struck a sympathetic chord which Rossetti reflected in the lush romanticism of such works as *The Day Dream.*

Du Maurier's Aesthetic jokes in *Punch* ended not with a drawing, but a comic sketch entitled *The Downfall of the Dado,* published on 21 November, 1881. A dado is an arrangement of wainscotting or decoration

around the lower part of the walls of a room, and much Aesthetic critical ink flowed on the difficult question of what one's dado should be. Perhaps because of its relationship to Dodo, and its connotation of stupidity, the word dado was found very amusing and it came to symbolize the sillier aspects of Aestheticism. In the sketch, Du Maurier imagines the style-crazed Aesthetes' return to normality. After declaring: 'We're much too sage to wear sage green', they break their blue

21

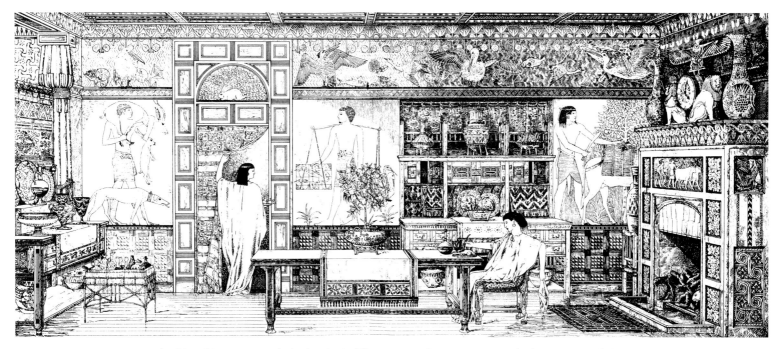

H. W. Batley (fl. 1860–80)
Study for a Dining Room
From *The Building News*,
26 June, 1878
Batley made several
attempts 'to adapt Egyptian
ornament and design to the
modern dining room'. In
this example, to quote
Batley: 'The furniture is
severe and heavy in form,
made in dark oak, with
ebony and ivory inlays, with
handworked tapestries for
the hangings, curtains and
coverings.' The seated lady
bears a marked resemblance
to Jane Morris!

and white china, tear up their Aesthetic lilies
and sunflowers, and sing:

We've cropped quite short our lengthy hair,
We've smashed up all our crockery-ware,
...We do not care about BURNE-JONES,
We worship not his maidens' bones,
And quite detest his 'subtle tones'
We mock a Dado do!
We now have lots of common sense,
We are not prone to take offence,
If people say we're not 'intense' –
Or even hint we're not 'too-too!'
E'en lilies now we don't adore,
We're sick of Art and what is more,
Vote BOTTICELLI is a bore
And mock a Dado do!
O mock a Dado, mock a Dado, mock a Dado, do!

They then all seize hatchets, pokers, chisels,
and forthwith proceed to demolish the Dado.

Although Du Maurier had finished
with Aestheticism as a comic theme, the
Movement had not yet run its course. Its
intellectual and visual diversity gave it great
appeal. Eclecticism reigned. Intense young
men and women made endless lists of the very

varied artistic topics which came into fashion.

List-making indeed became something
of an obsession. This was satirized brilliantly
in 1883 by the words in which the lovesick
Aesthetic ladies in Gilbert and Sullivan's *Patience*
disparage the crude colours of the uniforms of
their suitors, the Heavy Dragoons as: 'Red and
Yellow! Primary colours!' They suggest they
wear instead:

a cobwebby grey velvet, with a tender bloom
like a cold gravy, which, made [in the] Florentine
fourteenth-century, trimmed with Venetian leather
and Spanish altar lace, and surmounted with
something Japanese – it matters not what – would
at least be Early English!

This description (apart from the cold
gravy!) could have been taken from any of the
many books on interior decoration published
in the 1870s and 1880s. A particularly dotty
example of such a book was *A Series of Studies
for Domestic Furniture and Decoration,*
published in 1883 with designs in Egyptian,
Japanese and Jacobean styles, by the long and
justly forgotten H.W. Batley, who worked in a
kaleidoscopic variety of styles. His *Study for a*

William de Morgan
(1839–1917)
Tiles in the craft tradition,
1880s

Dining Room is straight from Thebes complete with dreamy Aesthetic ladies. It was designed in an attempt 'to adapt the various styles of architecture to modern interior decoration ... The walls are supposed to be painted in flat colourings, representing fish, flesh and fowl'...

Batley's was just one of a spate of books which popularized the Aesthetic concepts formulated by Charles Eastlake in his classic work *Hints on Household Taste*. In Mrs H.R. Haweis's *The Art of Beauty* (1878) the more practical aspects of interior decoration are covered. The secret, it seems, is based upon daring mixtures of colours: '... a room could have a dark blue ceiling and walls of Vandyck brown or be painted scarlet ... with black or sage green doors and wainscot'. She expands on these ideas in *The Art of Decoration* (1881), a compendious work consisting of three sections called *The Search After Beauty, A Retrospect of Rooms* and *General Applications*. It was followed a year later by *Beautiful Houses* which described the homes of distinguished artists of the day.

It is rewarding to imagine how a young London couple of Aesthetic tastes might have consulted such works and furnished their new home in the 1870s. Morris papers would have certainly looked ideal on the walls, but they were expensive and it might have been better to purchase Bruce Talbert's 'Frieze-Filling-Dado' wallpaper of circa 1877, a tripartite wallpaper neatly combining Japanese, Morrisian and classical elements. Such papers could be both hygienic and Aesthetic, particularly the embossed, washable type known as Lincrusta, which like the ceiling paper Anaglypta could be painted and varnished. The tiles in the conservatories might have been by William De Morgan, or variations on Japanese themes by Dr Christopher Dresser. These were available at the newly opened premises in Mayfair of

Thomas Goode & Co, designed by Ernest George and Peto, completed in 1876, and still today one of the best surviving examples of Aesthetic architecture. There could also be obtained the charming heads of nymphettes by W.S. Coleman, who was art adviser to Minton. Art pottery might have included Doulton's Lambeth faience, where great stress was placed on the 'graceful, appropriate and at the same time profitable employment for ladies'. The pottery work of the Martin Brothers and the Worcester Porcelain Company also in their very differing ways showed the pervasive influence of Japan.

The requisite Japanese lamp, screens, fans and other oriental bric-a-brac could, of course, have been obtained by visiting Messrs Liberty's new shop in Regent's Street. If really avant garde in taste, the young couple might have puchased the strikingly severe 'Anglo-Japanese' furniture of E.W. Godwin with its original handling of volume and mass. They were perhaps more likely to have bought furniture described as 'Hepplewhite', 'Sheraton' or 'Chippendale' of a type dating unmistakably from the late nineteenth century which now

Above: Ernest George and Peto
Thomas Goode & Co, South Audley Street, London, 1876
One of the most striking 'Queen Anne' shops in London, the building survives today unaltered right down to the blue and white Nankin vase set in a brick alcove in the facade's centre.

Left: E.W. Godwin (1833-86)
'Monkey' cabinet, 1876
Walnut, inset with four boxwood plaques
This cabinet was made for Godwin's own use, probably by William Watt. The carved boxwood panels and netsuke handles are Japanese in origin and may have been acquired from Liberty's East Indian Art Warehouse, which opened in Regent Street in 1876.

jostles for our attention in large second-hand shops specializing in 'antique and reproduction furniture'. Designed interiors could take the strangest forms. Walter Hamilton, the first historian of the Aesthetic Movement, writing in 1882, gives us a notion of what was considered fashionable or correct:

Chippendale furniture, dadoes, old-fashioned brass and wrought iron work, mediaeval lamps, stained-glass in small squares, and old china are held to be the outward and visible signs of an inward and spiritual grace and intensity.

By the 1880s the Aesthetic Movement had become a little old-fashioned but it did not lose all its adherents and its tenets held for many years. By 1896 anything was possible, and Mrs Panton[6] deplored 'the jumble of styles made by having an eastern-looking hall, an Old English dining room, a Queen Anne drawing room, and Moorish landing'.

This mixture of clashing styles and the speed of such eclectic change produced a feeling of world weariness which the critic, Raffles Davison, writing in the *Art Journal* in 1892, gave voice to in a tone which has been echoed down the following century by writer after writer:

Just when the Gothic house was losing its smartness when its piquancy had proved such a relief to the refined classic, we suddenly found that Queen Anneism was vastly better, and when that had been clearly revivified we found that Dutch and French Renaissance were more interesting; and now alas! some new prophet asks us to believe in the stiffest of all possible classics, even whilst one of the cleverest things in Francois Premier is mounting up the stairs in Berkeley Square.[7]

In 1986-7, the Metropolitan Museum, New York, staged a major exhibition on the subject of Americans and the Aesthetic Movement with a magisterial catalogue entitled *In Pursuit of Beauty*. The first sentence of the Preface defines both the parameters of the exhibition and the subject:

The term 'Aesthetic Movement' refers to the introduction of principles that emphasized art in the production of furniture, metalwork, ceramics, stained glass, textiles, wallpapers and books. During its height, from the mid-1870s through the mid-1880s, the Aesthetic Movement affected all levels of society in America. The catalyst for its widespread popularity was the Philadelphia Centennial Exposition of 1876. There, in numerous displays, many Americans, artists and craftsmen as well as the general public, were exposed to art objects from a great variety of nations and periods.

This definition interestingly makes no mention at all of painting, but poses a subject

Above and opposite above: Frederick E. Church (1826–1900) Interior and exterior details of Olana, 1888–9 The renowned American landscape painter Frederick Edwin Church travelled widely in the Middle East and elsewhere before purchasing a dramatic site high above the river Hudson in Upper New York State. The contents of the house provide far more than an eclectic mixture of different ethnic artifacts for the rooms re-interpret the visual experience of Islamic decorative art in an aesthetic form. Both the stencilling inside, with its debts to the ornamental lexicon of Owen Jones, and the decorative polychromy of the exterior form a harmonious entity. The house, with its breathtaking views, is one of the major achievements of the Aesthetic Movement.

Below left: William de Morgan
Vase, c.1880s
Lustreware
De Morgan designed tiles, dishes, vases and bowls decorated with a gallimaufry of fabulous beasts, sailing ships and exotic floral designs.

Below right: James Hadley (1837–1903)
Pair of Pilgrim flasks, 1872
Glazed earthenware
Showing scenes in a Japanese porcelain-manufacturing workshop, these flasks were produced by Royal Worcester.

worthy of the brush of Max Beerbohm, 'the exposure of art objects to the craftsmen and general public of America'. 'Art objects' alone, however, do not tell the whole story. Admittedly, the main achievement of the Aesthetic Movement was to place new and powerful emphasis upon the importance of the decorative arts, but painting was also a central concern of the Movement, necessitating a close examination of the work of such key figures as Burne-Jones, Albert Moore, Alma-Tadema, Leighton and Whistler in England, and Winslow Homer, William Merritt Chase, Thomas Dewing and Elihu Vedder in America.

A rewarding experience for students of the Aesthetic Movement is a visit to some of the surviving artist's studios of the era, in particular Olana, the summer home and studio of the great landscape painter Frederick Church. It was created chiefly in the 1870s, with a new wing added in 1888-9. A large red brick house, it stands high above the river

Hudson in Upper New York State, its porches, towers and balconies accentuated with colourful tiles. The floors of the hall are carpeted with Oriental rugs, and the walls glow with stylized stencil designs of Arabic floral patterns or black Assyrian figures, showing that Church was a keen student of the 112 plates in Owen Jones's *Grammar of Ornament*. An Egyptian bronze ibis, a brass Buddha, 'Hindoo' carvings, floors strewn with Oriental rugs provide a rich ethnic mix, the eclectic international style which was one of the great features of Aesthetic style.

Two features are pertinent to the story which follows: the frames containing butterflies, the iridescent symbol of immortality and the ephemeral nature of natural beauty; and a large blue and white china vase placed prominently on a corner of the second landing. The collection of such blue and white porcelain in both England and America was an important stage in the quest for new Aesthetic standards, as was the cult of Japan which not only provided an opportunity for staid Victorian ladies to become geishas for the evening by slipping on a kimono and picking up a fan, but also supplied an alternative to the tyranny of the Gothic style and the beginning of an exciting phase of Aesthetic design.

Below: Martin Brothers
Vase, 1889
Glazed earthenware
The Martin Brothers, who were based at Southall in London, produced some outstanding 'art pottery' showing Japanese themes.

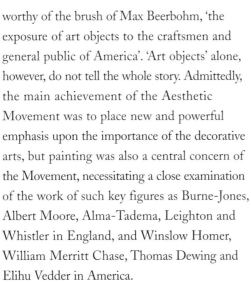

There's a joy without canker or cark,

There's a pleasure eternally new,

'Tis to gloat on the glaze and the mark

Of china that's ancient and blue;

Unchipped all the centuries through

It has passed since the chime of it rang,

And they fashion'd it, figure and hue,

In the reign of the Emperor Hwang.

ANDREW LANG, *BALLADES IN BLUE CHINA*, 1880

**Opposite: Ellen Clacy
(fl. 1870–95)**
*Lady Betty Germain's China
Closet, Knole*, c. 1880
Watercolour, 46.9 x 35 cm
Lady Betty Germain, a
connection of the Sackvilles
and close friend of Horace
Walpole, lived for some years
in the mid-eighteenth
century in the great
Elizabethan house of Knole.
There she formed a
collection of Chinese
porcelain which she housed
in a china closet. The
talented but little-known
watercolour artist, Ellen
Clacy, chose to take this as
the subject for this painting.
The identity of the Aesthetic
lady dressed in blue is not
known.

**Right: K'ang Hsi
(1662–1722)
Blue and white ginger jar
Porcelain, underglaze blue**

I feel an irresistible desire to wander, and
go to Japan, where I will pass my youth,
sitting under an almond tree, drinking
amber tea out of a blue cup, and looking
at a landscape without perspective.

LETTER FROM OSCAR WILDE, 1882

These two quotations were written at the height of the craze for blue and white porcelain and the cult of Japan, vogues which, though often satirized, played a highly significant role in the artistic life of High Victorian England.

Ever since Marco Polo's return to Venice with tales of the forbidden city of Peking in 1295, Europeans had delighted in the textiles, ceramics and, much later, wallpapers which found their way out of China on the Silk Route or via the various East India companies. In the eighteenth century a European craze developed for an exotic 'Chinoiserie' style, essentially a decorator's fashion.

Fantasy structures were erected in England such as the Kew Pagoda by Sir William Chambers dating from 1757–62, and the interior at Claydon House by the carpenter Mr Lightfoot. An amusing

Utagawa Kunisada (1786–1864)
A colour woodcut showing women imitating craftsmen as they carry out the various processes in the production of Japanese prints. These prints were to trickle into Europe and produce an Aesthetic revolution.

comment on the craze was made in 1756. 'Nay, so excessive is the love of Chinese architecture become, that at present foxhunters would be sorry to break a leg in pursuing their sport in leaping any gate that was not made in the eastern taste of little bits of wood standing in all directions.'

The romantic world of 'Far Cathay' took different forms, varying from the ever-popular narrative of the 'willow pattern' pictured on many thousands of ceramic wares, to the opulent exotic interiors of the beloved creation of George IV, the Brighton Pavilion, which did *not* amuse Queen Victoria who only visited it once and let it fall into neglect.

Such frivolity did not suit the earnest mood of the early Victorian era which triumphed in the engineering skills of Sir Joseph Paxton at the Crystal Palace and the severity of the all-pervasive Gothic Revival style. But in the 1860s, with the increased trade of tea clippers to the ports on the Chinese coast there began a craze for the collection of blue and white Chinese porcelain, which was to run parallel with a cult for the art of Japan. Both vogues, though often satirized, played a highly significant role in the artistic life of High Victorian England. The intelligentsia, surfeited with the universality of the Gothic Revival style, found in the art of China and Japan just the electrifying kick-start needed to trigger off the Aesthetic Movement. In the words of the popular song, the urge for 'long ago' gave place to the desire for 'far away'.

The origins of this vogue can be seen when on 31 March, 1853, the American Commodore Perry with four ships of war arrived in Edo (Tokyo) to open diplomatic relations. His arrival woke the sleeping beauty of Japan, and the effect was analogous politically to the fall of the Berlin wall in our own times. Artistically it can be

James Abbott McNeill Whistler (1834–1903)
Symphony in White, No 2: The Little White Girl, **1864**
Oil on canvas, 76.5 x 51.1 cm
'... Deep in the gleaming glass. She sees all past things pass', wrote Swinburne in his poem *Before the Mirror*. His words were inspired by this painting for which Whistler's mistress Jo Hiffernan posed. Although Swinburne praised the way in which her 'hand, a fallen rose, lies snow-white on white snows', he does not describe the Japanese fan she holds, nor the blue and white jar, the red lacquer bowl nor the azaleas, which have been used to accent the spatial ambiguity of the mirrored image of Jo's face.

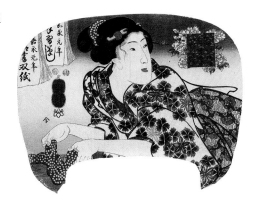

Right: Two fans
Above: Utagawa Kunisada
(1786–1864) also known as
Toyokuni III
Girl washing a patterned cloth,
1848
Below: Probably by Hiroshige
II (1826–69)
*The Bay at Kuoto in Kazusa
Province*, 1858

Opposite: Edward William
Godwin (1833–1886)
Cabinet, 1877–80
Ebonized mahogany, with
silver-plated fittings and
leather
This piece appears with other
furniture in the Anglo-
Japanese style in a catalogue
published by the cabinet-
maker William Watt in 1877.
It has frequently been
wrongly dated to 1867. At
least six cabinets of this
design still survive, and the
six-legged version in the
Bristol Museum is known to
have belonged to Ellen Terry.

compared to the impact of the discoveries at Herculaneum and Pompeii
in the 1730s, and the moment when peering into Tutankhamun's tomb
Howard Carter glimpsed 'wonderful things' hitherto unseen by modern
eyes. For over 200 years, since 1640, Japan had been virtually closed to
the outside world after a trade ban imposed by the Shogun Ieyasu
Tokugawa. The Japanese art and artifacts, brought back to Europe as a
result of the ending of this embargo, were to have a profound impact on
western art.

Shortly before 1853 there had been significant cracks in
the bamboo curtain surrounding Japan, and artifacts had begun to trickle
into the outside world. Throughout the Shogunate limited contacts had
existed with Europe via a small colony of Dutch traders on Deshima
island, Nagasaki. Prior to 1812 some prints were brought to Europe by
the head trader Isaak Thyssen, and in 1830 the doctor and naturalist
Philipp Franz von Siebold, as representative of the Dutch government,
ventured into the interior of Japan. His diaries record experiences along
the famous Tokaido road made just as Hiroshige was depicting it in the
famous *One Hundred Views* print series. Siebold's collection, chiefly curios
but including some *kakemono-e*, was bequeathed to the Leyden Museum.

At the 1851 Great Exhibition in the Crystal Palace a
very limited number of Japanese items was shown, as was the first
recorded English textile influenced by Japan entitled 'Japanese spots
and honeycombs'. A Dutch firm, F. Zeegers & Co, exhibited the first
Japanese screen to delight English eyes. In the next few years Japanese
prints and porcelain began to emerge in some numbers, and by 1854 an
exhibition of over 600 items of Japanese applied arts was held at the
Old Watercolour Society in London. With characteristic energy Henry
Cole acquired almost all the exhibits for the Museum of Manufactures,
the ancestor of the Victoria and Albert Museum. Two years later J.C.
Robinson, the museum's curator, waxed lyrical about this unique
collection: 'Japanese art ... is distinguished from [that of China] by a
more refined perception of the innate grace and beauty of natural
objects, especially of the floral kingdom, which are often reproduced as
decorative motives with wonderful spirit and truth to nature.'

There was little popular awareness of things Japanese
until the first extensive display at the Great Exhibition of 1862. Visitors
there could see lacquer, bronzes and porcelain brought to England by Sir
Rutherford Alcock, the first representative of the British crown at Edo
(Tokyo) in 1859. Alcock wrote a study of Japanese colour techniques,
working methods and artistic practice, entitled *Capital of the Tycoon*
(1863), which was among the first publications to contain reproductions
of Japanese woodcuts.

France signed a trade treaty with Japan in 1858, but as in England Japanese artifacts only started to make a great impression in the 1860s, although interest had begun earlier. The first work to make a stir were some of the fifteen volumes that comprise Hokusai's *Manga*. They were published between 1814 when Hokusai was fifty-four and 1878, twenty-nine years after his death. The word *manga* has been translated as drawing things 'just as they come', and the slim volumes do indeed provide a most glorious huggermugger of random sketches and great landscapes, alternating with comic scenes in the bath house, Sumo wrestlers preparing to enter the ring, labour-saving devices, tips on carpentry, exquisite birds, fish, plants, flowers and so on. It is like the motto of the *News of the World* – 'All Human Life is There'. Copies were passed eagerly from hand to hand in artistic circles when they first arrived in Europe. The exact date of their arrival is conjectural although

they first came to notice in 1856 in the hands of the printer of etchings, Delâtre, who showed them to both Whistler and Félix Bracquemond (1833–1914). In 1858 Bracquemond acquired the *Manga*, and introduced it to many other artists and writers including Fantin-Latour, Alfred Stevens, Burty, Champfleury, Degas and Monet, all of whom became influenced by it. Some years later in 1867 Bracquemond prepared careful copies of illustrations in the *Manga* of birds, plants, flowers and fish. He used these drawings for transfer prints with which to decorate a dinner service, the first western ceramic objects to show the influence of Japanese art.

Hokusai's *Manga* was also to be important in England. Japanese prints may have begun to enter England via the port of Bristol. They are first recorded in 1862 on the walls of the home of a talented young Bristolian architect and writer Edward William Godwin (1833–86), who became a leading figure of the Aesthetic Movement (see Chapter Eight). He particularly prized two slim volumes of Hokusai's *Manga* showing Japanese techniques of construction, joints and carpentry which proved immensely influential on his later career. From them in the 1870s he drew the inspiration for the design of his 'Anglo-Japanese' furniture, which comprised ebonized black sideboards and cupboards and reveals Godwin's profound understanding of Japanese concerns for space and volume, asymmetry, reticence and restraint. The prototype for these pieces was possibly the sideboard of 1867, bequeathed to the Bristol Museum by Edith Craig, the daughter of Godwin and Ellen Terry the actress. In her memoirs *The Story of my Life* (1933) Ellen Terry recalled the nursery: 'They were allowed no rubbishy picture books but from the first Japanese prints and fans lined the nursery walls'. The children wore tiny kimonos, 'while their English classic was Walter Crane', himself an admirer of things Japanese, as can be seen in *One, Two, Buckle My Shoe* (1869).

From an early date Godwin shared his Japanese enthusiasms with the great architect of the Gothic style (such as Cardiff Castle), William Burges, whose review of the 1862 exhibition in the *Building News* glows with enthusiasm: 'If the visitor wishes to see the real Middle Ages he must visit the Japanese Court, for at the present day the arts of the Middle Ages have deserted Europe and are only to be found in the East ...these hitherto unknown barbarians appear to know all that the Middle Ages knew but in some respects are beyond them and us as well.'

Some of Burges's collection of Japanese prints survive in the Victoria and Albert Museum, pasted into a scrapbook.

Above: Elkington & Company and Royal Worcester Porcelain Company
Tea set, 1875–7
Silver gilt and porcelain engraved with Japanese and European motifs

Below: Attributed to Christopher Dresser
'Cloissoné-style' vase, c. 1870s
Porcelain
In recent years Dresser's challengingly modern and original productions have been recognized as some of the most remarkable achievements of the Aesthetic Movement. With facility and flair he created metalwork for Elkington & Co and J. W. Hukin and Heath, ceramics for Minton & Co, the Linthorpe Art Pottery and other firms and the striking 'Clutha' glass for James Couper & Sons of Glasgow.

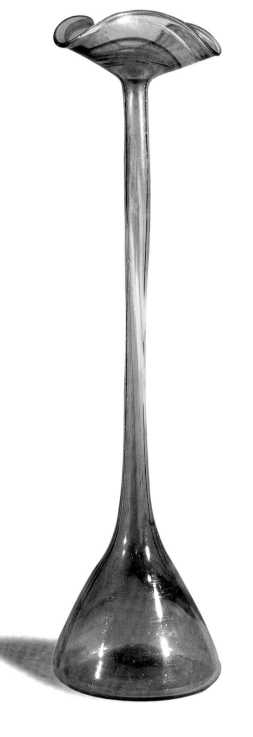

Christopher Dresser
'Clutha' glass, c. 1890s
Dresser's remarkable glass
shows the amalgamation of
assymetrical motifs from
both Japanese and Egyptian
prototypes.

To turn its pages is an exciting experience, enabling us to share vicariously with Burges and Godwin the thrill of seeing for the first time the exotic patterns and bold designs of Japan.

In May 1863, Burges chaired a meeting of the Architectural Association on 'Japanese Art'. A lecture on 'The Prevailing Ornament of China and Japan' was given by Christopher Dresser, a young man who was to play a remarkable role in the dissemination of knowledge of Japan. He had just become a Doctor of Philosophy at Jena University after first studying at Henry Cole's School of Design at South Kensington, where he had been particularly influenced by Owen Jones, the author of the *Chinese Grammar of Ornament*. A trained botanist, the infinite variety of natural patterns provided the basis for his successful career as a designer.

From the mid- to late-1860s Dresser designed for Wedgwood, Minton Coalbrookdale, and from the mid 1870s for Elkington & Co, the silverware manufacturers. Many of these early designs reflect a knowledge of Japanese export wares. In 1876 he went to Japan as representative for the South Kensington Museum and agent for Tiffany & Co, New York, visiting sixty-four potteries and dozens of manufacturers of different wares. He took hundreds of photographs, and advised the Japanese on their export trade. On his return he radically altered his own designs, particularly for pottery and his 'Clutha' glass, making them far more abstract as a result of his greater understanding of Japanese materials and aesthetics. In his 1882 publication *Japan, its Architecture, Art and Art Manufactures* he wrote: 'I firmly believe that the introduction of the works of Japanese handicraftsmen into England has done as much to improve our national taste as even our schools of art and public museums ... for these Japanese objects have got into our homes, and among them we live.' But in the 1860s such refined understanding still lay far ahead, and imitation of a more uncritical nature reigned in the porcelain companies Royal Worcester and Minton and the silversmiths Elkington & Co, which began to experiment with Japanese decorative motifs, including asymmetric arrangements of blossoms, fans, bamboos, birds and fish. The sparrow of Edo began surprisingly to feature upon that most British of design innovations, the Christmas card invented by Sir Henry Cole in 1843.

From the start of the 1860s, the interest of Godwin, Burges, and Dresser reveals that the British, as opposed to the European, reaction to the influence of Japanese art was to manifest itself in the *decorative*, rather than the *fine* arts. Another close friend of Godwin, Whistler, radically affected both artistic disciplines, to become the principal catalyst of the cult of Japan

Christopher Dresser
Twin-handled bowl, 1879
Electro-plating decorated
with Japanese motifs

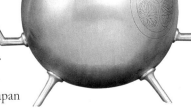

**Opposite: Kate Hallyar
(fl. 1883–98)**
Sunflowers and Hollyhocks,
**1889
Watercolour, 31.75 x 22.8 cm**

**Below: Jessica Hallyar
(1858–1940)**
Autumn Sunlight, **1891
Watercolour
Kate and Jessica Hallyar,
together with their sisters
Edith and Mary, studied art
under their father the
portrait and genre painter
James Hallyar. All four girls
ended up becoming artists.
It is intriguing to find both
Kate and Jessica using the
same sunflowers, Chinese
vase and Oriental carpet –
with such different, yet
commitedly Aesthetic,
results.**

and the Aesthetic Movement.

Whistler's character is as difficult to capture and pin down as the fluttering butterfly which he adopted as a signature. Born to trouble as the sparks fly upwards, as an artistic force he operated simultaneously as painter, wit, polemicist, etcher, aphorist, Aesthete, and became the one revolutionary figure in the English-speaking world regarded as an ally by Degas and Manet in their crusade against academic art. Here, it is valuable to examine him as a collector, not only of things Japanese, but also of Chinese 'blue and white' porcelain.

Collecting Oriental porcelain had become a passion in the seventeenth century, when wares were brought back to Europe by the various East India companies. Before Japan became isolated from the outside world the Dutch East India Company imported large quantities of porcelain, silks and lacquer which became greatly prized. These wares conjured up an exotic vision of 'Far Cathay' as a fairyland of the decorative arts. In the 1730s Augustus the Strong in Dresden renamed a palace as the Japanese Pavilion, furnishing it throughout with porcelain. Imported Chinese tea accompanied the porcelain and in England tea drinking was first made fashionable by Charles II's queen, Catherine of Braganza. The later monarchs William and Mary formed a choice collection of Chinese blue and white which they proudly displayed at Hampton Court Palace. By the nineteenth century the British passion for tea was no longer an aristocratic prerogative but a universal pleasure, and porcelain as well as tea was brought back from the coastal ports of China, although until Whistler's arrival 'blue and white' was not particularly prized.

What exactly was 'blue and white' porcelain? In China since the Ming period (1368–1644) a cobalt oxide pigment had been used for painting under a transparent glaze on fine white porcelain surfaces, which when fired at very high temperatures provided attractive results. This technique continued to be used by later generations of Chinese potters in the Ch'ing Dynasty (1644–1911). During the reign of K'ang hsi (1662–1722) particularly fine work was produced on vases and ginger jars using a motif of white prunus blossom against the background of a blue which has been aptly described as pulsating, irregularly divided by dark lines to suggest the cracked ice of the spring thaw. Such pots have been extensively copied ever since.

Whistler owned some examples of Ming fourteenth-century wares although most of his collection probably dated from the seventeenth and eighteenth centuries. His motives for collecting it were complex, including both the antiques lovers' delight in the chase, and a personal love of the colour blue, subtle variations of which hue appear

**Thomas Jeckyll (1827–1881)
Sunflower firedog design,
c. 1870
Cast iron, gilt bronze and
wrought iron
Jeckyll designed many
metalwork items in the
Japanese taste for the
company Barnard, Bishop
and Barnard of Norwich, the
most well known being this
'sunflower' firedog design and
the most remarkable the cast-
iron pavilion designed for the
Philadelphia Centennial
Exhibition of 1876.**

in so many of his paintings. But the most compelling motivation may have been appreciation of the consummate freedom of the brushwork. In Gilbert and Sullivan's *Patience* Bunthorne, its Aesthetic hero, is described: '... as such a judge of blue and white and other kinds of pottery from early Oriental down to modern terra-cott-ry'.

Always alert for new fashionable trends the ceramic industry of the day, seized with enthusiasm for Japanese themes, was busy producing 'other kinds of pottery' by the ton. Sprays of cherry blossom, sparrows, bamboos, and above all fan shapes were reproduced with prodigal abundance and combined in endless permutations. Floral motifs provided a common ground on which both cultures could meet. Victorian watercolours of primroses and violets, nosegays of roses and bunches of bluebells yielded place to the lilies and sunflowers which were already popularized by the Pre-Raphaelites, as well as chrysanthemums, peonies, cherry blossom and bamboo.

The sunflower was one of the earliest introductions from the New World, being first grown in Europe before 1569. It was greatly admired by artists who saw its face as an expression of the Renaissance concept of the Golden Section of Divine natural proportion. Van Dyck painted a memorable self-portrait with a single bloom. The sunflower owes its popularity in the Aesthetic era to its use by William Morris and Edward Burne-Jones, notably in the Oxford Union frescoes of 1857. The sunflower's bold colour and the ease with which its simple flat shape could be wrought into a formal pattern invested it with a potent visual appeal which led to it becoming what may be termed, to use a design cliché of the late twentieth century, virtually the 'logo' of the Aesthetic Movement. It appears as stucco ornament on red brick houses from Chelsea to Bedford Park and swamps the tiles which surround the stove in the Grillroom at the Victoria and Albert Museum, South Kensington, designed in the mid-1860s by Edward Poynter. Another striking example of its use occurs in two watercolours of the same aesthetic interior by the two Hallyar sisters Kate and Jessica, *Sunflowers and Hollyhocks* (1889) and *Autumn Sunlight* (1891). One of the most flamboyant and extensive decorative treatments utilizing sunflowers as a motif occurs in William Eden Nesfield's lodge at Kinmel Park, Denbighshire in 1868. But the use of the sunflower motif at its most striking can be seen in the designs by Thomas Jeckyll in cast and wrought iron for a famous pavilion in the Japanese style which he designed for international exhibitions at Philadelphia in 1876 and Paris in 1878. Jeckyll became virtually obsessed by the sunflower as a design motif, strikingly exemplified in his sunflower table top made for Barnard, Bishop and Barnard.

Design attributed to William
Eden Nesfield (1835–88) and
made by James Forsyth
(1826–1910)
Folding screen, 1867
Ebonized wood
Incorporating six panels with
twelve Japanese-inspired
paintings of flowers and
birds, this screen was given
by James Forsyth to the
architect Richard Norman
Shaw as a wedding present,
and is extensively inscribed
with marital good wishes.

The talented young Jewish Pre-Raphaelite painter Simeon Solomon was one of the most enigmatic figures of the Aesthetic Movement. He vies with Whistler for the claim of being the first western artist to paint a model holding a Japanese fan. In 1863 he wrote to Swinburne excitedly telling him of the collection of a friend, William Eden Nesfield, an architect and artist with an immense enthusiasm for Japanese art:

> ... it will be by no means difficult for you to meet him, for his rooms are in Argyll Street near mine, and he has a very jolly collection of Persian, Indian, Greek and Japanese things that I should really like you to see, so, if you care to go I will take you round to him when you call on me, he is an intimate friend of Albert Moore.

Like Simeon Solomon, Albert Moore was to produce some of the most distinguished Aesthetic paintings, and later in the 1860s was to become one of Whistler's closest associates. Reviewing Moore's painting, *Azaleas*, Swinburne waxed lyrical about 'the gentle mould of [the model's] fine limbs through the thin soft raiment; pale small leaves and bright white blossoms about her and above, a few rose-red petals fallen on the pale marble and faint-coloured woven mat ... a strange and splendid vessel, inlaid with designs of Eastern colour; another – clasped by one long slender hand and filled from it with flowers – of soft white, touched here and there into blossoms of blue'.

Flowers, one of the great shared delights of the cultures of England and Japan, also featured prominently on a six-fold screen designed in 1867 by William Eden Nesfield. It was made as a wedding present for his architectural partner Richard Norman Shaw with whom he shared offices from 1863 to 1876. The screen displays a highly sophisticated knowledge of Japanese motifs. Twelve Japanese painted panels depict birds perched on blossoming branches of chrysanthemums, lilies, pinks, peonies and magnolias. The panels are surrounded by incised ebonized wooden frames, separated at the top with strips of open fretwork and a band of gilded and carved motifs of Japanese origin.

Right above: Herter Brothers Cabinet, c. 1880 Ebonized cherry, inlaid and gilded woods
While the wardrobe (below) gets its effect by its dramatic simplicity this Herter Brothers cabinet (which was possibly used to hold sherry), is effective because of its far more elaborate decoration, carved dog's head finials and intricately inlaid central panel, showing an urn surrounded by the Japanese motifs of butterflies, cranes and plants, all effects which combine to make this one of the most significant items of Art Furniture produced on either side of the Atlantic.

Right below: Herter Brothers Wardrobe, 1880–5 Ebonized cherry, inlaid woods
This spectacular piece of furniture was one of the finest objects created by the Herter Brothers in New York. This famous firm was founded in the 1850s, at first offering customers Modern Gothic furniture in the 'Eastlake' style but moving on in the 1870s to their own individual Anglo-Japanese style for which the firm has become most famed. This wardrobe was appropriately owned by the actress and Broadway star Lilian Russell who must have enjoyed its dramatic black background, the remarkable golden oriental branches which grow from the cornice, and the fluttering leaves and flowers.

The screen is elaborately inscribed (in short lines) with the couplets:
All are Architects of Fate
Working on these walls of time
Some with massive deeds and great
Some with ornaments of Rhyme. RICHARD AND AGNES SHAW, 1867 AD

The gilded bands of asymmetric decoration are composed of the Japanese patterns *sayagata* (key fret motif), *uzumaki* (spirals), family crests known as *tomoe*, and the auspicious Asian symbol of the swastika, all handled with great technical flair. The question of where Nesfield and James Forsyth (who made the screen) can have acquired such knowledge is a fascinating one, and can perhaps be partially explained by a study of Owen Jones's *Grammar of Chinese Ornament* published in a limited edition of 300 in 1867. The more unusual motifs of the screen could also have been borrowed from Japanese ceramics and textile stencils. Such goods and screens and prints were obtainable at Farmer and Rogers Oriental warehouse in Regent Street, the owners of which had acquired the stock direct from the Great Exhibition of 1862. It was at this shop that Rossetti is reputed to have introduced Whistler to the manager Arthur Lasenby Liberty, who was later in 1875 to found his own famous firm.

For Rossetti, just as with blue and white, so it was with things Japanese. 'It was Mr Whistler,' wrote William Michael Rossetti, 'who first called my brother's attention to Japanese art: he possessed two or three woodcut books, some coloured prints and a screen or two.' Rossetti collected with discrimination and flair and made a deep study of Japanese 'mon' which he re-interpreted in his designs for book bindings, notably for the cover of Swinburne's *Atalanta and Calydon*. He also used a Japanese kimono (borrowed from his friend G.P. Boyce) to great effect in *The Beloved (The Bride)* of 1865. In November 1864 while in Paris, Rossetti visited Madame de Soye's famous shop at 220, Rue de Rivoli. Opened in 1862, it had become the haunt of all interested in Japanese art including Baudelaire and the Goncourt brothers, Zola, Manet, Degas, and of course Whistler. Rossetti bought four Japanese books but 'found that all the costumes were being snapped up by a French artist, Tissot, who it seems is doing three Japanese pictures, which the mistress of the shop described to me as the three wonders of the world, evidently in her opinion quite throwing Whistler into the shade. She told me, with a great deal of laughing, about Whistler's consternation at my collection of china.'

Liberty's, which for many years specialized in Oriental furnishings and fabrics, at the height of the Aesthetic period was one of the most important cross-pollinating centres of the movement where both Japanese art and products influenced by Japanese design could be found. This description by E.W. Godwin, in 1867, of the excitement aroused by the expected arrival of a new consignment of fans at Liberty's vividly conveys the atmosphere of the shop in those days:

> There was quite a crowd when we arrived. A distinguished traveller had button-holed the obliging proprietor in one corner; a well known baronet, waiting to do the same, was trifling with some feather dusting brushes, two architects of well known names were posing an attendant in another corner with awkward questions; three distinguished painters with their wives blocked up the staircase; whilst a bevy of ladies filled up the rest of the floorspace.
>
> Before I could catch the eye of the master of this enchanting cave, it was learned that the cases would not arrive till late in the evening. Almost in a moment the swarm of folk vanished, and I was free to pick my way from ground-floor to attics, for No. 218 Regent Street is from front to back and top to bottom literally crammed with objects of oriental manufacture.

Liberty's was to play an important role in the production in 1885 of Gilbert and Sullivan's *The Mikado*, which event ensured the popularity of the cult for Japan in England and America, by making gentle fun of it. The subsequent successful rush to New York by the official company to open before the pirated version and secure American copyrights is worth recording, if only because it led during the winter of 1885-6 to Madison Square Gardens housing a *Mikado* village with demonstrations of silk weaving, and subsequently the appearance of a *Mikado* room in every New York home of artistic pretensions.

A particularly remarkable example of such a room was the Japanese parlour of the William H. Vanderbilt house on Fifth Avenue, New York, created by the interior decorators and designers, the Herter Brothers, in 1883–4. Although Commodore Perry had broken the trade embargo in 1853, America had been slow to develop an enthusiasm for Japanese art. The artist John La Farge began importing Japanese prints in 1863 but it was not until the Philadelphia Centennial exhibition of 1876 that Japanese art became widely admired. The official catalogue echoed Burges's comment on the 1862 exhibition: 'The Japanese artisan is still very much like those of Mediaeval Europe ... being himself both artist and artisan.' Christian Herter, an eclectic society designer, was greatly taken by the Japanese works he saw there, and designed quantities of furniture in the Japanese manner produced by his family firm, Herter Brothers. Several pieces echo Godwin designs, but in the

James J. Tissot (1836–1902)
L'Eté (Summer), 1878
**Etching and drypoint,
37.6 x 20.8 cm
One of several depictions
by Tissot in differing media
of his mistress Kathleen
Newton. Here she is
silhouetted against an open
Japanese parasol.**

remarkable cabinet of 1880, Japanese and Gothic decorative themes are linked with superb effect to produce an outstanding example of 'American-Japanese' furniture. It is however surpassed by the restraint of the wardrobe, also of 1880, in which floral inlay of great distinction produces a work which ranks with the Nesfield screen. It was owned in the 1880s by the actress Lilian Russell, who starred in Gilbert and Sullivan's *Patience* in which Bunthorne the 'Aesthetic Sham' confesses that he does 'not long for everything that's Japanese'.

The figure of Bunthorne was in part based on Oscar Wilde, who later in 1882, adrift in San Francisco, fantasized about a visit to Japan in a letter to Whistler:

I feel an irresistible desire to wander, and go to Japan, where I will pass my youth, sitting under an almond tree, drinking amber tea out of a blue cup, and looking at a landscape without perspective ...

Wilde, for whom the word charisma might have been invented, owed the initial lift-off of his career to his passion for 'blue and white' which developed while still an undergraduate at Oxford. There, he was credited with the remark: 'I find it harder and harder every day to live up to my blue china', the first of many of his aphorisms to gain international celebrity. It scandalized the university, provoking some undergraduate 'hearties' to break up his porcelain collection.

For James Tissot (1836-1902), like Whistler, the 1860s, passed both in London and Paris, were some of his most creative years. In Paris he painted fashionable young girls with Japanese props, posed in his studio which was sumptuously decorated with Japanese objects including gifts from Prince Akitake who, after representing the Tokugawa government at the Exposition Universelle of 1867, stayed on in Paris for further education, including drawing lessons from Tissot. After Tissot settled in London in 1871 he continued to use accessories such as Japanese parasols in his portraits of his beautiful mistress Mrs Newton in the spirit of the Japanese tradition of *bijin-e*, that is, portraits of beauties. But his works also show a deeper knowledge of Japanese woodcuts by the use of the narrow vertical format of *hashira-e* pillar prints. This progression was by no means unique to Tissot. The influence of Japan manifested itself on two distinct levels. On first acquaintance many artists responded with delight to the sheer exoticism of the subjects. With further study came a deeper appreciation which led to a sympathetic assimilation of compositional devices and spatial relationships. A frequent initial reaction for artists was to dress a model in a kimono, giving her a fan to hold and painting her with a screen (or *kakemono*) as a background. Other artists who used 'the exotic approach' include Edouard Manet who made extensive use of fans in 1874 in his

Opposite: James J. Tissot
'En Gaine'– Children in a Garden, 1882
Cloisonné enamel vase
Tissot was one of the earliest collectors of Japanese art in France, and included in his personal collection both Chinese and Japanese *cloisonné* enamels. This interest may have led him to experiment in the medium himself. In 1882 he exhibited a group of over twenty pieces at the Dudley Gallery. Amongst them was this example which again shows Kathleen Newton silhouetted against a parasol.

Right: Claude Monet
(1840–1926)
La Japonaise, 1876
Oil on canvas, 241 x 142 cm
This portrait of Madame Monet in a Japanese costume standing in a room carpeted with *tatami* matting and backed by a wall covered with fifteen Japanese fans is one of many similar portraits by European and American artists. Indeed for half a century most painters' studios contained *uchiwa*, *Noh* masks and *netsuke* and of course a model wearing a kimono.

La Dame aux Eventails and introduced into the background of his *Portrait d'Emile Zola* of 1868 a colour woodcut of a Samurai by Toyokuni.

This initial response to the exoticism of the theme can be seen at its most joyous in Claude Monet's *La Japonaise* of 1876, showing his wife in a bold kimono against a wall, down which cascade fifteen colourful fans, a painting which met with immense success, being sold for 2,000 francs. Two years later he said:

We needed the arrival of Japanese albums in our midst, before anyone dared to sit down on a river bank, and juxtapose on canvas a roof which was bright red, a wall which was white, a green poplar, a yellow road and blue water. Before the example given by the Japanese, this was impossible, the painter always lied ... all one ever saw on a canvas were subdued colours, drowning in a half-tone ...[1]

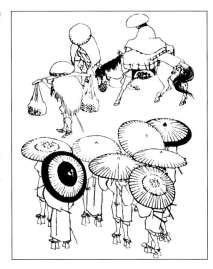

Monet collected Japanese prints throughout his life (they can be seen at his home in Giverny), and it may well be that Hokusai's *Thirty-Six Views of Fuji* showing the great volcano in different weather conditions and times of day inspired the sequence paintings so associated with Monet of haystacks, poplars, the façade of Rouen Cathedral, Westminster Bridge and waterlilies.

Degas, more successfully than any other European artist, assimilated the major lessons of Japanese dramatic composition, viewpoint and perspective such as cutting off figures by the picture frame. His studies of 'nude women bathing, drying themselves, combing their hair or having their hair combed' were directly inspired by Hokusai's *Manga*.

By 1900 many motifs of Japanese art had been adopted by western artists including the wave, rocks in the sea, the bridge, patterned backgrounds, fan-shaped compositions, stencils and the folding image of the screen. Even Renoir, most chauvinist of artists, used an idea from Hokusai's *Manga* for his painting *Les Parapluies* (c. 1881-5) despite his grumble: 'Japanese prints are certainly very interesting, as Japanese prints – in other words as long as they stay in Japan. A people should not appropriate what belongs to another race; in so doing, they are apt to make stupid mistakes. There would soon be a kind of universal art, without any individual characteristics ...'[2]

Japanese themes also abound in work by artists other than the Impressionists, spectacular examples being provided by the German Hans Makart, the Belgian James Ensor, and the Dutch artists Hans Breitner and Alfred Stevens.

In the English-speaking world Whistler, more than any other artist, showed in his enthusiasm for Japanese art a sympathetic empathy, which gives even his early paintings that merely use Japanese props a unique and special quality. In the most hauntingly beautiful of

Right above: Katsushika Hokusai (1760–1849)
Umbrellas
From the *Manga*, Vol 1, 1814
Colour woodcut, 18 x 12.5 cm

Right below: Pierre-Auguste Renoir (1841–1919)
Les Parapluies, c. 1881–5
Oil on canvas, 182 x 116 cm
This painting is one of the last of a series of large vertical modern-life subjects. Renoir worked on it twice, with a four-year gap in between. The umbrellas and background all belong to the second stage of its execution. Renoir, whose interest in Japanese art, was highly qualified, may nevertheless have been aware of Hokusai's useful compositional device of umbrellas in the rain.

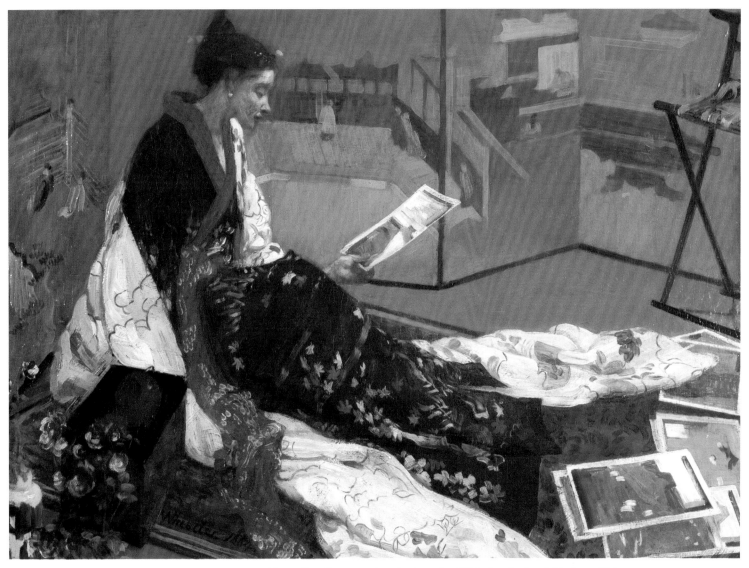

James McNeill Whistler

Caprice in Purple and Gold, No 2: The Golden Screen, **1864**
Oil on panel, 50.6 x 69.2 cm
Dressed in a kimono, seated on the floor, a model stares at the Japanese print in her hand. It is one of what appears to be a pile of landscape prints by Hiroshige. In the background is a screen, probably from the Tosa school, whose literary theme has been taken from the *Tales of Gengi.*

his earliest Japanese-inspired works, Whistler depicted his beautiful Irish mistress Jo Hiffernan as a model, notably in *Symphony in White, No. 2: The Little White Girl* (1864). She stands, clad in a voluminous white dress, her left arm leaning on a white marble mantelpiece with a pier glass, while her right hand hangs by her side holding a colourful Japanese fan. She gazes at a blue and white jar, a red lacquer bowl and some colourful azaleas, all reflected in the mirror, as is her face and some paintings with the characteristic wide golden frames which Whistler loved. Inspired by this painting Swinburne wrote a poem *Before the Mirror:*
'... Deep in the gleaming glass
She sees all past things pass ...'

In *Caprice in Purple and Gold, No. 2: The Golden Screen* (1864) the same model looks at a pile of prints by Hiroshige, clad not in a white dress but a kimono, her head dramatically silhouetted against a magnificent screen. In the following year Fantin-Latour painted *The Toast* showing Whistler wearing a kimono, while a testament of Whistler's deep-seated love of blue and white porcelain is provided by his *Purple and Rose; The* Lange Leizen *of the Six Marks* (1864). As he said in his *'Ten O'Clock'* lecture (1885): 'The story of the beautiful is already complete – hewn in the marvels of the Parthenon - and embroidered, with birds, upon the fan of Hokusai at the foot of Fujiyama'.

Whistler's words marked the height of popularity of the Japanese fan in 1885. Just under a decade earlier in 1876 Godwin had warned:

Either the European market is ruining Japanese art or the Japanese have taken our artistic measure and found it wanting; perhaps there is a little of both. Take for example the common paper fan of today and compare it with some imported here ten or even eight years ago. Those are for the most part lovely in delicate colour and exquisite in drawing, but most of today's fans are impregnated with the crudeness of the European's sense of colour, and immeasurably beneath the older examples.

But the craze continued and in its fixed form the cheap paper *uchiwa* were by the 1880s made literally in millions in Japan specifically for the export market. In 1891 the combined total of folding and rigid fans exported from Japan reached the astounding total of 15,724,048!

Like the spread of karaoke bars today, curio shops selling fans soon abounded. Fans were arranged upon dado-rails, pinned to walls, and as a writer in Oscar Wilde's journal *The Woman's World* observed in 1887: 'in the hot summers that have become the fashion, (we) fan ourselves, without regard to sex or condition, with Japanese fans.' As early as 1880, when George Du Maurier advised Frank Burnand to put 'Japanese sixpenny fans here and there on the walls' for the set of his play *The Colonel* satirizing Whistler, they had become an Aesthetic cliché. By 1888 when *Punch* began a series of cartoons, 'Our Japanneries' by Lika Joko (Harry Furniss), and then the Grossmith brothers' classic description of suburban life *The Diary of a Nobody* appeared in which Carrie Pooter beautifies 'The Laurels, Upper Holloway' by tacking up a few fans, it had become, to use the slang of the day, distinctly 'old hat'.[3] But some artists still enjoyed the craze, and Phil May, the *Punch* artist whose drawings of the London streets provide perhaps the nearest English equivalent to Hokusai's pictures of the floating world in the *Manga*, had a studio which may stand for many others:

The mantelpiece is peopled with little Japanese dolls, little bronzes and brasses, and figures carved in yellow ivory. These, with a few plaster casts of arms and legs which hang on the wall, a line of Japanese prints put around the ceiling 'to try an effect', a few Japanese lanterns hanging from the roof, some Japanese lay figures in armour standing round the walls, and a few

Weedon Grossmith (1854–1919)
'He is dead too'
From *The Diary of a Nobody*, 1894
George Grossmith was a leading singer in Gilbert and Sullivan's operettas from 1877 to 1889, creating the role of Pooh Bah in *The Mikado*. With his brother Weedon, he wrote a classic commentary on Victorian lower middle-class suburban life. *The Diary of a Nobody* first appeared in *Punch* in 1892 before being published independently two years later with Weedon's illustrations. Here we see the hero Mr Pooter overcome with embarrassment as his attempt to admire a family portrait is greeted with the reply 'He is dead too – my brother'. The main interest in the drawing arises from its record of the manner in which cheap Japanese fans were placed behind the paintings in suburban homes 'to make an effect'.

sketches are about all the decoration of this long sky-lit room.

Another great popular artist on the other side of the Channel also reflected an enthusiasm for Japanese knick-knacks in his work. Jules Chéret, the poster designer who taught Toulouse-Lautrec his craft, frequently shows Japanese toys, fans, and masks in his annual seasonal posters entitled *Etrennes* – literally festive gifts.

In Tennyson's poem *The Lady of Shallot* the spell is broken when she looks out of the window at the real world, rather than observing its reflection in a mirror. So it was for the Scottish painters E.A. Hornel and George Henry. Visiting Japan from 1893 to 1894 they stayed at Nagasaki, Yokohama and Tokyo where they were disappointed by an exhibition of works by Japanese artists who had gone to study painting in Paris and Munich, and in so doing had, in Hornel's view, 'learned their painting but lost their art!' For Henry the experience was a mixed blessing. A year later, suffering from a bad case of post-Japanese depression, he wrote to Hornel: 'I have so little heart for these d——d Japanese pictures that I am seriously thinking of chucking the whole thing up. I have not a bloody cent.' He also later recalled his visit to Japan in less than enthusiastic terms:

I painted landscapes there, both oils and watercolour, and figures, from the geishas, the most highly refined and educated women in Japan; and in both the same national feeling was visible, the absence of any strong contrast of colour. I had all my life been trying for strong colour, tartan landscape and vivid contrast.

In *The Dancing Geisha*, Hornel displays a very non-Japanese use of rich pigment.

The English painter Frank Dillon visited Japan in 1875 and on his return painted several interiors. Crowded with correct Japanese props including samisen, scrolls and sword racks (which he left to the Victoria and Albert Museum), they are obviously painstaking recreations of Japanese rooms, rather than depictions of the real thing.

Mortimer Menpes, Whistler's Australian assistant and biographer, also visited Japan in 1887 for eight months to learn 'all the methods of Japanese art'. On his return he exhibited 137 oils and forty prints he had created in Japan, in the Dowdeswell Galleries, in London's New Bond Street. The exhibition was visited by Oscar Wilde who, as always sharply aware of the pulse of fashion, posed the problem of the overkill effect of Japanese art succinctly in *The Decay of Lying* published in January, 1889:

... do you really imagine that the Japanese people, as they are presented to us in art, have any existence? If you do, you have never understood Japanese art at all. The Japanese people are the deliberate, self-conscious

Left above: **James McNeill Whistler** *Purple and Rose: The* **Lange Leizen** *of the Six Marks,* **1864 Oil on canvas, 92 x 61.5 cm In what is clearly the interior of a shop, a seated western girl, brush in hand, gazes intently at the beautiful jar resting in her lap. The '***Lange Leizen** of the Six Marks'* **refers to the decorative figures that form the maker's marks which appear on rare pieces of blue and white porcelain.**

Left below: **Edward Atkinson Hornel (1864–1933)** *Dancing Geisha Girls,* **1894 Oil on canvas**

Left: Henri de Toulouse Lautrec
Divan Japonais, **1893**
Lithograph, 78.8 x 59.5 cm
In 1893 the Café du Divan Japonais was transformed with dramatic Japanese lanterns and bamboo furniture and Lautrec was asked to design a new poster advertising its attractions. This provided him with an exciting opportunity to try out some Japanese compositional principles of dramatic cropping. The main figure is the dancer Jane Avril in an austere black dress, with the music critic Edouard Dujardin behind her. On the stage is the headless figure of the performer who can only be recognized as the singer Yvette Guilbert by her famous black gloves.

Opposite: Aubrey Beardsley (1872–1898)
The Black Cape, **1893**
From *Salomé*, 1894
The drawing has no connection with the play and is a caricature of the stylized fashions of the period.

creation of several individual artists. .... In fact, the whole of Japan is a pure invention. There is no such country, there is no such people. One of our most charming painters went recently to the Land of the Chrysanthemum in the foolish hope of seeing the Japanese. All he saw, all he had the chance of painting, were a few lanterns and some fans. He was quite unable to discover the inhabitants, as his delightful exhibition at Messrs Dowdeswells Gallery showed only too well. He did not know that the Japanese people are, as I have said, simply a mode of style, an exquisite fancy of art. And so, if you desire to see a Japanese effect, you will not behave like a tourist and go to Tokyo. On the contrary, you will stay at home and steep yourself in the work of certain Japanese artists and then, when you have absorbed the spirit of their style, and caught their imaginative manner of vision, you will go some afternoon and sit in the Park or stroll down Piccadilly, and if you cannot see an absolutely Japanese effect there, you will not see it anywhere.

As was so often the case, Wilde was at his most profound when most paradoxical, and it is impossible not to feel sorry for poor Menpes, who was also abused by Whistler, enraged by his disciple visiting Japan without his permission. Undeterred, Menpes continued to be a passionate advocate of Japanese decoration, and his home in a Mackmurdo house at 25 Cadogan Gardens, London was described as a 'dream of Oriental beauty' with themed peony, camellia and chrysanthemum rooms. On a second visit to Japan in 1896 he: 'gathered together the best artists and craftsmen that I could command ... ceiling, doors, wallcoverings and windows were finished completely ... by Japanese craftsmen. In two hundred packing cases their work was carried to London.' But in a few short years even Menpes had tired of the Japanese style and he sold the house in 1900, retiring to the sylvan delights of a Kentish fruit farm.

Yet Japanese art still had a powerful appeal for young artists. In 1892 Aubrey Beardsley wrote to his old headmaster, telling him excitedly about his discovery of 'a new style and method of work which is founded on Japanese art'. This method shows itself in his highly individual adaptation of a bold silhouette style and the flowing line, so fundamental an aspect of Art Nouveau, which can be seen at its most extreme in the dramatic *Black Cape*. Wilde's observation that the dress of fashionable women seen in a stroll down Piccadilly was absolutely Japanese in effect is vindicated by Beardsley's powerful image.

In Paris, Toulouse-Lautrec remained so enamoured of Japanese prints that he was prepared to exchange one of his own works for a coveted print, and sent to Japan for special inks and brushes. His favoured subject-matter – popular entertainers, dancers and dance halls, bars and restaurants, prostitutes and their activities – has many affinities with the subjects portrayed in Japanese prints. There are obvious parallels between Lautrec's stay in the brothels of Montmartre and Utamaro's in the 'Houses of Pleasure' in the Yoshiwara. The imaginative and total integration of image and lettering into one decorative and instructive whole in his posters also owes much to Japanese prototypes. His poster *Divan Japonais* advertised a café transformed in 1893 by lanterns and bamboo furniture into a Japanese setting. In the background the singer's head is cut off by the edge of the composition, in the manner of a Japanese print.

But the most far-reaching effect of the love of Japanese art was to be sparked off by a visit by the young Frank Lloyd Wright in 1893 to the Chicago World Colombian Exposition which contained a large Japanese display. This experience began his life-long love of the serenity of the arts of Japan, which led to the creation of some of the most dynamic and important buildings of the twentieth century.

The painter must also make of the wall upon which his work hung, the room containing it, the whole house, a Harmony, a Symphony, an Arrangement, as perfect as the picture or print which became a part of it.

E. R. AND J. PENNELL, *THE WHISTLER JOURNAL*, 1921

Opposite: James McNeill Whistler
The Peacock Room doors, 1876
Whistler created the peacocks on these shutters for the Dining Room of the shipping magnate F.R. Leyland. Their sweeping trains swirl in cascades of golden feathers silhouetted against a background of gold leaf when the shutters are folded at night. However, they were not part of the original commission, and Leyland wrote: 'The peacocks you have put on the back of the shutters may possibly be worth (as pictures) the £1,200 you charge for them but ... I certainly do not require them and I can only suggest that you take them away and let new shutters be put up in their place' ... But it was too late, for patron, painter and peacocks, since by then the battle of the Peacock Room had begun.

Right: Plate from *Keramic Art of Japan*, 1875
This book, by G. A. Ashley and J. L. Bowes, was an important source of inspiration for the Peacock Room.

In gorgeous plumage, azure, gold and green,
They trample the pale flowers, and their shrill cry
Troubles the garden's quiet tranquillity!
Proud birds of Beauty, splendid and serene,
Spreading their brilliant fans, screen after screen
Of burnished sapphire, gemmed with mimic suns
– Strange magic eyes that, so the legend runs
Will bring misfortune to this fair demesne ...

OLIVE CUSTANCE (LADY ALFRED DOUGLAS), *PEACOCKS: A MOOD*

James McNeill Whistler
Symphony in Flesh Colour and Pink: Mrs Leyland, **1871–4**
Oil on canvas, 207.9 x 92 cm
This is one of the most striking of all Whistler's early portraits of women. Mrs Leyland stands with her back to the spectator, a pose reminiscent of the work of Antoine Watteau who loved to portray the backs of women's necks. Whistler himself designed the elegant dress of pink and white chiffon with darker pink rosettes which set off Mrs Leyland's reddish hair. The decorative effect is heightened by the sprays of almond blossom and the patterned matting.

The Peacock Room was one of the greatest works of art produced in the Aesthetic style. It was initially conceived by the discerning patron F.R. Leyland as a showcase for Whistler's Japanese fantasy, a painting entitled *Rose and Silver: The Princess from the Land of Porcelain*. As in a fairy story the Princess would take her place in Leyland's great collection of porcelain. But this conception was to be transformed by the arrogant genius of Whistler into one of the most dazzlingly beautiful and innovative decorative schemes of all time. In the process both patron and artist were to quarrel and the architect of the room became insane and died in tragic circumstances. The ill luck proverbially associated with the peacock triumphed.

Nicknamed the 'Liverpool Medici' by Rossetti, who first introduced him to Whistler, F.R. Leyland was a self-made millionaire who had risen from office boy to wealthy shipowner and for a time became President of the National Telephone Company of England. Nineteenth-century Liverpool had a tradition of culturally enlightened merchant princes, a role which fitted Leyland to perfection, for he was both an accomplished amateur pianist, and an art lover with a discriminating eye both for Old Masters and contemporary artists.

Even before Leyland acquired his London home he commissioned Whistler to paint his portrait and the portraits of his wife and four children, generously paying in advance. Not all the commissions were fulfilled, but the portrait of Leyland, *Arrangement in Black:F.R. Leyland*, the first full-length male portrait Whistler painted, is a successful variation on Velasquez, whom Whistler admired.

Whistler became a frequent visitor to Leyland's home at Speke Hall, near Liverpool and a close, indeed intimate, friend of Mrs Leyland. In her portrait *Symphony in Flesh Colour and Pink: Mrs Leyland*, she stands, tall, elegant, her back to the viewer, her hands clasped behind her, her dress, designed by Whistler, sprinkled with rosettes which harmonize with the pink almond blossom and the patterned matting against the rose-hued wall.

For Leyland, with wealth, came the ambition to live the life of a Venetian merchant prince in London. He needed an appropriate setting to display the collections he had amassed of Old Masters and contemporary art using the advice of Murray Marks, the most cultivated dealer of the day. Leyland owned no less than nine works attributed to Botticelli, nine paintings by Rossetti, seven by Burne-Jones, and three by Albert Moore. As a setting for them he bought a London house, known as the Mansion, situated at 49, Prince's Gate.

Leyland commissioned Norman Shaw to re-model the house incorporating a famous gilded late eighteenth-century staircase which had been salvaged from Northumberland House, the palatial London home of the Percy family, before its demolition. Whistler was asked to paint a number of 'panels imitating aventurine lacquer, decorated with delicate sprigs of pale rose and white flowers in the Japanese taste' to fit near the staircase and harmonize with it. Whistler's friend Alan Cole saw them on 24 March, 1876 and noted: 'To Leyland's house to see Whistler's colouring of the hall – very delicate cocoa colour and gold – successful'[1]. These discreet decorations were odd harbingers of what was later to spring from his brush.

The interiors of the house were entrusted to Thomas Jeckyll (1827–81), the innovative 'Japanese' designer of cast-iron sunflowers, who had turned his attention to domestic work and recently designed a new wing for the house at 1, Holland Park of the well-known Aesthetic collector, Alexander Ionides, for which Jeckyll

Above and left: Dining Room, Study and Drawing Room in Leyland's house These photographs, which were taken by Henry Bedford Lemare on the occasion of the sale of the house and its contents after Leyland's death in 1892, reveal that the unusual pendant light fittings, designed by Thomas Jeckyll, were not confined solely to the Peacock Room, but were also installed in the Study and the Drawing Room. Note the sunflower firedogs (also designed by Jeckyll) in the fireplace.

had devised a billiards room, sitting room, bedroom and servants' hall, all in the 'Anglo-Japanese' manner. But for Leyland's home, Jeckyll turned for inspiration to a wider variety of sources, and in the Drawing Room and Dining Room introduced a fan-vaulted ceiling based on the Tudor ceiling of the Watching Chamber at Hampton Court Palace with distinctive octagonal light fittings reminiscent of Chinese lanterns. Originally lit by gas, by 1892 electric light bulbs illuminated the Old Masters in the Study (a Crivelli and Signorelli) and the Pre-Raphaelite paintings in the Drawing Room.

Photographs taken by Henry Bedford Lemare shortly after Leyland's death in 1892 and before the dispersal of the collection, provide glimpses not only of the Dining Room (subsequently known as the Peacock Room) but also of the Study and Drawing Room. They reveal that the pendant light fittings were not unique to the Peacock Room but used throughout the house.

The Study, like the Peacock Room, was panelled in Spanish leather, and the Drawing Room was hung with curtains of cherry red Genoa velvet on cloth of gold. Years later, Murray Marks claimed to be responsible for the Peacock Room being lined with the Spanish leather which he had suggested (and also purchased). He obtained the idea from Cyril Flower, later Lord Battersea, the sitter for one of Sandys's most Aesthetic portraits, who also had a Spanish leather-lined room to set off his blue and white porcelain.

The screen in the Drawing Room, designed by Norman Shaw, was suggested by the rood-loft of the cathedral at Bar-le-Duc, sold by Murray Marks to the Victoria and Albert Museum, where it still stands. The painting over the Venetian commode is Burne-Jones's *Merlin and Nimuë* painted for Leyland between 1873 and 1876. Leyland delighted in Burne-Jones's work and it is intriguing, in view of later events, to surmise whether he was ever aware of a watercolour in which Burne-Jones uses a single fairytale figure posed as a centrepiece in a collection of blue and white porcelain. Entitled *Cinderella* and painted in 1863, you can only tell that she is Cinderella by the patch on her apron, otherwise she too looks every inch a princess, bewailing the fact that she has to do the dusting!

The Rossettis in the Drawing Room are, from left to right, *Monna Rosa, Mnemosyne, The Blessed Damozel, Proserpine, Veronica Veronese* and *Lady Lillith*, the fruits of Leyland's long-term patronage of the artist. This was by no means an easy relationship, as Rossetti often became bored with specific commissions and never tired of playing one patron off against another. He was frequently asked to paint replicas of particularly spectacular 'stunners' – the vivid Pre-

Opposite: Edward Burne-Jones
Cinderella, 1863
Gouache, 67 x 31.5 cm
When exhibited in 1864 at the Old Watercolour Society, this charming picture was praised by the Pre-Raphaelite critic F. G. Stephens for its intense colour. One speculates whether Cinderella is holding her head because she has lost her shoe or at the thought of washing all the blue and white plates on the dresser.

Right: James McNeill Whistler
Rose and Silver: The Princess from the Land of Porcelain,
1864
Oil on canvas, 201 x 117.3 cm
When first exhibited at the Paris Salon in 1865, it bore the title *La Princesse du Pays de la Porcelaine*.

Raphaelite slang for beautiful models – a task
which he often left largely to his devoted studio
assistant Treffry Dunn. Leyland was also a major
patron of Albert Moore whose three paintings
had pride of place at the top of the stairs.

In 1865 the Paris Salon
exhibited Whistler's *Rose and Silver: The
Princess from the Land of Porcelain*, a work
which shows his increasing knowledge of
Japanese art, for this portrait of Christine
Spartali, daughter of the Greek Consul, is an
interpretation of woodcuts by Koryusai with a
geisha in long elegant robes. Leyland
subsequently acquired the painting, and
wished it to star as the centrepiece in a

sumptuous arrangement of his collection of blue and white porcelain.
By so doing the Princess would become truly what her title implied.

Leyland's collection of porcelain had largely been
formed by Murray Marks, who was a key figure of the Aesthetic
Movement. His business card claimed to be the result of a
collaboration between Whistler, who painted the pot and peacock's
feather, Rossetti, who designed the decorative background for the card,
and William Morris who designed the typography. Both Marks and
his rivals, the Duveen brothers, vied for the custom of a small group of
committed collectors who had been infected with a passion for blue and
white by the enthusiasm of Whistler and Rossetti. Amongst their
number were George Salting, F.R. Leyland and the distinguished surgeon
Sir Henry Thompson.

At a recherché supper to launch a catalogue of Sir
Henry Thompson's collection, with a text by Murray Marks and plates
by Whistler, an eminent critic of the day was quite carried away by the
occasion. 'He saw nothing, he could converse about nothing, but this
translucent "Blue". "Look at that!" he exclaimed, as a servitor
approached, carrying with extreme care, as he had a right to do, a
magnificent dish of the true brand. "Could France, could England
produce anything like it? Observe that exquisite pink on that lovely
blue!" The "exquisite pink" was pickled salmon.'

While Leyland did not indulge in such maudlin
sentiments, he did look forward with great excitement to the
realization of his dream of uniting Whistler's *Princess* with his
porcelain in an imaginative and inspired setting, the blue and white
forming a happy colour contrast with the sumptuous red leather

**Morris, Whistler and
Rossetti
Business card**
This trade card for the
famous dealer Murray Marks
is a unique collaboration
between Whistler who
painted the porcelain,
Rossetti who devised the
decorative Japanese
background and Morris who
designed the typography.

Frederick Sandys (1829–1904)
Lord Battersea, **1872**
Oil on canvas, 32.7 x 50.4 cm
Cyril Flower, Lord Battersea
(1843–1907) had extreme
Aesthetic tastes and was the
first to think of setting off
his collection of blue and
white porcelain in a room
lined with Spanish leather.
A friend and patron of
Simeon Solomon, Lord
Battersea bought *The Golden*
Stairs **from Burne-Jones.**
This portrait of him by
Frederick Sandys reveals the
artist's obsessive interest in
depicting hair, which he
drew and painted with
consummate skill.

already used elsewhere in the house. In April 1876, Mrs Leyland passed on to Whistler a fateful enquiry: 'Jeckyll writes what colour to do the doors and windows in the dining room ... I wish you would give him your ideas.'[2]

At last the *Princess* was hauled into position, the blue and white arranged on the shelves, and Whistler was asked to comment on the effect by Leyland. Whistler felt that the red flowers on the leather, which were painted not embossed, 'killed' the tones in his painting. Leyland gave permission for the flowers to be painted yellow and gold, and for the red border of the rug to be trimmed. Whistler was still not completely satisfied, and Leyland agreed to him adorning the wainscotting and cornice with a 'wave pattern'. In tones as gentle as a turtle dove Whistler wrote to Leyland:

Your walls are finished – they are to receive their last coat of varnish tomorrow – (indeed the men promised to do part this afternoon); and on Friday you can put up the pots [Leyland's porcelain]. The blue which I tried as an experiment was quite injurious to the tone of the leather – and so I have carefully erased all trace of it – retouching the small yellow flowers wherever required – leaving the whole work perfect and complete. The wave pattern above and below – on the green gold – will alone be painted in blue – and this I shall come and do on Friday – without interfering with the pots or the leather ... I just painted it as I went on, without design or sketch, it just grew as I painted.

The last words of this letter strike an ominous note in view of what was to follow. But fate intervened with business problems for Leyland. His fleet, the Leyland Line, was entering into the Atlantic trade, and he had to leave London to stay in Liverpool during the summer months of 1876, to supervise events. He left assuming the decoration of the room to be virtually completed. But Whistler, in his patron's absence, was inspired to a far more radical treatment of the room. He covered the ceiling with Dutch metal, imitation gold leaf, over which he painted a lush pattern based on peacock feathers. He gilded the walnut shelves and embellished the interior of the four wooden shutters with four gorgeous peacocks with vast sweeping trains derived from Japanese sources. As he wrote to the Pennells:

I just painted as I went on – without sketch or design – it grew as I painted. And towards the end I reached such a point of perfection – putting in every touch with such freedom – that when I came round to the corner where I had started, why, I had to paint part of it over again, or the difference would have been too marked. And the harmony in blue and gold developing, you know, I forgot everything in my joy of it![3]

At this point it is perhaps pertinent to ask *why*

Above, right and opposite: James McNeill Whistler *The Peacock Room, 1876–7* The primary source for the Peacock Wall is thought to be a Japanese print of 1804 entitled *Utamaro Painting a Ho-Ho Bird in One of the Green Houses.* It seems probable that Whistler painted the panel after his first quarrel with Leyland, when he realized that there was no chance of the wall being occupied by his *White Symphony: Three Girls*, as originally conceived.

Whistler should have selected the peacock as the dominant component in his decorative scheme for the room. Peacocks in both Japanese and western art are among the most painted of birds. The ancient belief that the peacock's flesh never decayed led to it becoming a Christian symbol both of immortality and Christ's resurrection, while in classical legend it is the attribute of Juno and the personification of pride – symbolism which Whistler would have appreciated.

The Pre-Raphaelites, attracted by its sonorous colours, often used it in paintings, Rossetti standing a large peacock next to King David in his triptych in Llandaff Cathedral. It is also amusing to recall that Rossetti kept peacocks in the back garden of his home in Cheyne Walk that screamed so loudly that a clause was inserted into the tenancy prohibiting keeping the birds. Burne-Jones used the motif in several frescoes, while a fine peacock appears in Arthur Hughes's painting *Silver and Gold*. Leighton, in the early 1860s, painted two works, *Girl Feeding Peacocks* and *Odalisque* (1862), that are amongst

the most interesting early examples of Aesthetic taste. Of *Odalisque* *The Times's* critic remarked: 'As a consummate illustration of the *dolce far niente* - an idyll for lotus eaters, the work leaves nothing to be desired'. The model is shown holding a fan of peacock feathers, while two butterflies hover towards the left, a Whistlerian parallel which needs no emphasis. Ceramic peacocks abounded, Minton producing a life-sized model of one in 1876 and William De Morgan returning again and again to the theme in his tile designs and bowls. Later, in 1878, Morris used the bird in one of the finest of his woven-wool tissues *Peacock and Dragon* and Walter Crane was to use the theme in the 1889 wallpaper *Peacock Garden*. But perhaps the most famous of all artifacts using the concept is Liberty's printed fabric *Peacock Feathers* designed by Arthur Silver in 1884. It was not only one of the most popular designs of its period, but it remains in production today, and has indeed become an instantly recognizable symbol for the firm.

Although Whistler did not know all these depictions

Right above: Arthur Silver
(1852-96)
Peacock Feathers, 1884
Roller-printed cotton
designed for Liberty's.

Right below: Walter Crane
(1845–1915)
Peacock Garden, 1889
Wallpaper block-printed by
Jeffrey & Co.

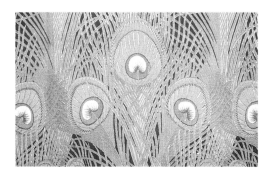

of the bird, he would certainly have been aware of two recent decorative room interiors using the peacock theme extensively. The earlier, dating from 1869, is the Dutch kitchen or Grillroom at South Kensington – now known as the Poynter room after its designer Sir Edward Poynter – where a frieze of peacocks surmounts the tiles which include two large panels above the grill depicting the bird. Even more important as a precursor was the fresco created by Whistler's friend Albert Moore for Frederick Lehmann's house in Berkeley Square in 1872. Surviving sketches in the Victoria and Albert Museum reveal that this room must have been a striking interior, although Moore's peacocks modestly trail their trains rather than flaunting them as do Whistler's. It is also worth pointing out E.W. Godwin's use of the peacock theme in the wall decorations of Dromore Castle in Ireland in 1867 and even more pertinently Godwin's block printed wallpaper *Peacock*, adapted directly from one of the Japanese *mon* studied with such delight by Godwin and Burges. Significantly this paper was originally printed on a bright *blue* ground which may have echoed in Whistler's memory, although it alarmed Godwin's landlady when he used it in his London lodgings in the early 1870s. This may have led Jeffrey & Co to subsequently produce it in the safer and more commercially successful 'Aesthetic green'.

While the painting of the Peacock Room progressed, artistic circles in London buzzed with stories about Whistler and his methods. It was said that he worked suspended from the ceiling in a hammock, blue paint on his hands, hair covered with flakes of gold leaf, using a brush attached to a fishing rod to touch spots too high to reach from a ladder.

Once it was finished, Whistler, a brilliant publicist and years ahead of his time in the manipulation of the media, held press conferences in the completed room. He even issued a pamphlet, privately printed for him by Thomas Way, copies of which were distributed to the public in several London shops, particularly Liberty's, and were intended to welcome people to Leyland's house.

In February 1877 Whistler held a press conference for critics. Amongst the high society guests who viewed the room were the Princess Louise and the Marquis of Westminster, Whistler's friend Alan Cole and his father, the redoubtable figure of Sir Henry Cole, the first Director of the South Kensington Museum, now the Victoria and Albert Museum. Alan Cole noted in his diary: 'Jimmy much disgusted at my father's telling him that, in taking so much pains over his work, and in the minuteness of his etched work, he really was like Mulready who was equally scrupulous' – analogous to telling Henry

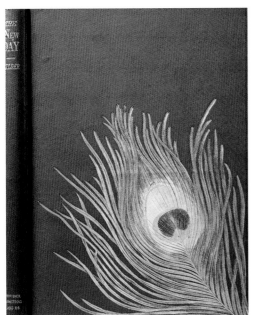

Moore that his work was like that of George Frederick Watts.

It says much for Henry Cole's continuing ability in old age to recognize outstanding talent even when it was controversial, that some years earlier in 1872, he had commissioned Whistler to create a mosaic called by Whistler *The Gold Girl* for the museum. Although the project was never realized, a study with a colour scheme of blue and gold may relate to it. A few years later, just before he died, Sir Henry the great Victorian administrator, posed for one and a half hours to Whistler for a portrait, although he said caustically that Whistler 'had merely touched the light on my shoes'.

Early in September 1876, elated with the progress of the decorations, Whistler wrote to Leyland:

Mon cher Baron – *Je suis content de moi!* The dining room is really alive with beauty – brilliant and gorgeous while at the same time delicate and refined to the last degree. I have *at last* managed to carry out thoroughly the plan of decoration I have formed – and I assure you, you can have no more idea of the ensemble in its perfection, gathered from what you last saw on the walls, than you could have of a complete opera, judging from a three finger exercise! – *Voila!* But don't come up yet – I have not yet quite done – and you mustn't see it till the last touch is on.[4]

Alas! a rude awakening awaited Whistler. Although the exact chronological sequence of events remains somewhat obscure, it is all too easy to imagine the row that ensued between artist and patron when at last Leyland saw the room. Leyland did *not* find it alive with beauty, and understandably was irate at the complete reversal of his own preferred colour scheme, and the resultant disappearance of the red Spanish leather (which had, after all, cost £1,000) under the brilliant blue and gold of Whistler's decorations. But what really rankled was Whistler's arrogance in inviting the general public into his home without asking permission. The whole affair was undoubtedly exacerbated even more by Whistler's growing intimacy with Mrs Leyland, to whom the artist had written in December 1876 about the Peacock Room: 'It is something quite wonderful and I am extremely proud of it. As a decoration it is thoroughly new and most gorgeous though refined. Tell Freddie that I think it will be a large sum but even then barely pays for the work'.[5]

The large sum which Whistler had in mind was 2,000 guineas. It is difficult to give an impartial account of the agreement which had begun on informal friendly terms, and had become exacerbated by misunderstandings on both sides. Initially Leyland refused to pay and suggested that Whistler should take away the doors. Later, after consulting with Rossetti, he offered Whistler the

Left above: E. W. Godwin *Peacock*, 1873
Wallpaper made by Jeffrey & Co
Whistler almost certainly saw it printed on a bright blue ground when visiting Godwin's rooms in the early 1870s.

Left below: Helena De Kay Gilder
Cover for *The New Day*, 1876
Inspired by Helena de Kay, this book of love sonnets was Richard Watson Gilder's first published work. The couple married in 1874 and in 1876 de Kay designed the binding for the book.

sum of £1,000. Whistler had already received £400 and now received £600 as 'payment in full'. Today many cannot remember the confusion in pre-metric days which often arose from the difference between pounds (twenty shillings sterling) and guineas (twenty-one shillings). As recently as the 1960s auction houses conducted sales in guineas, but in Whistler's day only tradesmen were paid in pounds, gentlemen's fees were settled in guineas. The prickly artist felt deeply insulted, accepting it with a very bad grace, replying: 'I have *enfin* received your cheque – shorn of my shillings, I perceive! – another fifty pounds off. *Bon Dieu*, what does it matter! The work alone remains the fact – so that in some future dull Vasari you may also go down to posterity like the man who paid Caravaggio in pennies.'[6]

Remarkably, Whistler was still allowed in the house and on the blank wall opposite *The Princess*, where Leyland had at one stage planned to hang Whistler's *The White Symphony: Three Girls* the artist took his revenge, although the sequence of events, and the extent to which Whistler's paintings were a sudden improvisation remains conjectural. Like a great actor he may have carefully rehearsed the apparently spontaneous 'ad lib'. It is worth recalling that in 1873 Whistler had suggested the theme of peacocks for an unrealized decorative scheme for Aubrey House, W.C. Alexander's house in Camden Hill. The Peacock Room provided the ideal opportunity to bring these ideas to fruition. He painted two magnificent peacocks, one representing the patron, under his claws a pile of silver coins, the disputed shillings, while the other bird, the artist, shrieks a proud defiance. Whistler definitely intended the two-peacock panel as a commentary on his relations with Leyland. In 1877 after he had been forbidden entry into the house he wrote to Mrs Leyland on 6 July: 'I refer you to the Cartoon opposite you at dinner, known to all London as *L'Art et L'Argent* or the Story of the Room.'[7]

The romantic liaison between them continued, provoking another furious outburst from Leyland on 17 July: 'I am told you were seen walking about with my wife at Lord's Cricket Ground. It is clear that I cannot expect from you the ordinary conduct of a gentleman. If I find you in her society again I will publicly horsewhip you.' After more exchanges of similar vehemence the correspondence came to an end on 27 July. In 1879 Frances and Frederick Leyland separated. The peacocks, traditional harbingers of bad luck, had asserted their sway.

Whistler had acknowledged Jeckyll's work on the room by writing to the monthly magazine *Academy* early in September 1876: 'If there be any quality whatever in my decoration, it is due to the

A. H. Mackmurdo
(1851–1942)
Cover for *Wren's City
Churches*, 1883
The most attenuated of all
peacocks shriek their
defiance at the edge of the
title page of this celebrated
precursor of the swooping
curves of Art Nouveau.

inspiration I may have received from the graceful proportions and
lovely lines of Mr Jeckyll's work about me.' Whistler had not
consulted Jeckyll on the full extent of the changes. The designer had
already suffered several disappointments due to circumstances
depriving him of the credit for certain of his works. He had hoped for
great acclaim for his decorative schemes for Leyland and when he saw
the obliteration of the gilded Spanish leather adorned with
pomegranates and flowers, and the defacement of his walnut panels
and shelves, it was too much for his mind. He went home, and was
found babbling of fruits and flowers and peacocks, while he feverishly
worked at gilding the floor of his bedroom. He died soon afterwards in
an asylum – an event upon which Whistler is said to have commented:
'That's the effect I have upon people'.

Whistler was always very conscious of the extent of his

James McNeill Whistler
Symphony in Blue and Pink,
c. 1870
Oil on canvas, 46.7 x 61.9 cm
This is one of the *Six Projects*
which Whistler made for a
frieze of figures
commissioned by F. R.
Leyland in 1867. These
projects, though never
completed, marked a turning
point in Whistler's career,
enabling him to synthesize
his various interests in
Japonism, classicism, and
the analogies between music
and painting into a coherent
aesthetic of his own.

own genius, and was fully aware that circumstances had combined to make him achieve not only his personal triumph of interior decoration, but a masterpiece of international importance. He wrote to his mother from Venice in the spring of 1880:

> I went to a grand high mass in St Mark's and very swell it was – but do you know I couldn't help feeling that the Peacock Room is more beautiful in its effect! – and certainly the glory and delicacy of the ceiling is far more complete than the decorations of the golden domes make them. That was a pleasant frame of mind to be in you must acknowledge – and I am sure you are not surprised at it!

The room's later influence was to be widespread, taking forms as diverse as the shrieking defiance of the two birds on the edge of A.H. Mackmurdo's famous proto Art Nouveau design for his book *Wren's City Churches* of 1883, the work of Aubrey Beardsley, and Endell's Art Nouveau façade of 1897 for an atelier in Vienna.

Deprived of his most generous patron, Whistler admitted that he had 'never had any luck' after the Peacock Room, ultimately holding Leyland responsible for his bankruptcy in 1879 and the enforced sale of his new home, the White House, Chelsea. According to Pennell, when Leyland and the committee of creditors made an official inspection of the White House in 1879, they were confronted by three satirical paintings ridiculing Leyland's love of money and addiction to frilled shirts, one portraying him as a hideous peacock, playing the piano and sitting on the White House, entitled *Gold Scab: An Arrangement in Filthy Lucre.*

It is a tragic irony that such an enlightened patron should be largely remembered in the unflattering roles of curmudgeonly

Right: James McNeill Whistler
Arrangement in Black: F. R. Leyland, **1874**
Oil on canvas, 191.5 x 90.7 cm
This painting was started at Leyland's home, Speke Hall, near Liverpool in August, 1870 and described by the sitter as 'my own martyrdom'.

Philistine and cuckold devised for him by Whistler. Yet Leyland was far from being the avaricious, grasping 'Eruption in Filthy Lucre' portrayed by Whistler after their dispute, but was a man of great refinement. Despite the controversy and personal hurt it is to his eternal credit that Leyland kept the room as Whistler left it, and made no attempt to erase the visual satire from his walls. He continued filling the shelves with porcelain until his death aged sixty in 1892. It is worth recalling that their relationship was not always so acrimonious, and indeed Whistler owed Leyland, who was a keen amateur musician, a considerable intellectual debt for the general title given to his series of paintings, the Nocturnes, as he acknowledged in a letter: 'I can't thank you too much for the name nocturne as a title for my moonlights. You have no idea what an irritation it proves to the critics and constant pleasure to me – besides it is really charming and does so poetically say all I want to say and *no more* than I wish.'[8]

Anticipating Monet and Pissarro, Whistler was one of the first artists to think in serial terms of motifs and the whole question of his choice of musical titles for his paintings is an extremely intriguing one. As early as 1863 when his *White Girl* was exhibited at the Salon des Refusés in Paris, the critic Paul Mantz had described it as *'la symphonie du blanc'*. Whistler's friend Swinburne, seeing the painting on a visit to the artist's studio, complained that a critic could not capture the qualities of such a painting, and declaring that a musician or a poet could do it better judgement, wrote a rather fine poem *Before the Mirror (Verses Written Under a Picture)* which Whistler admired and pasted on to the frame. Later Swinburne praised some paintings by Whistler's friend Albert Moore by stating that in them: 'The melody of colour, the symphony of form is complete', and then analyzed three paintings from the *Six Projects* which he had seen in Whistler's studio. Musical analogies again abound, the pictures are themselves 'instruments', their 'main strings' strike 'varying chords of blue and white, not without interludes of the bright and tender tones of floral purple or red'. In two of the 'arrangements' the sea sets the dominant note, while the human figures sustain 'the symphony or (if you will) the antiphony'.[9]

These recurring analogies may have led Whistler to the decision to give the first of his paintings a musical name, the *Symphony in White, No 3* of 1867, which has its title printed prominently at the bottom left of the canvas. It was not however until the 1870s that Whistler began to elaborate a system of musical terms as nomenclature. In doing so he may also have recalled that Gautier, whom he read closely, had written a poem entitled *Symphonie en Blanc Majeur*, and may also have known Murger's novel *La Vie de Bohème* in which

Left above: James McNeill Whistler
Nocturne: Blue and Silver: Chelsea, **1871**
Oil on wood, 50.2 x 60.8 cm
The first of the 'Nocturnes'. In a letter Whistler's mother recalled watching it being painted: 'I hung over his magic touches till the bright moon faced us from his window and I exclaimed "Oh Jamie dear it is yet light enough for you to see to make this a moonlight picture of the Thames."'

Left centre: James McNeill Whistler
Nocturne: Blue and Gold: Southampton Water, **1872**
Oil on canvas, 50.5 x 76.3 cm
One of the first two Nocturnes to be exhibited. After it was shown at the Dudley Gallery in 1872, Whistler wrote to Leyland expressing this thanks for the title 'Nocturne' and reporting that the pictures were 'a great success'.

Left below: James McNeill Whistler
Nocturne: Blue and Silver: Cremorne Lights, **1872**
Oil on canvas, 50.2 x 74.3 cm
The lights and frequent firework displays of the pleasure gardens at Cremorne attracted Whistler like a moth. Rowed by his followers the Greaves brothers, he would drift near the gardens from twilight to dawn. Walter Greaves drew a series of sketches of Whistler at Cremorne enjoying the Gardens which he celebrates in this Nocturne and, more famously, in the *Falling Rocket*.

one of the characters composes a *Symphonie sur L'influence du Bleu dans les Arts*. It was however left to Walter Pater in 1877 to write the most celebrated passage on the relationship between painting and music when he expressed his belief that 'all art continually aspires to the condition of music'.[10]

Although we do not know to what extent Whistler was aware of these intellectual concepts, we do know that he was not himself musical. Yet prompted initially by Leyland's suggestion, he evolved a whole series of musical terms as titles for his works, adding 'Arrangements', 'Harmonies', 'Notes' and 'Variations', to 'Symphonies' and 'Nocturnes'. Such titles, like Swinburne and Pater's words, demonstrate the Aesthetic belief in synaesthesia, the interrelationship of the arts, a conviction that all artistic mediums have common areas of impact and harmonic unity. They also point the way to abstraction.

While Leyland may be given the credit of initially thinking of the title 'Nocturne' for these hauntingly beautiful paintings, the motif of the Thames as a pictorial theme, may, like the Aesthetic Movement itself, owe something to the initial inspiration of Gautier, who in 1852 described the river as: 'the main thoroughfare of London ... the moving panorama which ceaselessly occurs is something so novel and grand that one cannot tear oneself away from it'. Certainly Whistler, Gautier's disciple, passed long hours contemplating the river either from his Chelsea window or skimming along the Thames at twilight in a skiff rowed by the follower Walter Greaves, who himself painted haunting if somewhat naive Nocturnes, and who once observed: 'To Mr Whistler a boat was always a tone, to us it was always a boat'.

For Whistler the final word came some years later in his *'Ten o'clock'* lecture given in 1885, when of his Nocturnes he said memorably:

And when the evening mist clothes the riverside with poetry, as with a veil, and the poor buildings lose themselves in the dim sky, and the tall chimneys become campanile, and the warehouses are palaces in the night, and the whole city hangs in the heavens, and fairy land is before us – then the wayfarer hastens home; the working man and the cultured one, the wise man and the one of pleasure, cease to understand, as they have ceased to see, and Nature, who, for once, has sung in tune, sings her exquisite song to the artist alone, her son and master – her son in that he loves her, her master in that he knows her.

Although after 1877 Whistler was never to see his masterpiece, the Peacock Room, again, he had not yet finished with

James McNeill Whistler and
E. W. Godwin
Butterfly Cabinet, 1877–8
This cabinet was designed
by E. W. Godwin as the
central feature of the
William Watt stand at the
Universal Exhibition, Paris
in 1878. It was made by
William Watt in bright
mahogany with painted
decorations of butterflies
and Japanese cloud motifs in
yellow and gold by Whistler.

the peacock as a decorative theme. It made a spectacular reappearance in the room on which he collaborated with Godwin at the 1878 Paris International Exhibition. This was a stand for the furniture maker, William Watt, entitled by Whistler *A Harmony in Yellow and Gold*, although decried by one critic as 'an agony in yellow', and another as the 'Primrose Room'. One American visitor vividly described the effect: 'yellow on yellow, gold on gold, everywhere. The peacock reappears, the eyes and the breast feathers of him, but whereas in Prince's Gate it was always blue on gold, or gold on blue, here the feather is all gold, boldly and softly laid on a gold-tinted wall ... The feet to the table legs are tipped with brass, and rest on a yellowish-brown velvet rug. Chairs and sofas are covered with yellow, pure rich yellow velvet, darker in shade than the yellow of the wall, and edged with yellow fringe.'[11]

The originality of 'The Butterfly Suite', the major feature of the stand, can be visualized from the surviving central cabinet, originally designed as a fireplace of bright mahogany with a painted decoration of Japanese cloud motifs and butterflies in shades of yellow and gold. The lower part was immediately converted from a fireplace to a cupboard with doors painted by Whistler, the form in which it survives today.

Confrontation, the adrenaline of a row, seems to have been a necessary part of Whistler's creative activities. The Peacock Room incident embodies the central tenet of his Aesthetic credo – the supremacy of the artist's opinion over that of collectors or patrons, a theme which recurs in the dispute between Whistler and Ruskin over the latter's criticism of Whistler's *Nocturne in Black and Gold*.

This dispute had its beginnings early in 1873 in Oxford, the city of dreaming spires, where the Slade Professor of Art, John Ruskin, had delivered his third lecture on Tuscan art. Always prone to digression and invective, and possibly alluding to a painting exhibited in 1872 entitled *Harmony in Grey* he said: 'I never saw anything so impudent on the walls of any exhibition in any country as last year in London. It was a daub, professing to be "a harmony in pink and white" (or some such nonsense); absolute rubbish, and which had taken about a quarter of an hour to scrawl or daub – it had no pretence to be called painting. The price asked was two hundred and fifty guineas.'

Whistler did not immediately learn of this tirade. When Ruskin returned to the attack four years later a pyrotechnic display of awesome power was to be ignited. The smouldering fireworks of the trial would burn both artist and critic.

Cheap builders are possessed with the idea that red brick, a blue pot and a fat sunflower in the window are all that is needed to be fashionably aesthetic and Queen Anne. *THE QUEEN*, JUNE 1880

James McNeill Whistler
The Artist's Studio, **1865**
Oil on millboard,
62.2 x 46.3 cm
Whistler planned, but never
completed, a large painting
of the interior of his studio
showing his models and
friends Albert Moore and
Fantin Latour. Both this
preliminary study and one
surviving in Chicago omit
the friends. The seated
model is Jo Hiffernan,
Whistler's mistress. On the
left Whistler's porcelain
collection shimmers in the
dusk.

The atmosphere in Albert Moore's studio was described by his pupil Graham Robertson as 'dominated by cats born abruptly in coal scuttles or expired unpleasantly behind canvases'. When on one occasion, accompanied by Whistler, Robertson visited Moore:

We found him in his desolate workroom solemnly painting, surrounded by a circle of spoutless, handle-less jugs each holding a large cornucopia of brown paper.

Whistler was instantly fascinated by the jugs and could think of nothing else, but he remembered Moore's dislike of being questioned. He edged nearer to me. 'What are the jugs for?' he asked in a whisper. 'The drips,' said Albert Moore laconically. 'The drips?' whispered Whistler. 'What drips? Ask him.' Luckily at this moment a fat water drop oozed from the ceiling and fell with a plop...The roof leaked.[1]

The picturesque squalor described by Robertson is traditionally associated with lonely artists' studios in both Paris and London. But the reality in the second half of the nineteenth century was far more varied, although exact parallels between the two cities are not possible. Throughout the period Queen Victoria presided over an

empire upon which the sun never set, while France suffered traumatic reversals of fortune, the transition from the Second Empire to the bloodstained beginnings of the Third Republic. In 1867 under Napoleon III, Paris gloried in the Universal Exhibition at the Champs des Mars. Three years later, reduced to rubble after the ravages of the Franco-Prussian war, the siege of Paris and the Commune, the historic heart of the city lay in ruins. Bridges were destroyed, the Bois de Boulogne had been stripped of trees, and as Théophile Gautier wrote in 1871: 'No clatter of vehicles, no shouts of children, not even the song of a bird ... An incredible sadness invaded our souls.' The sadness was caused not just by the effects of the siege, but by the peculiar bitterness of civil war – the fact that Paris, torn in two jagged halves by the horrors of the Commune, had fought itself to a bloody standstill, leaving violent animosities between suburbs which, over a century later,

Right above: Gustave Doré (1832–1883)
Over London By Rail
From *London: A Pilgrimage,* 1872
It is salutary to recall that only a dozen stops on the District line railway from Bedford Park stood the dirty back-to-back tenements of the London slums.

Right below: M. Trautschold (fl. 1880–90)
Tower House and Queen Anne's Grove in Bedford Park, 1882
Colour lithograph, 22.5 x 35.4 cm
This is the most famous of all early views of Bedford Park showing the developer Jonathan Carr's large freestanding house in a big garden, and a number of cherry trees in blossom providing the requisite Japanese note.

are still vivid in folk memory.

In England in early June 1871 the painters Camille Pissarro and Claude Monet, then refugees from war-torn Paris, made plans 'to return to France as soon as possible ... it is only when you are abroad that you realize how beautiful, grand and hospitable France is ... Oh! how I hope everything will be all right and that Paris recovers her supremacy!'

Artistically speaking, Pissarro's hopes were soon realized, for by 1878 the city had recovered enough to stage yet another of the great exhibitions which have so influenced the artistic landscape of Paris. In the British section one of the more memorable exhibits was a Queen Anne house in the Rue des Nations, designed by Norman Shaw. Its 'red brickwork, white stone balcony, fluted pilasters, elaborately moulded panelling and ornate cornices' led the journalist George Augustus Sala to rhapsodize about 'this ghost of an old English town house of the first years of the eighteenth century ... peopled with the ghosts of Sir Roger de Coverly and Tristram Shandy'.[2] The building was a small three-storeyed structure, but it was not actually constructed of red brick! Its presence at the exhibition demonstrates the potency of Norman Shaw as one of the most charismatic architectural names of late Victorian London. Shaw was to design in the fashionable Queen Anne style, not only sumptuous studios for the stars of the Royal Academy, but also an Aesthetic suburb at Bedford Park, the prototype of the 'garden suburb'. It was built in the late 1870s, a few years after the publication in 1872 of *London: A Pilgrimage* by Gustave Doré. In it is depicted *Over London by Rail*, a nightmare vision of back-to-back housing, with tiny back yards in which washing hanging out to dry is besmirched by the soot of the trains on the gigantic viaducts. It is important to remember the proximity of the slums to the leafy lanes of the Aesthetic suburb of London.

Paris not only excelled in the field of exhibitions, it could also claim to be the cultural capital of the world, where artists and students were counted in their thousands, while in London the artistic community was numbered only in hundreds. As early as 1845, Henri Murger's novel, *Scènes de la Vie de Bohème*, charted a Bohemia in which both poverty and student life were greatly romanticized. Nearly fifty years later, failing eyesight led the cartoonist Du Maurier to turn to writing novels. In *Trilby*, serialized in 1894, he looked back nostalgically to his student years in the 1850s in the Latin Quarter when he had shared a studio with Whistler, Thomas Armstrong and Edward Poynter.

The moral attitudes of the two novels present a

fascinating contrast. In Murger's Bohemia love affairs are conducted with amoral Gallic zest while in Du Maurier's novel the heroine is the seventeen-year-old model, Trilby, whose innocence enables her to pose 'in the altogether'... 'Truly, she could be naked and unashamed'. Yet once she comes under the influence of the British students all is changed. The novel's hero Little Billee retreats in horror when he finds her posing in the nude, 'suddenly a quick thought pierced her through and through ... Could it possibly be that he was *shocked* at seeing her sitting there?'

Such a reaction reminds us that in the 1850s only married students at the Royal Academy were allowed to draw from the female nude model under the instruction of the academician J.C. Horsley (who earned the inevitable nickname of 'Clothes Horsely'). The chill winds of British morality were to blow strongly throughout these years. But exciting news of activities in the French capital was provided by the young Irishman, George Moore, in his *Confessions of a Young Man* published in 1888. Stylistically an exotic cocktail of Pater and Flaubert, it first brought some mention of Verlaine, Rimbaud, Mallarmé and the great artists of the Impressionist movement (Moore was also a friend of Manet) across the Channel.

Nowhere are comparisons between the two cities more intriguing than in the growth and variety of artistic areas and artists' studios, particularly since several important artists were active in both capitals. The range and variety of studios were remarkable. In both Paris and London a distinction must be made between the large and imposing studio homes of the successful masters of the Salon and the Royal Academy; the large public teaching studios through which generations of young aspiring students coped with their varied initiations to art; the comfortable suburban studios of successful illustrators; and the more or less picturesque garrets of the poor novice.

A view from just such a garret window is described at the beginning of Du Maurier's *Trilby*. The hero looks down on to 'the old houses opposite, some of which were being pulled down, no doubt lest they should fall of their own sweet will. In the gaps between he could see discoloured, old, cracked, dingy walls, with mysterious windows and rusty iron balconies of great antiquity – sights that set him dreaming dreams of mediaeval French love and wickedness and

BRITONS IN PARIS

FIRST ENGLISHMAN: "Where shall we go?"
SECOND ENGLISHMAN (*who does not know that 'relâche' means that the piece is taken off*): "Let's go to the Eden and see 'Relâche'!"

Opposite: Phil May
(1864–1903)
Britons in Paris, **1891**
Morrissy columns are still a
familiar feature of the
Parisian streets.

Above left: Jules Chéret
(1836–1932)
Eldorado Music Hall, **1894**

Above right: Jules Chéret
Palais de Glace, **1896**
Chéret's unique gifts were
particularly well adapted to
advertising places of popular
entertainment.

crime, bygone mysteries of Paris.'

The old mediaeval Paris was to be replaced by the wide avenues with which Baron Haussmann transformed the face of the city. The large blocks of apartments which lined both sides of the *grandes boulevards* not only created new aerial viewpoints for Impressionist painters such as Pissarro and Monet, but their walls also provided perfect sites for the new flamboyant posters of Jules Chéret.

The main difference was that Paris lived in public. Many Parisians took all their meals, even the *petit déjeuner*, in one of the innumerable cafés which had sprung up everywhere. At the hour of the aperitif half the population sat at little tables on the pavement watching the other half go by. Chéret's posters earned him the praise of Manet who described him as the 'Watteau of the streets' and of Degas, who dubbed him 'the Tiepolo of the boulevards'. Indeed, in an interview with the English critic Charles Hiatt, Chéret maintained that for him posters were not necessarily a good form of advertising but they made excellent murals! It was his great achievement to take the visual language of popular folk art, add the delicate colours of the butterfly wings he kept by him as he worked, and produce a new art form. His posters of the 1890s were aptly described by Crauzat as 'a hooray of reds, a hallelujah of yellows and a primal scream of blues'.

While Paris lived its life in the open on the boulevard,

71

James J. Tissot (1836–1902)
L'Esthetique, 1883–5
Oil on canvas, 64 x 44.5 cm
This composition was the
second in a projected series
showing the pastimes of
'foreign' women living in
Paris. The Aesthetic lady
resting on a visit to the
Louvre is pictured below a
window looking out to the
Pavillon Sully. Before her is
La Rotonde de Mars, a large
classical vase.

using its cafés like clubs or debating societies, by contrast, in London
artistic life flourished behind the closed doors of respectable suburbs.

The advent of the sweetness and light of the Queen
Anne style did not meet with universal approval. William Morris in a
lecture extolling the virtues of the Gothic Revival delivered at
Birmingham in March, 1884 criticized:

... the worthy people who started with regenerating the arts by
imitating the thirteenth century have grown older and have more or less sunk
in their ideals and are prepared to put up with the quaint bourgeois trimness
of a Queen Anne house.

Despite Morris's strictures concerning 'quaint bourgeois
trimness', the Queen Anne style had surprisingly begun to emerge in the
architectural offices of the Gothic Revival architect, G.E. Street, in
which worked Philip Webb and the young Norman Shaw. With their
contemporaries W. Eden Nesfield, E.W. Godwin, J.J. Stevenson and
J.P. Sedding they enjoyed the imaginative freedom offered by the new
architectural fashion. Its very lack of fundamental principles was its
great attraction. Young architects could add their own individual voice
to an architectural style which had relatively little to do with the
sobriety of early eighteenth-century architecture. Their works survive
throughout Britain in colleges at Cambridge, in town halls at
Leicester, Northampton, Congleton and Wakefield, in stately homes at
Denbighshire, in vicarages at Scarborough, in churches in Sloane
Street and in Board Schools up and down the land.

The originality of the new style derived from a vigorous
classical eclecticism based on Christopher Wren, with a stress on
asymmetry and flexibility leading to a mixture of red brick and white
painted sash windows, Dutch gables, steep roofs, curving bay
windows, wooden balconies enlivened with stucco and brick panels in
which putti struggled, nymphs writhed and sunflowers and lilies
bloomed exultantly.

The most notable examples of the style appear in several
artists' colonies in London in which Aesthetic credos found fertile soil.
A list of their residents reads like an honours board of Aestheticism
and it is rewarding to examine the inhabitants and their aims.

Of course not all artists were convinced 'that the reign of
good Queen Anne was culture's palmiest day' as Gilbert put it. In the
studios of Sir Lawrence Alma-Tadema, Albert Moore and Lord
Leighton, we can glimpse at what might be facetiously described as
'Everyday Life in Greece, Rome, St John's Wood and Kensington' for
their choice of classical Hellenic subjects. The very word 'aesthetics'
derives from the Greek and among the cultural features of the

Sir Lawrence Alma-Tadema (1836–1912)
Two details of a couch, 1893
Mahogany, satinwood, ebony and cedar with mother-of-pearl inlay and brass mounts
The upholstery is modern and the leather straps original. It is possible that this couch was made by Johnstone, Norman & Co in London, who made several pieces of furniture for Alma-Tadema. It is one of a pair designed as props by Alma-Tadema for the studio in his house in Grove End Road. One side is closely based on an ancient Roman bronze seat excavated at Pompeii, the other side is Egyptian.

movement was an interest in Attic Greek vases, Tanagra figures, and an appreciation of the Elgin marbles. More daring Aesthetic women adopted the Greek 'chiton' worn by the models for Albert Moore's paintings.

In the late Victorian era, even the name St John's Wood, the home of George Eliot and her lover George Lewes, was redolent of sexual impropriety. Its small villas shielded by high walled gardens provided a *'rus in urbe'* seclusion, ideal for clandestine activities. There was the discreet establishment where Swinburne could indulge his masochistic taste for the delights of the rod and the apartment where Holman Hunt painted *The Awakened Conscience*, depicting a kept woman overcome by shame – in short, it provided a retreat for all those authors, artists, bohemians and demi-mondaines who wanted a safe spot away from public scrutiny. Among them could be found James Tissot who in about 1875 settled in Grove End Road with his beautiful but tubercular Irish mistress, Kathleen Newton. Deeply in love, Tissot painted her delicate features obsessively for six years, and even after her death in 1882 continued to paint her for two or three more years as if she were still alive.

Tissot eventually returned to Paris and began in a series of eighteen large paintings undertaken between 1883 and 1885 to record Parisian women of different social classes, encountered as if by chance at their pursuits. In each painting the gaze of the principal figure catches the eye of the spectator as though in real life. We surprise them Aesthetically dressed visiting the Louvre, attending a smart lunch after a private view on *le vernissage* (varnishing day), or out shopping. The series presents a glimpse of the ordered high society of the Paris in which the young Marcel Proust was to grow up. It was a world tied to the socially ordained cycle of activities circumscribing a drive in the Bois de Boulogne, a lunch in the centre of the city, a visit to the dressmakers or an opening of an exhibition in the afternoon, a little discreet flirtation between the evening hours of five and seven, as a precursor to a night out at the theatre or Maxims.

In London some of the most popular of all society parties were those given by the immensely hospitable artist Sir Lawrence Alma-Tadema (1836–1912). He was of Dutch birth and acquired his taste for antiquity when studying art and archaeology in Antwerp. A visit to London, in 1862, to see the International Exhibition, gave him his first contact with the Elgin marbles and the great Egyptian collections of the British Museum. The following year he married and on his Italian honeymoon became fascinated by Roman remains and the excavations at Pompeii. He had found his

Sir Lawrence Alma-Tadema
An Earthly Paradise, 1891
Oil on canvas, 86.4 x 165.1 cm
This painting shows the
Pompeiian side of the couch
which is in use as a studio
prop.

life-long mission: 're-animating the life of the old Romans'.

      In the late 1880s he created a remarkable house in Grove
End Road. It was the former home of Tissot, who in several paintings
had depicted a number of features in the garden that also appealed to
Alma-Tadema, notably the colonnade beside a pond. Alma-Tadema
enlarged the house into a spectacular Roman palace, surmounted by an
artist's palette as a weather-vane. Above the doorway, modelled on one
in Pompeii, was the word *'Salve'* ('Welcome'), and on the door a
knocker made of a bronze Roman mask. Rainspouts were in the shape
of lions' heads. Once inside, the visitor to one of his famous 'At
Homes' would be awed by the polished aluminium dome over the vast
galleried marble-floored studio. Alma-Tadema loved to paint himself
as a Roman emperor, a costume he often wore at fancy dress parties.
An example is *A Roman Garden* in which he descends the stairs into a
lararium, a Pompeiian courtyard with a well-tended garden filled with
poppies, and (one of his very rare anachronisms) sunflowers, which
were unknown in the ancient world. The woman is his second wife
Laura and the two girls are his daughters by his first wife.

      When knighted in 1899, Alma-Tadema declared: 'I have
always endeavoured to express in my pictures that the old Romans
were human flesh and blood like ourselves, moved by the same

passions and emotions.' Such an aim is easy to satirize, and his works have been dismissed as mere 'Five o'clock tea Antiquity' – anecdotal genre situations which placed 'Victorians in togas' in the settings of Ancient Rome. For Roger Fry in 1919, who equated late Victorian London with the decadence of the last days of the Roman Empire, remarking 'Pompeii was a thoroughly Victorian city', there were obvious parallels in the carefully researched mirror of antiquity reflected in his Roman works and the life of upper middle-class society of late nineteenth-century England. Like the figures in Alma-Tadema's paintings, British high society enjoyed a privileged lifestyle of numerous servants, flirtation and art connoisseurship at the heart of a great Empire.

Such works also provided an additional frisson for their nouveau riche owners, for by displaying them they could show evidence of classical leanings, if not a classical education, by the representations of tepidariums, frigidariums and apodyteriums. Such subjects also allowed the aesthetic and enjoyable appreciation of titillating female nudes. The subjects portrayed were usually either Pompeiian or Roman, although on twenty occasions Alma-Tadema ventured upon an Egyptian theme.

Theatrical productions also played a highly important part in the development of the Aesthetic Movement. In the 1880s Alma-Tadema designed costume and scenery for two spectacular productions of Shakespeare's *Cymbeline* and *Coriolanus* for Sir Henry Irving, the great actor manager, and two further classical settings *Hypatia* and *Julius Caesar* for Herbert Beerbohm Tree, and a sensitive interpretation of Maeterlinck's *Pelléas and Melisande*. Versions of the costume worn by Ellen Terry as Imogen in *Cymbeline* became very fashionable, as did other Liberty dresses 'à la Tadema'. For although Aesthetic ladies might plaster their walls with Japanese fans, they actually wished to look like ancient Romans or Greeks, and eagerly pounced upon striking costumes like the one described in *The Pictorial World* in 1880 as 'a Greek chiton of fawn-coloured Indian cashmere over a bodice and divided skirt of terra-cotta ottoman, with antique ornaments and belt ...'

As 'props' Alma-Tadema designed two studio seats decorated on one side with Egyptian and on the other with Pompeiian ornament. The latter is based on a couch excavated from Pompeii in 1868 and can be seen in *An Earthly Paradise*. But whether Roman or Egyptian, such themes provided Alma-Tadema with the freedom to depict nudes to his heart's content, despite inevitable occasional criticisms, like the alarm aroused by *The Sculptor's Model*. Its exhibition

"O. W."

"O, I feel just as happy as a bright Sunflower!'
Lays of Christy Minstrelsy.

Æsthete of Æsthetes!
What 's in a name?
The poet is WILDE,
But his poetry 's tame.

Above: Interior of 18, Stafford Terrace, Kensington The home of Edward Linley Sambourne.

Opposite: Edward Linley Sambourne (1844–1910) *Oscar Wilde* From *Punch*, 25 June, 1881

Right: Kate Greenaway (1846–1901) *My House is Red* From *Under the Window*, 1878 The publisher Edmund Evans's home at Leybourne, at Witley in Surrey, was the model for the house.

at the Academy in 1877 led the Bishop of Carlisle to write to the portrait painter George Richmond: 'My mind has been considerably exercised this season by... Alma-Tadema's nude Venus ... [there may] be artistic reasons which justify such exposure of the female form ... In the case of the nude of an Old Master, much allowance can be made, but for a living artist to exhibit a life-size almost photographic representation of a beautiful naked woman strikes my inartistic mind as somewhat if not very mischievous.'

The troubled Bishop was however in a minority, for in 1882 the Grosvenor Gallery staged a successful exhibition of 287 of his paintings. 'How Marbelous!' quipped *Punch* on seeing the work of the leading exponent of painting marble, blue skies, and exotic blossoms like azaleas. Amongst the most spectacular of all his works is *The Roses of Heliogabalus* which depicts the psychopathic Emperor suffocating his guests at an orgy, under a cascade of rose petals. The blossoms depicted were sent to Alma-Tadema's studio weekly from the Riviera for four months in the winter of 1888.

Not far away from St John's Wood in Fitzjohn's Avenue, Hampstead, in a Queen Anne house designed in 1872 by Norman Shaw, lived the great specialist on Egyptian rather than Roman themes, Edwin Long, who painted *The Babylonian Marriage Market*. This painting was sold at Christies in 1881 and made the record price for a work by a living artist of £6,615 – a record which lasted for ten years. Long's house contained a twenty-five-foot square central 'Spanish' patio, filled with tropical plants, adjoining the vast studio with its inglenook, screened pipe organ, anteroom for sitters and separate models' entrance.

Norman Shaw practised his daring picturesque grouping of solids and voids in his own house in Hampstead, built in 1875, and in one built ten years later for the writer and illustrator Kate Greenaway, at 39 Frognal, Hampstead, which is less assertive than his other Hampstead houses. Although variety of depth and surface texture are gently achieved by the use of a corner balcony and tile hangings, Shaw believed in matching design to client, so the resultant structure resembled a dolls' house. Kate Greenaway's admirer John Ruskin disapproved, saying: 'I am aghast at the house in Hampstead and quite resolved that you shan't live in London', but she paid no heed, living there until her death in 1901. One of Kate Greenaway's more emetic verses begins:

My house is red – a little house

A happy child am I

I laugh and play the livelong day
I hardly ever cry ...

George Du Maurier, who lived further up the hill in
Hampstead, had a rather more realistic view of children's behaviour,
revealed in his cartoon *The Height of Aesthetic Exclusiveness* which
appeared on 1 November, 1879, and in which four girls dressed in Kate
Greenaway costumes, carrying emblematic peacock feathers and
sunflowers, grimace at more conventionally dressed children, whose
mother enquires:

'Who are these extraordinary looking children?' to which 'Effie'
replies: 'The Cimabue Browns, Mamma. They're *Aesthetic*, you know?'
Mamma: 'So I should imagine. Do you know them to speak to?' Effie: 'Oh
dear no, Mamma – they're most *exclusive*. Why, they put out their tongues at
us if we only *look* at them!'

There was a darker side to the cult for peacock feathers.
They became a kind of materialised 'pass word' by which people 'of the
same feather' could recognize each other, and men could confess the
sins which they so vividly imagined and wrote about, but seldom really
committed, while women could sink into a trance-like pose reminiscent
of the mediaeval never-never land of the Pre-Raphaelites. This latter
meaning is hinted at in Du Maurier's cartoon depicting *Aesthetic Love
in a Cottage*. Miss Bilderbogie tells Mrs Cimabue Brown about her
love for Peter Pillcox. On being asked: 'Never mind *how* but where are
you going to live?' she replies: 'Oh in dear old Kensington, I suppose –
everything is so cheap there, you know! Peacock feathers only a penny
a-piece.'

One famous Aesthetic resident of 'dear old Kensington'
was Du Maurier's colleague at *Punch*, Linley Sambourne (1844–1910),
much of whose work is still preserved at his home at 18, Stafford
Terrace, Kensington, where, like a fly in amber, the Aesthetic interior
has survived virtually untouched. It is as if Sambourne has just slipped
out to attend one of the convivial weekly lunches at the famous *Punch*
table. Rich stained glass designed by Sambourne depicts sunflowers in
blue and white vases, owls and swallows. Along the frieze shelves
stands an impressive collection of blue and white ceramics, an
intriguing mixture of Chinese and Delftware. The walls are lined with red
and gold embossed papers and dull gold dadoes and skirtings, upon
which hang in serried rows Sambourne's own drawings and those of his
fellow *Punch* cartoonists John Leech, Charles Keene and Sir John Tenniel.
The work of neighbours such as Luke Fildes, Walter Crane and Marcus
Stone, can also be seen, as well as watercolours by Kate Greenaway,
and fans ornamented by small drawings by such eminent Victorian

Below: James J. Tissot
Frederic, Lord Leighton, 1872
Watercolour, 30.3 x 18.8 cm
The caricature for which this
is the original artwork
appeared in *Variety Fair* on
29 June, 1872 and is subtitled
A Sacrifice to the Graces. It
captures the future president
of the Royal Academy at a
rare unguarded moment
propped against a door jamb
in a languid pose expressive
of one worn out by a hectic
social whirl.

Right: George Aitchison
(1825–1910)
Design for a wall elevation
in the Arab Hall at Leighton
House, 1880

**Frederic, Lord Leighton
(1830–96)**
The Garden of the Hesperides,
1878
**Oil on canvas, 169 cm
diameter**
Leighton's painting shows a
pagan Garden of Eden with
the three daughters of
Hesperus reclining gracefully

in Hera's orchard on Mount
Atlas. They are protected by
the dragon Ladon, whom
Leighton has transformed
into a snake. Two of the girls

are singing a lullaby to
Ladon, while the third is
languorously asleep. Later
Hercules will steal the

apples and change the
course of history but for
the moment all is peace
and tranquillity.

79

artists as Frith, Watts, Millais and Alma-Tadema.

Half a mile away at Holland Park stand the studio homes of the most successful artistic figures of the day; William Burges's Tower House at Melbury Road, Holman Hunt's residence, Sir Luke Fildes' house, and, most memorable of all, in Holland Park Road, the home from 1866 to 1895 of the 'High Priest of the cult of Eclectic Beauty', Lord Leighton, which was designed by his friend George Aitchison. From its studio emerged such masterpieces as *The Garden of the Hesperides* and a steady stream of paintings of girls with names like Italian songs – Biondina, Teresina, Caterina, Rubinella – varied by the occasional painting of a Greek girl entitled *Wide Wandering Eyes*, or a German girl described as a *Liede Ohne Worte*.

Leighton, like Alma-Tadema, was extremely hospitable and many famous parties were given in the exotic setting of the house which resembled a scene from *The Arabian Nights*. Passing through a small entrance lobby embellished with that potent Aesthetic symbol, a proud peacock (stuffed), and a statue of Icarus by Alfred Gilbert, the visitor passed into the Arab Hall hung with Islamic mediaeval tiles from Rhodes, Damascus, and Cairo. These Leighton both collected, and acquired through the help of friends, such as the explorer Sir Richard Burton, who wrote in 1871 from Damascus regretting that: 'The bric-a-brac dealers have quite learnt their value and demand extravagant sums for poor articles. Of course you want good specimens.' The tiles collected were augmented by others produced by William De Morgan and subtly incorporated to form a single sumptuous Oriental court. Under a great gilt dome, a fountain played in a pool cut from a solid block of black marble in which swam Japanese goldfish and into which, on more than one occasion, distinguished guests, deep in conversation, fell. Walter Crane created the mosaic frieze, incorporating the inevitable peacocks, while around the walls was an inscription from the Koran in flowing Arabic calligraphy, and high up in the dome, windows with *mashrabiyya* screens added an exotic note.

Leighton House remains today one of the most impressive Aesthetic interiors open to the public. The experience of visiting it can be compared with that of entering Gustave Moreau's studio at 14, Rue de La Rochefoucauld (now the Gustave Moreau Museum). Unlike Leighton House, which lacks really large and spectacular examples of Lord Leighton's works, most of Gustave Moreau's greatest paintings, which are too large to move, can still be seen in the two elegant studios linked by a magnificent staircase, providing us with a moving glimpse of the great Symbolist painter's life work.

Val Prinsep (1838–1904)
Honey Queen, **1859**
Oil on canvas, 58.4 x 33 cm
Prinsep, who helped to paint the Oxford Union frescoes, provided the link between the Pre-Raphaelite world of Rossetti, Burne-Jones and Morris and the Olympian world of Leighton, the Pattle sisters and G. F. Watts. In 1884 he married Frederick Leyland's daughter.

Near Leighton House, on the edge of Holland Park, was Little Holland House where Sara Prinsep created one of London's leading salons. Sara was the oldest of the seven formidable Pattle sisters (known collectively as 'Pattledom'). Their 'open house every Sunday afternoon', was described irreverently by Du Maurier:

It's a nest of prœraphaelites, where Hunt, Millais, Rossetti, Watts, Leighton etc. Tennyson, the Brownings and Thackeray etc. and *tutti quanti* receive dinners and incense, and cups of tea handed to them by these women almost kneeling.

Sara's son, the painter Val Prinsep, was a universal favourite, whose early *Honey Queen* reflects his friendship with Rossetti and Morris. He married F.R. Leyland's daughter Florence in 1884. Sara's permanent house guest, who 'came to dinner, but stayed for twenty years', was George Frederick Watts. It was probably Watts's presence at Little Holland House that first attracted Leighton to the area, for they were close friends, sharing numerous interests in common.

The oldest of the Pattle sisters was Julia Margaret Cameron, whose life was passed in India with her husband, an administrator, until she returned aged nearly fifty and took up photography with passionate enthusiasm, admitting that even, 'From the first moment I handled my lens with a tender ardour'. In Kensington, Mrs Cameron met virtually all the leading intellectual figures of the day, most of whom she managed to lure before her camera at her home at Freshwater, on the Isle of Wight, to the lasting benefit of posterity. Du Maurier recalled meeting G.F. Watts there, and how they talked about 'the beauty of the Elgin Marbles and the desirability of growing as like them as possible.'

Mrs Cameron virtually invented the 'close up', taking a series of soft-focused portraits of remarkable sensitivity of such figures as George Frederick Watts, Robert Browning and Thomas Carlyle. 'When I have had such men before my camera,' she wrote in 1874 in *Annals of My Glass House* (published in 1889), 'my whole soul has endeavoured to do its duty towards them in recording faithfully the greatness of the inner as well as the features of the outer man.' The poet Alfred, Lord Tennyson (who lived nearby on the Isle of Wight at Farringford House) was a frequent, if reluctant, sitter protesting mildly that one portrait made him look like 'a Dirty Monk'. A great admirer of Tennyson's poetry, Cameron also made a series of photographs, one of which is *Merlin and Vivien* illustrating his poem *The Idylls of the King*, which dealt with the legendary story of King Arthur of Avalon and the Knights of the Round Table, also a favourite theme of

Left above and centre:
Clementina, Viscountess Hawarden (1822–65)
Two photographs of her daughters
Lady Hawarden's photographs were mostly taken in her photography room on the first floor of her house in Prince's Gate, South Kensington. They are distinguished by her remarkable gifts for lighting her sitters whom she posed with great imagination.

Left below: **Julia Margaret Cameron (1815–1879)**
The Passing of Arthur
From *Idylls of the King*, 1859

Albert Moore (1841–1893)
Blossoms, **1881**
Oil on canvas, 147.3 x 46.4 cm

Rossetti, Morris and Burne-Jones. She enjoyed interpreting some other Pre-Raphaelite themes such as *Beatrice* and *St Cecilia*.

Not far from Kensington in the large stucco houses of Thomas Cubitt's Belgravia, Julia Margaret Cameron's contemporary, Lady Hawarden, also produced a number of haunting Aesthetic photographs which recall the sensual visual poetry of such later Pre-Raphaelite painters as Frederick Sandys or Simeon Solomon. Many portray two of her daughters either alone or in an empty room, reclining on a bed, reflected in a tall mirror, or standing outside the room looking in through the closed windows.

This last image has a mysterious power, and parallels one of the most captivating of Holman Hunt's works, the portrait of his son *Master Hilary – The Tracer* painted in 1886, at Draycott Lodge, Fulham. It shows Hilary tracing at the window a design by Walter Crane (another Kensington resident) from *The Baby's Opera: A Book of Old Rhymes With New Dresses*, engraved and colour printed by Edmund Evans in 1877. The design shows a shepherd and two shepherdesses listening to a tune played by Tom the piper's son. Hilary is clad in 'Aesthetic' dress of blouse, knickerbockers and stockings, and the painting is executed in the appropriate hues of 'greenery-yallery' for the Grosvenor Gallery, where it was first exhibited.

In about 1871 Ruskin wrote to Burne-Jones, who lived at The Grange, North End Road, Fulham: 'Nothing puzzles me more than the delight that painters have in drawing mere folds of drapery and their carelessness about the folds of water, or clouds, or hills, or branches. Why should the tuckings in and out of muslin be eternally interesting?' Poor Ruskin always had his problems when discussing the veiled female form. For the late Pre-Raphaelites such as Burne-Jones and artists of the Aesthetic Movement like Albert Moore, the study of draperies and the nude were among their chief preoccupations, and were metaphors for passive or concealed sexuality.

From 1877 until 1891 Albert Moore lived near Leighton and Watts in Holland Lane. His peaceful work was surprisingly revolutionary in the context of its time. He very consciously rejected painting pictures which contained a narrative or story, posing figures in a manner inspired by ancient Greek sculpture. In 1868 his *Azaleas* prompted Swinburne to identify Moore with the theory of art for art's sake: 'the melody of colour, the symphony of form is complete: one more beautiful thing is achieved, one more delight is born into the world; and its meaning is beauty; and its reason for being is to be'.

Moore's *Blossoms* reveals Japanese and Classical Greek

influence, the figure's pose recalling an antique Venus whilst the light colours of the robe and flowers are an exercise in Japonaiserie. The shortened foreground is a device which he shared with his friend Whistler. His pupil Graham Robertson wrote:

> The technical perfection of his pictures fascinated me; the rather uninteresting Graeco-West Kensington young women who invariably appear in them did not appeal very strongly; they were a little monotonous in their calculated loveliness, but if one could only paint like that.

Moore was not interested in archaeological reconstructions of the past and was often criticized for absurd combinations of Chinese vases, Japanese fans, Greek costumes and modern European musical instruments or sports equipment. The critic Cosmo Monkhouse's defence of him on this charge in 1885 is an interesting statement of Aesthetic principles:

> The ... complaint which supposes that Albert Moore intends to give us pictures of Greek life and fails, implies a total misconception of the aim of his art ... He seeks only after beauty ... Remembering such criticism as applied to his work, he has been known to utter the astonishing dictum 'Anachronism is the soul of Art'.

Round the corner from Leighton in Melbury Road lived William Holman Hunt, Luke Fildes, William Burges, Herkomer and Phil May, creator of *Guttersnipes*, whose studio was crammed with Japanese art. Not far away in Addison Road, Charles Debenham would build in 1906 his remarkable house completely covered in William De Morgan tiles.

Holland Park and Kensington did not have the monopoly of artists' homes in London for Chelsea, the artistic heart of London, saw the emergence of a colony of leading artistic figures. Since Turner's day artists had loved to live in close proximity to the river. In October 1862 Rossetti moved into 16, Cheyne Walk, which George Meredith, a fellow tenant described as: 'A strange, quaint grand old place, with an immense garden, magnificent panelled staircases and rooms, a palace'. Nearby was the old wooden Battersea Bridge, soon to be immortalized by Whistler.

Rossetti, gloomy after the suicide of his wife Lizzie Siddal, at first welcomed the fun of sharing the house with Meredith and Swinburne. However, the latter's drunken delight in sliding naked down the bannisters of the staircase in pursuit of Simeon Solomon 'dancing all over the studio like a wild cat' was, Rossetti declared, 'enough to drive me crazy'. Rossetti's fellow tenants moved out within a year or so, leaving Rossetti with his 'housekeeper' and model Fanny Cornforth, to find pleasure in the creation of his extraordinary

menagerie of animals in the garden, including kangaroos, wombats and salamanders, gazelles, an Indian bull and the notorious peacocks. Inside the house he began to collect antiques with equal frenzy and variety, acquiring a female portrait by Botticelli, Delft tiles, mirrors of all shapes and sizes, four-poster beds, and of course a large and important collection of blue and white porcelain.

      The main artist settlement in Chelsea was to be in Tite Street. Among its most notable residents were Whistler, and Carlo Pellegrini, who as 'Ape' for *Vanity Fair* drew entertaining caricatures of such figures as Oscar Wilde, another Tite Street resident, no longer clad in velvet jacket and knee breeches, but in evening dress which makes him appear every inch a lounge lizard.

      The south side of Tite Street, as depicted in *The British Architect*, 14 May, 1880, shows Whistler's controversial White House on the extreme right, and on its left Godwin's studio tower. On the left of the picture is Godwin's house for Archibald Stuart-Wortley

Atkinson Grimshaw (1836–93)
Summer, **1875**
Oil on canvas, 63 x 75.6 cm
As well as painting a series of 'Moonlights' which were admired by Whistler, Grimshaw also set out in 1875 to paint a series based on Tissot's favourite theme of 'the fashionable woman' entitled *Il Penseroso, In the Pleasaunce, Spring* and the present example *Summer*, which is notable for the Japanese fans above the door and the blue and white Chinese porcelain.

enriched by tile-hung gables. Whistler's commission for the White House led to Godwin building a number of important buildings in Tite Street, although sadly only number 44, Tite Street, the home of Oscar Wilde's friend Frank Miles and Godwin's Tower House, number 46, remain today.

One of the main attractions for Whistler in his choice of Tite Street as a home was its proximity to his beloved river Thames. Again and again he returned to the subjects of motionless barges seen at dusk, by the bridges and warehouses of the Thames. One little known but haunting example actually takes the Japanese form of a two-fold screen *Blue and Silver: Screen With Old Battersea Bridge.*

Not far away in Manresa Road, the Yorkshire painter Atkinson Grimshaw (1836–93) had a studio in the 1880s, visited by Whistler who remarked with uncharacteristic modesty: 'I considered myself the inventor of Nocturnes until I saw Grimmy's moonlit pictures'.

Working at dusk or at night Grimshaw painted the rain and mist, the puddles and smoky fog of late Victorian industrial England with great poetry. Some of his finest works are of his home town, Leeds, but he also painted Glasgow, Liverpool, Scarborough, Whitby and London. Equally memorable are Grimshaw's delightful studies *Il Penseroso* (1875), *In the Pleasaunce* (1875) and *The Rector's Garden: Queen of the Lilies* (1877) of Aesthetic ladies armed with the requisite Japanese fans, parasols or lilies enjoying the pleasures of a summer's day, and thus demonstrating Grimshaw's control of a bright as well as a sombre palette.

One of the most extensive areas of London given over to the Queen Anne style is the Cadogan estate, which was wittily dubbed by Sir Osbert Lancaster as 'Pont Street' Dutch, after its principal thoroughfare. Nowhere else is red brick redder, stepped Dutch gables more varied nor terracotta ornamentation more extreme. To understand the role of the Queen Anne style in the Aesthetic Movement one has only to walk along Pont Street and around Hans Place or Cadogan Gardens, visiting the Cadogan Hotel, famed for its guests Lily Langtry and Oscar Wilde, who was in Osbert Lancaster's memorable phrase 'called away from it on urgent business', a yellow book under his arm, to Bow Street Police Station. Not far away in Harrington Gardens, South Kensington, is one of the most impressive houses in this Dutch gabled style, built in 1884 for W.S. Gilbert, partly with the profits from *Patience* produced two years earlier.

Surprisingly, the most famous of all the artist colonies, often referred to as a village, was by far the most suburban, Bedford

Park. It was developed in the 1870s and 1880s by a shrewd property developer with artistic interests, Jonathan T. Carr. His brother was a Director of the Grosvenor Gallery and his sister-in-law was involved in the movement for rational dress reform and against tight lacing and is generally assumed to have been the original model for Du Maurier's Mrs Cimabue Brown.

Lennox Gardens, London SW3 An example of the architecture of the Cadogan Estate. Developed in the late 1880s, it was wittily dubbed 'Pont Street Dutch' by Sir Osbert Lancaster in the 1930s.

The idea of an artistic village was not without some interesting precedents. The picturesque qualities of cottages featured greatly in the watercolours of Birket Foster who initially commuted to and from St John's Wood to paint countless scenes of rural life before taking a cottage at Witley in Surrey. Witley became the nucleus for a distinguished group of homes, including those of Tennyson, Sir Henry Cole, Richard Redgrave, George Eliot, the colour printer Edmund Evans, Kate Greenaway, Fred Walker and the watercolour painter Helen Allingham, who excelled even Birket Foster himself in her pursuit of cottage subjects. Birket Foster's large house at Witley, 'The Hill', was extensively decorated by William Morris and Burne-Jones, with such themes as St George and the Dragon, the life of St Frideswide, and tile groups of Cinderella, Beauty and the Beast and the Sleeping Beauty. In some rooms stained-glass windows were installed, at the suggestion of Charles Keene, the *Punch* cartoonist, which depicted musical scores of madrigals and carols, so that visitors, one imagines, could break into a 'round' or a 'catch' without the trouble of searching for sheet music !

Bedford Park, although far from being a rural idyll like Witley, can claim to be the first garden suburb, prototype of Bournville, Port Sunlight, Letchworth, Hampstead and Welwyn, or developments abroad such as Tuxedo Park, New York. It was situated, to the west of London near Turnham Green station on the District line, an unlikely setting for an 'aesthetic Elysium', yet from the beginning it was far more than just a housing estate. It comprised not only nearly 500 houses but a 'Queen Anne' art school, church, club, shop, inn ('The Tabard') and sports facilities.

Ecologically, Carr was ahead of his time. In laying out the estate he took great care to retain the great elm trees which stood

Aubrey Beardsley
A Comedy of Sighs, **1894**
This poster was
commissioned by the famous
Bedford Park *femme fatale*
Florence Farr in her capacity
as manageress of the Avenue
Theatre. *Punch* **made fun of**
the poster, calling it the 'ave a
new' poster.

on the site:

The first thought of the proprietor of these hundred acres was how to spare the greatest number of trees and build artistic houses among them that might look as though they were surrounded by the growth of centuries. Here there is a medlar by the roadside, there the street curves so that it may not disturb a noble elm, and in fact, the position of the trees may have decided those of the houses.

Today when we walk down the still leafy roads of Bedford Park, it is hard to realize that these familiar-looking red brick, gabled houses with large bay windows were considered highly original when built, that to people of that time they appeared highly controversial, and that architectural students used to visit them, as today we might visit recent buildings by Richard Rogers or the late James Stirling.

Carr's choice of architects was up to the minute. E.W. Godwin, Carr's first architect, developed a twin-gabled motif from rural cottages, which was in its time a sharp departure from the clumsy gimcrack Gothic dormers then widely used. But most of the houses were designed by Norman Shaw.

For once, even Walter Hamilton, so often qualified in his admiration of Aesthetic innovations, was full of approval:

In architecture the Queen Anne style is favoured by the aesthetes, and on the really beautiful Bedford Park estate, one of the chosen homes of the 'select', only houses built after that manner are permitted to be erected … Even the names on the door-posts have a touch of poetry and quaintness about them: Pleasaunce, Elm-Dene, Kirk Lees, Ye Denne for example.

For those Aesthetically aware middle-class intellectuals, Norman Shaw provided a quaintly 'olde worlde' village setting in which, in the words of one of the many satirical poems on the suburb: 'they could sit and read Rossetti there by a Japanesy lamp'.

That was by no means the only activity open to Bedford Park residents. A bewildering variety of lectures could be attended at the club on such themes as literature, science and art. On 27 January, 1883, for example, the founder of the suburb Jonathan Carr, could be heard on a particularly enthralling theme entitled *The harm aestheticism has done to the spread of art*. After making a distinction between true Aestheticism, or the seeking of beauty, and false Aestheticism characterized by Oscar Wilde, Carr continued: 'It was not blue and white china, or peacock's feathers, that constituted the word aestheticism.' He praised the work of Burne-Jones and Rossetti and concluded by urging those who had attained 'a little prettiness around them in the uphill walk of life not to stop and rest, but to persevere for something better, and something nobler', apt advice from the founder of an Aesthetic colony to his little flock.

Food for the mind of this useful and uplifting nature could be supplemented by a game of lawn tennis on the two courts in the grounds of the adjoining Tower House, or by attending a service conducted by Moncure Conway (1832–1907), an American clergyman and author, once described as 'being so broad-minded as to have ended up with virtually no mind at all'. It was he who, on first visiting Bedford Park in the 1870s, had exclaimed, 'Angels and Ministers of Grace! Am I dreaming? Right before me is the apparition of a little red town made up of the quaintest Queen Anne houses.' It was no dream and he became one of the suburb's most famous residents, although the ultimate accolade must surely go to the Yeats family: J.B. Yeats, the portrait painter and his two sons Jack and the poet W.B. Yeats.

Camille Pissarro (1830–1903)
Bath Road, **1897**
Oil on canvas, 54 x 65 cm
In May 1897 Camille Pissarro came to London to visit his son Lucien who was recovering from a stroke and was living at 62, Bath Road, Bedford Park. This picture was painted from the front window of the house.

Another famous visitor was Camille Pissarro who stayed with his son Lucien at Bedford Park in the 1890s and painted several local views of the Bath Road and nearby Kew Gardens. Other residents of note included the captain of the voluntary fire brigade, the dashing H.M. Paget, an eccentric illustrator who has left a record of the notable production of *A Sicilian Idyll* by Dr J. Todhunter the local dramatist, much admired by W.B. Yeats. The lead was taken by Florence Farr, the femme fatale of Bedford Park who scrawled across the back of a photograph of herself reclining in a hammock the words: 'Do I inspire thee?', which she sent to the eminently respectable Dr Todhunter. His reply is only to be guessed at. Florence Farr numbered George Bernard Shaw amongst her admirers, and it was said of her that she was prepared to commit adultery on principle, as a protest against double standards. She was said to have remarked, presumably in a languid way, to Yeats: 'When a man begins to make love to me I instantly see it as a stage performance.' As manageress of the Avenue Theatre later in her career, she commissioned one of Aubrey Beardsley's greatest posters for *The Comedy of Sighs* and *Land of Heart's Desire.* Beardsley also illustrated her book *The Dancing Faun* with a caricature of Whistler as a satyr.

Virtually as Whistler withdrew from the London scene,

**John Singer Sargent
(1856–1925)**
Carnation, Lily, Lily, Rose,
1887
Oil on canvas, 174 x 153.7 cm
On 10 September, 1885
Sargent wrote from
Broadway, Gloucestershire:
'I am trying to paint a
charming thing I saw the
other evening. Two little
girls in a garden at dusk
lighting paper lanterns hung
among the flowers from rose
tree to rose tree.' The
picture was a great success
when it was exhibited at the
Royal Academy in 1887.

John Singer Sargent (1856–1925) moved in. Born in Florence, the son
of a Bostonian doctor, Sargent's career resembles that of a character in
one of the novels of Henry James. After studying art in Florence and in
Paris under Carolus Duran, he had a studio in Paris from 1880 to 1884,
but left after the scandal caused by the exhibition of his portrait of
Madame Gautreau at the Salon. Sargent brought with him the *plein air*
techniques which he shared with his friends the Impressionists. But
shortly after settling in England Sargent was to paint one of the most
beautiful of all paintings showing Aesthetic qualities, *Carnation, Lily,
Lily, Rose*, an entrancing vision of little children and Japanese lanterns
created on a warm summer night. When we look at it we can also recall
those exciting evenings in Bedford Park when ladies in fancy dress,
mounted on bicycles hung with Japanese lanterns, wobbled their way
into the strange history of the Aesthetic Movement.

'It is your best work, Basil, the best thing you have ever done,' said Lord Henry languidly (referring to the portrait of Dorian Gray). 'You must certainly send it next year to the Grosvenor. The Academy is too large and too vulgar. Whenever I have gone there, there have either been so many people that I have not been able to see the pictures, which was dreadful, or so many pictures that I have not been able to see the people, which was worse. The Grosvenor is really the only place.' OSCAR WILDE, *THE PICTURE OF DORIAN GRAY*, 1890

Opposite: James McNeill Whistler
Arrangement in Grey, Self-Portrait, 1871–3
Oil on canvas, 74.3 x 52.9 cm

Right: John Ruskin
Self-Portrait with a Blue Neckcloth, 1873
Watercolour, 35.2 x 25 cm

The Whistler versus Ruskin libel case epitomizes the unending nineteenth-century battle between conservative criticism and innovative artistic departures, between pragmatic Philistinism and Aesthetic principles.

The case really starts with the opening exhibition at the 'greenery-yallery, Grosvenor Gallery' which came to symbolize the Aesthetic Movement for the general public. But before describing the famous clash between the upstart forty-four-year-old artist and venerable fifty-nine-year-old critic, it is necessary to explain just why a Grosvenor Gallery, willing to nail Aesthetic colours to its masthead, was so necessary in the art world of the 1870s, and to describe the activities of its artistic precursor the Dudley Gallery.

In the 1860s virtually all recognized centres for the exhibition of works of art were hostile environments for artists of Aesthetic tendencies. Both the charismatic leader of the older generation of Pre-Raphaelite painters, Dante Gabriel Rossetti, and the younger master of medieval dreams, Edward Burne-Jones, boycotted the overcrowded walls of the Royal Academy. At the conservative venues of the New and Old Watercolour Society the traditional landscape role of the watercolour reigned supreme, although it was at the Old Watercolour Society that in 1864 Burne-Jones made his debut. His works, one of them *Cinderella*, had a powerful effect on the young Walter Crane. For him it was as though:

The curtain had been lifted, and we had had a glimpse into a magic world of romance and pictured poetry, peopled with ghosts of 'ladies dead and lovely knights' – a twilight world of dark mysterious woodlands, haunted streams, meads of deep green starred with burning flowers, veiled in a dim and mystic light, and stained with low tones of crimson and gold.[1]

Burne-Jones continued to exhibit at the Old Watercolour Society, although his work was regarded with suspicion by the critics. In 1869 the *Art Journal* condemned: 'This art which has assuredly not the breath of life, the health of nature, or the simplicity of truth: it belongs to the realm of dreams, nightmares and other phantasms of diseased imagination'.

The following year, 1870, Burne-Jones showed *Phyllis and Demophöon* in which not only was the figure of Demophöon naked and with visible genitalia, but Phyllis was recognizably given the features of Maria Zambaco, the beautiful Greek girl with whom Burne-Jones was currently conducting a fairly well-publicized affair. Complaints were made about the undraped nude male figure and Burne-Jones removed the painting and resigned. Apart from two paintings shown at the Dudley Gallery, he ceased to exhibit until the

Edward Burne-Jones
Phyllis and Demophöon, **1870**
Gouache, 91.5 x 45.8 cm
The story (taken from Ovid)
recounts how Phyllis was
metamorphosed into an
almond tree. Here she is
embracing her lover on his
return. The model for
Phyllis was Burne-Jones's
mistress Maria Zambaco.
Burne-Jones, with his
favoured themes of the
Romaunt of the Rose **and the**
Sleeping Beauty **and his love**
of flowing draperies, was
closely identified with the
Aesthetic Movement
throughout his career.

Grosvenor Gallery opened in 1877. Reviewing *Phyllis and Demophöon*, the *Art Journal* critic commented acidly: 'Mr Burne-Jones … stands alone: he has in this room no followers; in order to judge how degenerate this style may become in the hands of disciples, it is needful to take a walk to the Dudley Gallery'.

Who were the artists at the Dudley Gallery that other

Alfred Sacheverell Coke
(fl. 1869–c. 1893)
Eros and Ganymede, **c. 1875**
Watercolour, 20.6 x 27 cm

critics facetiously dubbed 'the legendary', 'the archaic' or 'the loathly' school, the 'mystico-mediaeval or romantico-classic' group? And what made the Dudley Gallery such a key Aesthetic venue?

Since it opened in 1865 at the Egyptian Hall, opposite the Royal Academy, the Dudley had a resolute policy of independence. 'The Water Colour Societies reserve their walls entirely for Members', complained its manifesto. The Dudley, in contrast, eschewed membership, and held truly open exhibitions. It soon attracted regular exhibitors of the calibre of Albert Moore, Frederick Sandys, Frederick Walker and especially Simeon Solomon, who exhibited annually works with such esoteric classical titles as *Antinous Dionysius* and *Sacramentum Amoris*, a painting which he sold to F.R. Leyland. The Dudley Gallery was strictly reserved for watercolour paintings, however, and the Royal Academy remained the major arbiter of public taste, the visual arena where reputations were won or lost. Solomon therefore continued to exhibit his oil paintings at the Royal Academy, and in 1867 his painting *Bacchus* gained a eulogy from his friend Walter Pater in *Greek Studies* who saw in it: 'the god of the bitterness of wine … of things too sweet … the sea water of the Lesbian grape become somewhat brackish in the cup …' When more works of similar Aesthetic tendencies featured annually at the Royal Academy the reviewer of the *Art Journal* in 1871 described the advent

of a new school of painting:

> The brotherhood cherish in common, reverence for the antique, affection for modern Italy; they affect southern climes, costumes, sunshine, also a certain *dolce far niente* style, with a general sybarite state of mind which rests in Art and Aestheticism as the be-all and end-all of existence.

Among the members of this group were such figures as Robert Bateman, Edward Clifford and Alfred Sacheverell Coke – whose *Eros and Ganymede* possesses just the frisson of Hellenic sexual ambiguity in mythological guise which had such potent appeal for Aesthetic taste.

When rejected by the Royal Academy such artists were faced with great difficulties, since liberal dealers, such as the Old Bond Street Gallery which exhibited Walter Crane's *Love's Sanctuary* were rare. The days of commercial galleries being in the vanguard of advanced taste had not yet dawned. Large mixed public exhibitions provided the unavoidable path to fame. Admittedly there was one major exception to this rule, an artist who became famous although he virtually never exhibited – Dante Gabriel Rossetti. The vicious criticism of Robert Buchanan had deeply upset Rossetti, who saw enemies everywhere and relied on individual wealthy and discerning patrons. When asked to exhibit at the new Grosvenor Gallery he replied:

> What holds me back is simply that lifelong feeling of dissatisfaction which I have experienced from the disparity of aim and attainment in what I have all my life produced as best as I could ... Your scheme must succeed were it but for one name associated with it – that of Burne-Jones – a name representing the loveliest art we have.

The auspicious opening event took place on 1 May, 1877, at 135, New Bond Street. May Day is traditionally given over to the celebration of the worker and organized labour, but this occasion was devised for high society to enjoy high art in its most extreme form. A glamorous private view was attended by every section of the Victorian establishment from politicians to the aristocracy. Two days earlier, an exclusive dinner party held in the restaurant had been attended by the Prince and Princess of Wales. For months, newspapers and journals had vied with each other in describing the sumptuous Renaissance grandeur of the building, and the Palladian doorway, salvaged from the demolished church of Santa Lucia in Venice and incorporated into the façade by the architect W.T. Sams.

Once inside, visitors entered an imposing hall, flanked by green Genoa marble columns, before ascending a fifteen-foot staircase to the picture galleries on the first floor. The galleries were lined with gilded Ionic pilasters, salvaged from the foyer of the old Italian Opera House in Paris, which were placed at intervals around

Opposite: Walter Crane
Love's Sanctuary, 1870
Oil on canvas, 77.3 x 54.8 cm
When first exhibited, this evocative Italianate Quattrocento pictorial exercise was criticized as being irreverent with its explicit ritualism echoing the sensuous aestheticism of Simeon Solomon's *Acolytes Censing*. **The picture depicts a handsome young male pilgrim kneeling in prayer before an altar, on which stands the icon-like portrait of Walter Crane's betrothed Mary Frances Andrews. The altar is an elaborate mixture of a celebration of the mass and pagan sacrifices to Venus which are variously symbolized by the illuminated missal, singers and musicians, the smoking censer and the flight of doves.**

Left: Joseph Middleton
Joplin (1831–84)
Sir Coutts Lindsay outside the Grosvenor Gallery, 1883
Watercolour, 53.5 x 18.9 cm

walls covered with a rich red silk damask and a dado of dark olive green velvet. The ceiling, painted a dark blue, was decorated with various phases of the moon and stars by Whistler. Conveniently sited in the heart of Mayfair, luxuriously fitted out, and provided with a good restaurant, it became crystallized in the public mind as *the* venue at which to see avant-garde art. The lavish furnishings of Oriental rugs, luxuriant potted plants on console tables, and movable Italian chairs led one critic, Agnes D. Atkinson, writing in *The Portfolio* to rhapsodize: 'This is not a public picture exhibition but rather a patrician's private gallery shown by courtesy of its owner.'

Such puffs were the result of a masterly publicity campaign devised by the Gallery's creator Sir Coutts Lindsay (1824–1913), who had spent £150,000 on building the Gallery on the site of three houses in New Bond Street. He was a wealthy dilettante amateur artist and poet, whose stunning good looks kept him constantly involved in affairs of the heart before and after his marriage in June 1864 to Blanche Fitz-Roy, a connection of the Rothschilds. Her formidable aunt, Charlotte de Rothschild, described the progress of the match in language worthy of Wilde's Lady Bracknell, commenting acidly on Coutts's eligibility, age, looks, income and over-artistic tastes. After their marriage Coutts Lindsay and Blanche entertained together, in a domestic setting apostrophized in a 'thank you' letter, in verse, by Lord Goshen who wrote:

'as one of the Guests

Who have basked in your aesthetic home,

So steeped in art, that even every rose

Seems bent on blooming in a perfect pose.'

Coutts Lindsay's initial motive in starting the Grosvenor (largely financed by his wife's fortune) was prompted by his own unfortunate experiences in exhibiting his paintings at the Royal Academy. He decided to open a gallery where artists should be invited to exhibit: 'artists whose works have not been so much known ... as I would have wished', as he explained to guests at the inaugural banquet. Many established artists accepted, and the 209 paintings and sculptures in the inaugural exhibition included works by G.F. Watts, Albert Moore, James Tissot, Alphonse Legros, Gustave Moreau and also surprisingly by Richard (Dicky) Doyle, the noted painter of fairies, as well as Coutts Lindsay's own works. But the exhibition was dominated by two famous artists, Edward Burne-Jones and Whistler.

Graham Robertson in *Time Was* vividly describes the

Right: Sir Coutts Lindsay (1824–1913)
Self-portrait, **1864**
Oil on canvas, 76.2 x 91.4 cm
The picture on the easel is probably *A Knight and his Daughter*, **which Coutts Lindsay exhibited at the Grosvenor Gallery in 1879.**

Opposite: James McNeill Whistler
Arrangement in Grey and Black, No 2: Portrait of Thomas Carlyle, **1872–3**
Oil on canvas, 171.1 x 143.5 cm
Carlyle admired Whistler's famous portrait of his mother, the *Arrangement in Grey and Black, No 1*, **and the artist adopted a similar profile composition for the seventy-eight-year-old philosopher, whose cheerful 'And now, mon, fire away' was the prelude to many sittings. This was the first painting by Whistler to enter a public collection when it was purchased by Glasgow in 1891.**

impression made by their work:

> The general effect of the great rooms was most beautiful and quite unlike any ordinary picture gallery. It suggested the interior of some old Venetian palace, and the pictures, hung well apart from each other against dim rich brocades and among fine pieces of antique furniture, showed to unusual advantage. I can well remember the wonder and delight of my first visit. One wall was iridescent with the plumage of Burne-Jones' angels, one mysteriously blue with Whistler's nocturnes, one deeply glowing with the great figures of Watts, one softly radiant with the faint, flower tinted harmonies of Albert Moore. Here, too was the sombre work of Legros, the jewelled fantasies of Gustave Moreau ... here at last were the pictures of Burne-Jones and Whistler for all to see ...

In the centre of the south wall hung the *Seven Days of Creation*, flanked by *The Mirror of Venus* and *Vivien and Merlin*. All were impressive but the *Beguiling of Merlin* wrought the most potent spell:

> The Whistler nocturnes did not as yet say much to me beyond – blue – blue – the intense but tender blue of twilight seen through the windows of a lamp-lit room.

> I was still a little boy, and a Burne-Jones is far easier to appreciate than a Whistler ... Burne-Jones' art is the exquisite accompaniment to another's voice, Whistler's is the song itself.

Whistler had four Nocturnes on view. Two bore the same title *Nocturne in Blue and Silver* (one then owned by Frances Leyland, Leyland's wife, who remained friendly with Whistler), one *Nocturne in Blue and Gold*, and what was to become one of the most controversial paintings entitled *Nocturne in Black and Gold*. Also on show were the famous portrait of Carlyle and some other portraits.

Whistler's aims in the Nocturnes are perhaps best described in a letter he wrote in 1868 to Fantin-Latour:

> It seems to me that colour ought to be, as it were, embroidered on the canvas, that is to say the same colour ought to appear in the picture continually here and there, in the same way that a thread appears in an embroidery, and so should all the others, more or less according to their importance. Look how well the Japanese understand this ...

This statement helps to explain why Whistler's Nocturnes are the most moving and profound expression of his indebtedness to Japanese art. But the public which could enjoy a pretty girl in exotic robes looking at porcelain found the Nocturnes far more difficult. Whistler resignedly said of his *Old Battersea Bridge: Nocturne in Blue and Gold* (1865): 'There is mystery here. The people don't want it. What they like is when the east wind blows, when you can look across the river and count the wires in the canary bird's cage on the other side.' The painting is indebted to such Japanese prints as

Hiroshige's *Moonlight at Ryogoko*, just as the 'falling rocket' Nocturne parallels a moment caught in Hiroshige's *Spring Fireworks Over Edo*.

John Ruskin, a far older, and generally considered a far wiser, visitor than fellow artist Graham Robertson, found Whistler's Nocturnes not only difficult to appreciate but positively objectionable. For thirty years he had dominated art criticism ever since the publication in 1843 of the first volume of *Modern Painters*, with its famous advice to artists that: 'They should go to nature in all singleness of heart, and ... walk with her laboriously and trustingly, having no other thought but how best to penetrate her meaning; rejecting nothing, selecting nothing, and scorning nothing.' These criteria became not only Ruskin's personal yardstick but as the simplified motto, 'Truth to Nature', a defining principle of British art. The artists he supported all conformed to Ruskin's highly personal interpretation of these rules, which enabled him to accept both the minute painstaking detail of Millais and the subjective abstraction of Turner. Ruskin's opinions expressed in *Modern Painters* could make or break the reputation of an artist. As early as 1856 *Punch* carried this verse written by 'A Perfectly Furious Academician':

I takes and paints,

Hears no complaints,

And sells before I'm dry;

Till savage Ruskin,

He sticks his tusk in,

Then nobody will buy.

NB. Confound Ruskin; only that won't come into poetry – but it's true.

By 1877 Ruskin's powers as a critic were even more formidable. He held the prestigious post of Slade Professor of Art at Oxford, but had just taken a year's leave in Italy to revise a new edition of *The Stones of Venice*, and find tranquillity for his highly strung mind. Ruskin's over-active social conscience led him to regard his role as teacher of art as a self-indulgence. He published a series of letters entitled *Fors Clavigera*, expressing his thoughts not only on artistic but also on social and economic concerns, expressing views which were often widely circulated in other publications. He visited the Grosvenor Gallery on 22 June, having been abroad for the opening, dining afterwards with the Burne-Jones.

In his extensive critique of the exhibition in *Fors Clavigera*, Ruskin fulminated at the presence of Sir Coutts Lindsay's own paintings, accusing him of being 'at present an amateur both in art and shopkeeping. If he intends to manage the Grosvenor Gallery rightly, he must not put his own works in it until he can answer for their quality:

Above: James McNeill Whistler
Nocturne in Blue and Silver: The Lagoon, Venice, **c. 1879–80 Oil on canvas, 50.4 x 65.2 cm**

Left: Whistler at work in his studio in 1886 before a portrait of his mistress, Maud Franklin. He may be preparing his 'sauce' (a runny mixture of copal, turpentine and linseed oil which he used in painting his Nocturnes).

if he intends to be a painter, he must not at present superintend the erection of public buildings, or amuse himself with their decoration' which, he complained 'is poor in itself; and very grievously injurious to the best pictures it contains, while its glitter as unjustly veils the vulgarity of the worst'.

We are left in very little doubt as to which paintings Ruskin considered the best and which the worst. Tissot is chided for his 'mere coloured photographs of society', although 'their dexterity and brilliance are apt to make the spectator forget their conscientiousness'. Ruskin has kinder words to say about Millais's portraits, although he laments that his painting of rocks is poor. If only Millais had:

remained faithful to the principles of his school when he first led its onset. Time was, he could have painted every herb of the rock, and every wave of the stream, with the precision of Van Eyck, and the lustre of Titian.

But real praise is reserved for Burne-Jones alone: 'simply the only art-work at present produced in England which will be received by the future as "classic" of its kind – the best that has been, or could be ... I *know* that these (works) will be immortal as the best thing the mid-nineteenth century in England could do.'

Comparisons are then made between the faults or mannerisms of Burne-Jones as revealed in his *Days of Creation* and those of Giotto, Masaccio, Luini, Turner, Bellini and Carpaccio. He continues:

Lastly, the mannerisms and errors of these pictures, whatever may be their extent, are never affected or indolent. The work is natural to the painter, however strange to us; and it is wrought with utmost conscience of care, however far, to his own or our desire, the result may yet be incomplete. Scarcely so much can be said for any other pictures of the modern schools: their eccentricities are almost always to some degree forced; and their imperfections gratuitously, if not impertinently indulged.

Then come the fateful lines, a condemnation of Whistler's *A Nocturne in Black and Gold: The Falling Rocket* with the now notoriously offensive words:

For Mr Whistler's own sake, no less for the protection of the purchaser, Sir Coutts Lindsay ought not to have admitted works into the gallery in which the ill-educated conceit of the artist so nearly approached the aspect of wilful imposture. I have seen, and heard, much of cockney impudence before now, but never expected to hear a coxcomb ask two hundred guineas for flinging a pot of paint in the public's face.

Ruskin's clouded mind was prone to swing abruptly from passionately-held intellectual convictions to sentimental bathos. This famous number of *Fors Clavigera* concludes with a mawkish description extolling the beauties of a chromolithograph depicting the horse who had recently won the St Leger, with his companion, a kitten. Whistler sued Ruskin for libel, and the case was tried in November 1878, although Ruskin, suffering from a mental breakdown, was unable to appear. The case marked an important turning point in the history of art, and the beginning of forms of art as various as conceptualism and abstraction.

Artistic controversies have always provided ideal opportunities for humour and satiric comment. Public interest in the case led to the rapid adaptation of a French farce *La Cigale*, by Meilhac and Halévy, which had satirized Degas and Impressionism, its target now being changed to Whistler. Entitled *The Grasshopper*, it was staged

Clockwise from top left:
Utagawa Hiroshige
(1797–1858)
Spring Fireworks over Edo,
35.3 x 24 cm
This was a favourite theme
of Hiroshige, who used the
subject again on some fan
prints of the 1840s.

Utagawa Hiroshige
Moonlight at Ryogoko
From *Famous Views of Edo*,
1857

James McNeill Whistler
*Nocturne in Blue & Gold: Old
Battersea Bridge*, 1872–3
Oil on canvas, 68.3 x 51.2 cm

James McNeill Whistler
*Nocturne in Black and Gold:
The Falling Rocket*, 1875
Oil on wood, 60.3 x 46.6 cm
Both these well-known
Nocturnes show Whistler's
debt to Japanese prints and
in particular to the work of
Hiroshige.

in December 1877 at the Gaiety Theatre. The plot involves an 'artist of the future' called Pygmalion Flippit, who names Whistler as his master, and produces a painting entitled *Dual Harmony*, representing a blue ocean beneath a burning sky. When hung upside down it showed a vast sandy desert under a blue and cloudless sky. Surprisingly the victim seems to have quite enjoyed the piece, which was put on with his co-operation. It was, after all, as his friend Alan Cole remarked, 'a tremendous puff for Whistler', during the months when he needed all the public support he could muster before the case came to trial in November 1878.

When read today the whole proceedings of the case are reminiscent of a Gilbert and Sullivan operetta. Indeed Gilbert himself, always alert for new comic material, had breakfast with Whistler on the morning of the first day of the trial, although sadly he was not present at a scene which could have been perfect material for his pen, the inspection of the works shown at the Grosvenor by Ruskin's lawyers. This took place in Whistler's new studio at The White House. Dinner was served by the bailiffs who had taken over the house pending payment of outstanding bills. One can also imagine the patter song Gilbert might have written for star witness Frederic Leighton who, having volunteered to give evidence on behalf of Whistler, in the end rather characteristically could not attend, as he had to go to Windsor to be knighted.

Gilbertian farce continued to prevail at the trial where the pictures were unceremoniously passed from hand to hand in the heavy fog which deepened the gloom of the candlelit court. One painting hit the head of a balding gentleman, and appeared liable to fall out of its frame, before it reached the witness box. Whistler, on being asked whether the painting was his, inserted his monocle, and paused theatrically before responding: 'Well, it was once. But it won't be much longer if it goes on in this way.' The inevitable jokes about paintings being upside down or the right way up were made, notably concerning *Nocturne in Blue and Silver*, Whistler's evocation of Battersea Bridge, which the judge carefully explained to the jury was a representation of Old Chelsea Church.

The trial took place on 25 and 26 November, 1877. Ruskin was not present owing to ill health, but was significantly represented by the establishment figure of the Attorney General, Sir John Holker. The cut and thrust of his cross-examination brings the case vividly to life:

Holker: Did it take you much time to paint the *Nocturne in Black and Gold?* ... How long do you take to knock off one of your pictures?

Whistler: Oh, I 'knock one off' possibly in a couple of days – (laughter) – one

THE NEWEST THING IN WALL-PAPERS.

Dealer. This is artistic, sir. A nocturne in blue and silver. Starlight at Stepney, treated decoratively. P'raps you read what Mr. Frith said about our goods at the Whistler trial, sir! Awfully down on Whistler. Brought us a lot of custom.

N.B.—In the course of this case Mr. Frith, R.A., in giving his opinion of Mr. Whistler's pictures said there was a beautiful tone of colour about them, but they did not represent any more than could be got out of a piece of wall paper.

AN APPEAL TO THE LAW.

Naughty Critic, to use bad language! Silly Painter, to go to Law about it!

Above top: *The Newest Thing in Wallpapers* From *Judy*, 11 December, 1878

Above bottom: Linley Sambourne *An Appeal to the Law* From *Punch*, 7 December, 1878 The jury (on the right) are portrayed as Winsor and Newton paint tubes.

day to do the work and another to finish it.

Holker: After partly painting a picture, do you put it up to mellow? (laughter)

Whistler: I do not understand.

Holker: Do you ever hang these pictures up on the garden wall?

Whistler: Oh I understand now. I did not put up *Nocturne in Black and Gold* or any other picture to 'mellow'.

(This exchange relates to widely reported accounts of the artist literally hanging his canvases out to dry like washing. There was truth in these allegations for a neighbour in Chelsea recalled 'seeing the nocturnes set out along the garden wall to bake in the sun'. The Nocturnes were painted with lavish resource to Whistler's 'sauce' – highly diluted oil paint used to establish the prevailing tone of colour, and Whistler sometimes left them out even in bad weather saying, 'it takes the gloss off them, that objectionable gloss which puts one in mind of a new hat'.)

Holker: The labour of two days is that for which you ask two hundred guineas?

Whistler: No, I ask it for the knowledge I have gained in the work of a lifetime. (Applause)

Holker: What is the peculiar beauty of that picture?

Whistler: I daresay I could make it clear to any sympathetic painter, but I do not think I could to you, any more than a musician could explain the beauty of a harmony to a person who has no ear.

Holker: Do you not think that anybody looking at that picture might fairly come to the conclusion that it has no particular beauty?

Whistler: I think there is distinct evidence that Mr Ruskin did come to that conclusion ... No artist of culture would come to that conclusion. I have known unbiased people to recognize that [the Nocturne] represents fireworks in a night scene.

Albert Moore (Witness for Whistler): I consider the pictures beautiful as works of art: I wish I could paint as well. There is one extraordinary thing about them, and that is that he has painted the air, which very few artists have attempted ...

One reluctant witness on behalf of Ruskin was the famous painter of cross-sections of Victorian social life, William Powell Frith (1819–1909). His *Private View at the Royal Academy* painted three years later in 1881, provides us with one of the most famous glimpses of High Victorian society at play, including a group of Aesthetic ladies clustered round Oscar Wilde, one of whom is Ellen Terry. Examined concerning the *Nocturne in Blue and Silver*, Frith responded:

There is a beautiful tone of colour in the picture of Old Battersea Bridge, but the colour does not represent any more than you could get from a bit of wallpaper or silk ... a pretty colour that pleases the eye, but nothing more ... the nocturne in black and gold is not in my opinion worth two hundred guineas.

During an exchange on Ruskin's views on Turner's works, counsel, witness and judge resorted to comic crosstalk worthy of a music hall routine.

Frith: I believe Mr Ruskin has a great estimate of Turner's works. I think Turner should be the idol of all painters ...

Counsel: Would you call Turner's *Snow Storm* a mass of soapsuds and whitewash?

Frith: I think it very likely I should. (Laughter) When I say that Turner should be the idol of painters, I refer to his earlier works and not to the period when he was half crazy and produced works about as insane as the people who admire them. (Laughter)

Judge Huddlestone: Somebody described one of Turner's pictures as lobster salad. (Laughter)

Frith: I have heard Turner himself speak of some of his productions as nothing better than salad and mustard. (Laughter)

A very different mood prevailed when Burne-Jones also gave evidence in support of Ruskin. The judge asked: 'You are a friend of Mr Whistler, Mr Burne-Jones, I believe', to which the witness replied: 'I *was*: I don't suppose he will ever speak to me again after today.' For Burne-Jones asserted that the *Nocturne in Black and Gold* was not a serious work of art. Asked to give his reasons he replied:

First, the subject itself. It is difficult to paint night, I have never seen one picture of night that was successful. This is only one of a thousand failures that artists have made in their efforts at painting night. The other two nocturnes look like night – they have a beautiful tone like night, especially the one of the bridge.

Asked whether any of the pictures he had discussed revealed any mark of labour, Burne-Jones replied:

Yes, in Mr Whistler's pictures I see marks of great labour and artistic skill. Mr Whistler gave infinite promise at first, but I do not think he has fulfilled it. I think he has evaded the great difficulty of painting by not carrying his pictures far enough. The difficulties in painting increase daily as the work progresses, that is the reason so many of us fail. We are none of us perfect. The danger to art by the plaintiff's want of finish is that men who come afterward will perform mere mechanical work, without the excellencies of colour and unrivalled power of representing atmosphere which are displayed by the plaintiff, and so the art of the country will sink down to mere mechanical whitewashing.

His statement to Defence counsel strikes an uncharacteristically unpleasant note, revealing a personal animosity to

James McNeill Whistler
The Doorway, c. 1880
Etching and drypoint,
29.2 x 20 cm
A Renaissance doorway in
the Palazzo Gussoni. This
etching, which was executed
from a gondola, was selected
for the 'First Venice Set'
issued by the Fine Art
Society in 1881.

Whistler's aims:

The point and matter seems to me to be this, that scarcely any body regards Whistler as a serious person ... He has never yet produced anything but sketches, more or less clever, often stupid, sometimes sheerly insolent, but sketches always. Not once has he committed himself to the peril of completing anything. For all artists know that the difficulty of painting lies in the question of completion ... I think Mr Ruskin's language is justified on the grounds of the scandal that the violent puffing of what is at best a poor performance brings upon art ... if anyone caring as Mr Ruskin does for the question of art ... could think this meaningless scribbling should be looked upon as real art ... art would be at an end.

In Ruskin's instructions to his Defence Counsel, he justifies his remarks by stating:

The public would at once recognize the coxcombery of a composer, who advertised a study in chiaroscuro for four voices, or a prismatic piece of colour in four flats, and I am only courteous in supposing nothing worse than coxcombery in an artist who offers them a symphony in green and yellow for two hundred pounds.

He concludes by stating that he is pleased the action has been brought because it gives him the opportunity to retire from public life.

After two days of legal argument, the jury declared a verdict in Whistler's favour, but awarded only a derisory farthing's damages (the smallest coin of the realm) and no costs. This precipitated his bankruptcy in May the following year, for the sum of £3,000, which forced him to sell his studio at The White House.

Both plaintiff and defendant suffered as the result of the case. Although his popularity was so great that his costs were paid by a public subscription organized by the Fine Art Society, Ruskin endured much mental distress even before the case came to trial, retiring to Coniston where in February 1878 he sank into his first major attack of insanity.

It was impossible to depress Whistler for long and soon after his bankruptcy in May his fortunes improved. The Fine Art Society, with remarkable even-handedness, advanced him the £150 necessary to take him to Venice for three months to produce a set of twelve etchings, with the option of buying the plates for £700 on his return.

While in Venice Whistler also painted some relatively little-known Nocturnes in oil of which *The Lagoon, Venice: Nocturne in Blue and Silver* is a fine example. Sickert recorded Whistler using large housepainter's brushes (favoured by twentieth-century action painters) for the large sweeps of colour in such works. He returned in November

Left above: John Ruskin at
Brantwood, 1880s

Left centre: Queen Mildred
and her Maidens at
Whitelands College, 1904

Left below: Anna Richards
*May Day Procession of Queen
Eva*, 1902
Watercolour

1880 and the Venice set was exhibited the following month in one of the carefully orchestrated settings which Whistler loved, followed soon after by his Venice pastels in February 1881. The first setting was described by Godwin:

First, a low skirting of yellow gold, then a high dado of dull yellow-green cloth, then a moulding of green gold, and then a frieze and ceiling of pale reddish brown.

In the pastel exhibition, white and yellow were the dominant note, the wall was white with yellow hangings, the floor was covered with pale yellow matting, the couches were pale yellow serge, and the cane-bottomed chairs were painted yellow. There were yellow flowers in yellow pots and a white and yellow livery for the attendants who at the private view wore yellow socks. The assistants wore yellow neckties. Whistler distributed yellow favours, 'wonderful little butterflies', to his friends.

Characteristically all these innovations led to argument on who was responsible for the expenses. Whistler wrote to the managing director of the Fine Art Society:

Useless my dear Huish! quite useless ...You know that the yellow man's wages do not come out of my pocket ... he was one of the elements of the Exhibition – like the hangings and various arrangements in canary – I shall neither pay for the man – not his socks, nor his hose, nor anything that is his.

The show prompted satiric verses in *Punch*:

Strangely adorned is the Gallery,
Done up in gamboge and white,
Even the flunkey is 'yallery',
Made a most exquisite fright.
We may be thought supercilious,
But, if the truth must be told,
It looks consumedly bilious,
This new 'arrangement in gold '...

Yet not all his exhibition settings were variations in yellow – one of the most subtle of all his colour schemes was for an exhibition entitled 'Notes, Harmonies, Nocturnes', held in 1884 in a gallery decorated with rose-coloured walls, a white dado, white chairs and pale azaleas in rose flushed jars.

Thus Whistler found solace, ironically among the stones of Ruskin's Venice and in the orchestration of arrangements in colour. These were not confined solely to exhibition settings. A.H. Mackmurdo, founder of the Century Guild recalled Whistler persuading the impresario Richard D'Oyly Carte:

to make his drawing room at Adelphi Terrace a harmony in yellow. He painted the grand piano an old gold colour with traces here and there of complementary greys and greens... When Whistler had his one man show of paintings I helped him in arranging his attractive schemes. Drawings hung in white frames on white walls; floor covered in white matting. The slightest touches of colour in a drawing shone out and caught the eye at once.

In 1891, fourteen years after the trial, Whistler finally had the satisfaction of selling the controversial Nocturne for 800 guineas, and was understandably eager for the news to be heard that his stand had been vindicated and that: 'the Pot of paint flung into the face of the British Public for two hundred guineas has now sold for four pots of paint, and that Ruskin has lived to see it'.

Balm for Ruskin's troubled mind took a very different form. Early in January 1880, Ruskin found a work of art far more to his taste, a Christmas card of a little girl by Kate Greenaway. He wrote a fan letter immediately to the artist telling her that: 'To my mind it is a greater thing than Raphael's *St Cecilia*.' Three years later Ruskin delivered a lecture in Oxford on her work entitled 'Fairyland' and they met for the first time. Their relationship rapidly blossomed into exchanges of pretend baby talk, the formality of 'Dear Miss Greenaway' becoming by August 1883 'Darlingest Kate'.

Kate Greenaway, who revived the Regency period as the Pre-Raphaelites had the Middle Ages and Alma-Tadema classical antiquity, was once questioned by Ruskin about the creation of her illustrative works:

Do you only draw pretty children out of your head? In my parish school there are at least twenty prettier than any in your book [of illustrations] but they are in costumes neither graceful nor comic – they are not like blue china – they are not like mushrooms – they are like – very ill-dressed angels. Could you draw groups of them as they are?

Again and again Ruskin returned to the task of encouraging Kate Greenaway to draw from nature, setting her as subjects, wild flowers such as shamrocks, studies of 'rocks, moss and, ivy', found in walks near Brantwood, and prepared ornithological specimens such as a kingfisher. He also begged her (without success) to make studies from the nude. 'As we've got so far as taking off hats, I trust we may in time get to taking off just a little more – say, mittens – and then – perhaps – even – shoes – and (for fairies) even stockings – and – then – '.

Such a distressing letter recalls aspects of Ruskin's life also revealed in his autobiography *Praeteria* as a tragedy of passionate yet unconsummated love, a tragic record of the life of an emotional tantalus. The mental flaws from his upbringing by his over-possessive parents left

Edward Burne-Jones
King Cophetua and the Beggar Maid, 1884
Oil on canvas, 290 x 136 cm
The subject derives from a poem in Percy's *Reliques*, which is printed from Johnson's *Crown Garland of Goulden Roses* of 1612 and entitled *Song of a Beggar and King*. It concerns a king of Africa, whose aversion to women was overcome by a beautiful beggar girl. The composition was inspired by Crivelli and the figures by Mantegna's *Madonna della Vittoria*. When exhibited in Paris, decadent poets enthused, especially over the girl's feet '*ivoire tache de sang*'.

him with deeply disturbed psychological problems which manifested themselves in distressing sentimentality.

In 1865, addressing women in *Sesame and Lilies* he rhapsodized: 'queens you must always be; queens to your lovers; queens to your husbands and your sons; queens of higher mystery to the world beyond, which bows itself down, and will for ever bow, before the myrtle crown and the stainless spectre of womanhood.'

These words reflect Ruskin's curious and highly personal delight in the celebration of May Day, and the crowning of Queens of the May. He made an early attempt to promote such an event at Winnington Hall, a girl's school in Cheshire which he often visited between 1859 and 1868, and featured in his book *Ethics of the Dust*, but was thwarted by the parents of a girl who suspected his motives. But in 1881 he was given a new opportunity to indulge this dream by the principal of another institution for training young girls to be teachers – Whitelands College, Chelsea.

Ironically, the approach, like the libel case, arose from one of Ruskin's essays in *Fors Clavigera*, Letter 80, *A Letter to Young Girls*. The principal of Whitelands, John Faunthorp, wrote to Ruskin asking for permission to reprint the piece in a standard reading book for use in elementary schools. Ruskin immediately became deeply interested in Whitelands and presented a set of his works to the newly formed college library, and later other books and pictures. When asked to present a copy annually of his book *Proserpina* as a prize Ruskin replied:

Very thankfully I will give the annual *Proserpina* but not as a prize ... I have a deep and increasing sense of the wrong of all prizes and every stimulus of a competitive kind ... [but] I believe the recognition of an uncontending and natural worth to be one of the most solemn duties alike of young and old. Suppose you made it a custom that the scholars should annually choose by ballot, with vowed secrecy, their Queen of May? and that the elected Queen had, with other more important rights, that of giving the *Proserpina* to the girl she thought likeliest to use it with advantage?

Ruskin wrote this letter on 25 January, 1881. Sadly a second attack of insanity in February 1881 prevented him from actually visiting Whitelands College, but with sensible modifications from Faunthorp and others, the ceremony evolved in the next year or two and remains much the same today. Each year the Queen is elected by secret ballot, using Ruskin's instructions so that *the likeablest and loveablest* is elected. The Queen is given a complete set of Ruskin's thirty-eight books to give away as presents, keeping for herself a copy of his *Sesame and Lilies* or *Queen of the Air*. She is also given a cross (one of the earliest was designed by Burne-Jones) and a dress. The

Edward Burne-Jones
The Golden Stairs, 1872–80
Oil on canvas, 277 x 117 cm
This painting was known at first as *The King's Wedding* and then as *Music on the Stairs.* The model for the bodies of the girls was an Italian called Antonia Caiva, the heads were portraits of Aesthetic ladies, including May Morris, the fascinating Laura Tennant, Frances Graham and Margaret Burne-Jones. This was one of the first of his large-scale works and Burne-Jones was asked from all over the world for an explanation of its theme, but refused to supply one. It may have inspired Gilbert's chorus of lovesick maidens in *Patience*.

first one was designed by Kate Greenaway whom Ruskin asked to represent him at the ceremony in 1896.

Whitelands College has now moved to Putney, taking with it its eight stained-glass windows designed by William Morris and Burne-Jones. The ceremony of the May Queen's procession now takes place on the nearest Saturday after May Day, and it is a lovely sight to see the Queens of all ages wearing their dresses in a procession to the Maypole. As it is now a co-educational establishment some recent Queens have been male, and instead of dresses they are given embroidered waistcoats (the Whitelands girls once embroidered a waistcoat for Ruskin). To see the celebrations of May Day at Whitelands is to experience one of the most remarkable evocations of the Aesthetic Movement.

The subsequent history of the Grosvenor Gallery follows very much the declining fortunes of Aestheticism, as the final decade of the century ushered in the spirit of the *fin de siècle*, and its moment passed. In the 1880s, paintings by Alma-Tadema, Walter Crane, Fairfax Murray, Spencer Stanhope, Albert Moore and J.M. Strudwick were shown regularly. Every summer Burne-Jones exhibited tall yet relatively narrow paintings, which showed to great advantage on the lofty walls of the Grosvenor. Their format may derive from the artist's extensive experience in designing stained-glass windows. The first of these was *The Annunciation*, shown in 1879, the most austere of all the artist's treatments of the theme. *The Golden Stairs*, shown in 1880, was the labour of four years. Most of the figures on the staircase carry musical instruments, and this may exemplify Burne-Jones's belief in Pater's dictum that 'all art consistently aspires towards the condition of music'. When first exhibited one critic described how:

the figures troop past like spirits in an enchanted dream, each moving gracefully, freely and in unison with her neighbours ... What is the place they have left, why they pass before us thus, whither they go, who they are, there is nothing to tell.

In 1883 the rooms were lit by 'smokeless' electric light, an exciting novelty, and the *Wheel of Fortune* was exhibited to great acclaim, followed the year after by *King Cophetua and the Beggar Maid*, where it was seen by the artist Simeon Solomon, socially ostracised because of a homosexual scandal. He had become a 'drop out' living in St Giles Workhouse near Tottenham Court Road, from which he frequently emerged for a day out. In a letter he describes a visit to the Grosvenor Gallery with the exotic poet and satanist Count Stanislaus Stenbock, which is a revealing Aesthetic document:

I received a letter from Count Stenbock asking me to go to him as soon as possible... he received me with a low and truly Oriental salute.

Aubrey Beardsley
Caricature of Whistler,
c. 1893–4
Pen and ink, 20.1 x 10.7 cm
Beardsley admired and was greatly influenced by Whistler's Peacock Room, which he visited with his sister Mabel in 1891. This bold but malicious drawing suggests that little love was lost between the two men, although on seeing the drawings for *The Rape of the Lock*, Whistler said: 'Aubrey, I have made a mistake: You are a great artist.' At this Beardsley burst into tears.

He had on a magnificent blood red silk robe embroidered in gold and silver. He was swinging a silver censer before an altar covered with lilies, myrtles, lighted candles and a sanctuary lamp burning with scented oil ... The air was so heavy with incense, sandalwood and the scent of flowers that I felt quite faint. His appearance was that of a tall, graceful intellectual looking girl, and although he is not exactly good looking, his eyes and expression are very beautiful; he began to talk about everything that interests me, and played beautiful religious music on the piano and harmonium ... He then went to get shaved and buy more flowers. We then went to the Grosvenor where I much enjoyed myself. The Cophetua is wonderfully beautiful and good with the exception of the disagreeable colour of the drapery the maid is sitting on ...

The same year as the exhibition of Burne-Jones's *King Cophetua and the Beggar Maid* (1884), Whistler sent in for exhibition a portrait of Théodore Duret, an art critic which prompted Sir Coutts Lindsay to write to the artist: 'The work is so incomplete, so slightly made out I cannot accept it at the Grosvenor. I wish my dear Whistler that you would do yourself and me more justice and not send work that cannot do you credit.' Not content with alienating Whistler, Sir Coutts also fell out with Burne-Jones, who disapproved of the constant letting out of the rooms. Burne-Jones's strong feelings led him to transfer his allegiance to the New Gallery, which opened its doors in 1888 in Regent Street.

The New Gallery managers, Charles Hallé and Joseph Comyns Carr, had both resigned from the Grosvenor when its changes in management made it less sympathetic to artists. The gallery successfully advocated both symbolist and decorative work, housing in 1888 the first exhibition of the Arts and Crafts Exhibition Society with 'pyramids of De Morgan tiles ... glorious tapestries from Merton Abbey ... cartoons by Burne-Jones for stained glass ...' The New Gallery's success led to the closure of the Grosvenor Gallery in 1890 (just too late to have actually exhibited Basil Hallward's portrait of Dorian Gray!). It had played a remarkable role in the history of English art and its very name had become a legend.

Wilde once said that Whistler's Nocturne was worth looking at for about the same time as a real falling rocket, that is about a quarter of a minute. In the '*Ten O'clock*' lecture of 1885, alluding to Wilde and putting the vulgarity of popular aesthetics in its place, Whistler warned: 'And now from their midst the Dilettante stalks abroad, the amateur is loosed. The voice of the aesthete is heard in the land and catastrophe is upon us.'

The voice of the Aesthete was soon to be heard in the 'land of the free' during the travels of Oscar Wilde in America.

111

To understand it cling passionately to one another and think of faint lilies. W.S. GILBERT, *PATIENCE*, 1881

And when one thinks that once people mocked at stained glass attitudes! They are the only attitudes for the clothed. LETTER FROM OSCAR WILDE, 1900

Alfred Concanen
(1835–1886)
The High Art Maiden music
cover, c. 1880
Sheet music was a popular
gift during courtship and its
covers often vividly reflected
the visual concerns of the
Victorian era. This Aesthetic
lady stands in front of a row
of Japanese fans lost in
admiration at the sunflowers
in a vase on a 'what-not'
covered in 'artistic pottery'.
Alfred Concanen, one of the
unsung artistic heroes of the
Victorian era, produced
many hundreds if not
thousands of fine covers.

Nonsense perhaps, but oh ! what *precious* nonsense!

W.S. GILBERT, *PATIENCE*, 1881

The latest developments in contemporary art have always formed a reliable and staple subject for humour. The remarkable thing about the satirical comment upon the Aesthetic Movement is that it is remembered more vividly than the subject satirized. The Movement's serious intent was often ignored and it was much ridiculed for its affectations. Look up the words 'Aesthetic Movement' in many a dictionary of art and you will often find a reference to Gilbert and Sullivan's *Patience* which includes the lines:
I'm a greenery-yallery, Grosvenor Gallery
Foot-in-the-grave young man ... A
Francesca di Rimini, niminy, piminy,
'Je-ne-sais-quoi' young man ...

Controversies, such as the Peacock Room scandal and the Ruskin-Whistler libel case, put the personalities involved into the public arena. Satire and Aestheticism became inextricably linked, first in cartoons in *Punch* and then in novel form, notably in W.H. Mallock's *The New Republic* of 1877, which satirizes Walter Pater as Mr Rose. Oscar Wilde was victimized in Rhoda Broughton's *Second Thoughts* of 1880 as a 'flaccid limbed', 'long pale poet' who writes 'sweet-sick poems' which 'should be read ... to the low pale sound of the viol or virginal, with a subtle perfume of dead roses floating about, while the eye is red with porphyry vases and tender Tyrian dyes'. More damagingly he was satirized in 1894 as Esmé Amarinth in Robert Hitchin's *The Green Carnation*. Most memorable of all was his *alter ego* Bunthorne, the fleshly poet in Gilbert and Sullivan's *Patience*. Gilbert's sparkling satire on the soulfully intense, despairing droop of the Aesthetes was the climax of a long series of jokes made on the subject in the preceding decade.

Throughout its 150-year history the editors and cartoonists of the magazine *Punch* felt it their duty to lampoon affectation and fashionable folly. The Aesthetic Movement, with its exaggerated hyperbole of language and the bizarre costumes worn by its adherents, provided an ideal target. What on earth, they asked, on behalf of their Philistine readership, did the word Aestheticism mean? Had it not in its original and general sense, implied an attachment to Aesthetic principles? How did it come in the 1870s and 1880s to be applied to 'the worship of the lily and the peacock's feather'?

Such rhetorical questions were posed and answered with great effect in the lengthy captions then in vogue, ideally suited for making fun of the affected metaphors and hyperbole of Aesthetic speech. But surprisingly George Du Maurier whose name is so associated with the subject, was not the first to see its comic potential,

Right above: George Du Maurier (1834–1896)
An Impartial Statement in Black and White
From *Punch*, 9 April, 1881

Right centre: George Du Maurier
The Cimabue Browns
From *Punch Almanack*, 1880

Right below: George Du Maurier
A Love Agony
From *Punch*, 5 June, 1880

that honour going to the finer draughtsman but lesser wit Charles Keene. On 29 August, 1868 Keene's cartoon showed an artist named 'Fadsby', a martyr to the decorative art of the nineteenth century, imploring his landlady to remove two Staffordshire chimney ornaments from his mantelpiece categorizing them as 'fictile abominations'. These are difficult words to appear in the caption of a joke in a comic weekly paper, and already indicate that satire of the Aesthetes was to concentrate particularly on their affected use of language. But Keene's heart was not really in the subject and although on 7 October, 1871 he portrayed a nephew with Aesthetic tastes discussing his carpets with a Philistine uncle under the title *A Thing of Beauty*, it is not until Du Maurier first tackles the subject in 1874 that humour really ignites.

Du Maurier's enigmatic personality is a puzzling one. Although himself an artist, he became the most powerful 'Philistine' critic of Aestheticism. As a young man, before losing the sight of one eye, he had been a fellow student with Poynter, Thomas Armstrong, and Whistler at Gleyre's academy in Paris, experiences which he would later use in his novel *Trilby*. For more than thirty years, week after week he was to draw a 'social' cartoon for *Punch*. Towards the end of his career he gave his thoughts on this exacting work:

... the illustrator in black-and-white ... must not hope for any very high place in the hierarchy of art. The great prizes are not for him! But if he has done his work well, he has faithfully represented the life of his time; and for that reason alone, his unpretending little sketches may ... have more interest for those who come across them in another hundred years, than many an ambitious ... canvas.

Du Maurier's words were prophetic, and certainly his Aesthetic cartoons for *Punch* did achieve the permanent interest for which he hoped. They appeared during the significantly short time span of the eight years from 1874 to 1882 when Aestheticism was at the height of fashion.

He chronicles every aspect of the Aesthetic style of costume which could be seen in all drawing rooms with a pretension to culture. For men it consisted of knee breeches, loose flowing tie and velvet jacket – a modification of the French romantic artist costumes described in Henri Murger's novel of 1845, *Scènes de la vie de Bohème*. The Aesthetic Woman daringly wore no corsets, but a loose robe emblazoned with embroidered sunflowers, flat shoes, and hair brushed forward over the eyes in emulation of a female model in a Burne-Jones or Rossetti painting.

Indeed his cartoons in *Punch* were at first aimed not at individuals but types, and their affected use of language. To this end he invented an Aesthetic family, the Cimabue Browns, and their friends the dilettantes Mr and Mrs Ponsonby De Tomkins, who all deeply admire the painter Maudle (painter of maudlin and sentimental love agonies) and poet Postlethwaite, characters possessing thinly-veiled references to Solomon, Whistler and Wilde. The Cimabue Browns, like the similar imaginary high-powered media family the Stringalongs (who also lived in N.W.5) created by Alan Bennett and so effectively visualized by Marc Boxer a century later, represent the 'intellectual' pretensions of Hampstead at their most extreme. Du Maurier dubbed his Aesthetic family the Cimabue Browns because of the immense acclaim which had greeted Leighton's painting of *The Triumphant Procession of Cimabue's Madonna through the Streets of Florence* when first exhibited at the Royal Academy in 1855.

An early example of Du Maurier's work is *Reciprocity* (16 January, 1875) a witty comment on Whistler's use of musical terminology in the titles of his paintings. The caption reads: 'The Arts are borrowing each other's vocabulary – Painting has its 'Harmonies' and 'Symphonies': Music is beginning to return the compliment.'

A series of compliments are showered on a clever pianist, congratulating him on the colour in his fortissimos, roundness of modelling in his pianissimos, perspective in his crescendos, chiaroscuro in his diminuendos etc, etc, etc.

Lengthy though such captions are, it was (and still is) far easier to glean the concerns of the Aesthetes through Du Maurier's cartoons than by reading Swinburne or Pater, or by attending the type of party given by an artist like Henry Holiday, painter of the famous *Dante meeting Beatrice*, stained-glass designer and keen supporter of dress reform for women. Such gatherings were:

THE PASSION FOR OLD CHINA.

full of weird people, women in cotton frocks of faded hues, made wide at the hips & tight at the feet like Turkish trowsers [*sic*] – and lank draperies of all sorts ... Miss Holiday fiddled, and a youth with anaemic face & hair played the piano, & someone, in a nasal voice, sang a long, long pseudo mediaeval ballad about a King's daughter & a swineherd, with an idiotic & melancholy refrain. It felt so completely high art[1].

Du Maurier's drawing *Flippancy Punished* of 14 April, 1877 portrays just such a party at the Cimabue Browns, as does *A Refined Aesthetic Exquisite* of 16 March, 1878. These drawings still retain their wit. Amongst the funniest are those which ridicule the craze for collecting blue and white china which appeared in *Punch* between 2 May, 1874 and 30 October, 1880. *Acute Chinamania*, *Punch Almanack* (1875) depicts a distraught woman contemplating some broken pottery. One of her daughters tries to comfort her: 'Mamma! Mamma!

THE SIX-MARK TEA-POT.

Æsthetic Bridegroom. "IT IS QUITE CONSUMMATE, IS IT NOT!"
Intense Bride. "IT IS, INDEED! OH, ALGERNON, LET US LIVE UP TO IT!"

Opposite above: George Du Maurier
Acute Chinamania
From *Punch Almanack,* **1875**

Opposite below: George Du Maurier
Passion for Old China
From *Punch,* **2 May, 1874**

Above: George Du Maurier
Six-Mark Tea-pot
From *Punch,* **30 October, 1880**

Don't go on like this, pray!'
'What have I got left to live for?'
'Haven't you got me, Mamma?'
'You child! You're not unique!! There are six of you – a complete set!!'

The plain walls hung simply with plates depicted in this cartoon may be a reference to Whistler's austere notions on room decoration. Another famous cartoon entitled *The Passion For Old China* (2 May, 1874) depicts a young couple cradling a six-mark china teapot. The husband speaks: 'I think you might let me nurse that teapot a little now, Margery – you've had it to yourself all the morning you know!'

But the most famous of all the china mania cartoons was to provide Wilde, for whom the word charisma might have been invented, with the initial lift-off to his career. His passion for 'blue and white' had developed while still an undergraduate at Oxford, where he was credited with the remark: 'I find it harder and harder every day to live up to my blue china', the first of many of his aphorisms to gain international celebrity. It scandalized the university, provoking criticism from the pulpit of St Mary's, Oxford, where Dean Burgess denounced a time: 'When a young man says not in polished banter, but in sober earnestness, that he finds it difficult to live up to the level of his blue china, there has crept into these cloistered shades a form of heathenism which it is our bounden duty to fight against and to crush out, if possible.'

From such promising early notoriety reputations are made, and soon the aphorism became widely celebrated in Du Maurier's cartoon of *Punch,* 30 October, 1880, *The Six-Mark Tea-pot* depicting an affected newly married couple. The Aesthetic Bridegroom speaks: 'It is quite consummate is it not?'
The Intense Bride replies:
'It is, indeed! Oh, Algernon, let us live up to it!'

Again and again *Punch* turned to Oscar for a laugh, a reviewer hailing the publication of a slim volume of Wilde's poems as 'Swinburne and Water' but praising its appearance, 'the cover is consummate, the paper is distinctly precious, the binding beautiful and the type is utterly too'[2]. When Wilde visited the Grosvenor Gallery in a coat shaped like a cello, *Punch* broke into verse:

The haunt of the very aesthetic,
Here come the supremely intense,
The long-haired and hyper-poetic,
Whose sound is mistaken for sense.
And many a maiden will mutter,

When Oscar looms large on her sight,
'He's quite too consummately utter,
As well as too utterly quite.'

     A well-leaked presentation of
an amaryllis to the legendary beauty Lily
Langtry led to reports suggesting that Wilde
strolled down Piccadilly indulging in small arm
exercises with sunflowers, in a manner that set
the seal on a sensational 'public image'. As
Wilde later remarked: 'To have done it was
nothing, but to make people think one had
done it was a triumph'. The incident prompted
several cartoons by Du Maurier in *Punch*,
notably Jellaby Postlethwaite's portrayal as
Narcissus swamped by drooping lilies in Maudle's
painting *A Love Agony* 5 June, 1880, and *An
Aesthetic Midday Meal* 17 July, 1880, in which
Postlethwaite contemplates a lily in a glass of
water in lieu of lunch.

     Gilbert used this material in
the final lines of *Patience* when Bunthorne's
fate is revealed – he alone of all the cast must
remain single although everyone else plunges
into matrimony:

... Single I must live and die
I shall have to be contented
With a tulip or Lily!

(Takes a lily for buttonhole etc) although elsewhere he confesses that
as an aesthetic sham: 'A languid love for lilies does not blight me'.

     Although these cartoons did so much to prepare the
ground for the libretto of W.S.Gilbert's *Patience*, Du Maurier was
himself to help its main theatrical rival for the public's attention. This
was another skit on the Aesthetes, *The Colonel*, an adaptation of a
French farce by F.C. Burnand, the editor of *Punch*, to whom Du
Maurier, a loyal member of the magazine's staff, sent a wonderful story
describing how Wilde once came down to breakfast in a country house
looking drawn and haggard, explaining that he had been sitting up all
night with a sick primrose.[3] Du Maurier used this incident himself in
a skit and drawing which appeared in *Punch* on 25 December, 1880. In
it Postlethwaite's determination 'to sit up up all night with a lily', is
amusingly superseded by an even braver resolve:

     I sat up all night with a Botanical Dictionary, and hit upon the

Right above: *The Colonel
Waltz* **music cover, 1881
Sheet music was a
popular gift, and its
covers would often
provide a visual souvenir
of a successful show.
An intense Aesthetic
lady, lilies, sunflowers
and peacock feathers
frame a scene from the
successful comedy.**

Right below: Scene from
The Colonel
From *The Illustrated
Sporting and Dramatic
News*, **19 February, 1881**

very flower at last – the Utter Blossom! The Perfect Thing!!... Good Philistines, every one you are the witnesses to the fact that I ... in a snowstorm at mid-winter, nine thousand feet above the level of the sea at considerable personal risk ... am SITTING UP ALL NIGHT WITH AN EDELWEISS!

F.C. Burnand, sensing a theatrical bonanza, opened *The Colonel* at the Prince of Wales Theatre in February 1881, just two months before *the* smash hit of the year dealing with the same theme, *Patience*. A few months later *The Colonel* achieved the ultimate Victorian accolade of success, royal approval, in what might be described as the strange story of how Queen Victoria *was* amused.

In 1881 Queen Victoria was staying as usual at Balmoral for the summer. Within driving distance was Abergeldie Castle, which since his marriage the Prince of Wales had made his home during the grouse shooting season. Twenty years had passed since the demise of Albert, the Prince Consort, and at last the Queen was persuaded that a little light might penetrate the gloom of her widowhood and was encouraged to visit Abergeldie Castle for the evening to attend a theatrical command performance. The curtain rose. On to the stage came the figure of Lambert Stryke, a thinly veiled caricature of the young Oscar Wilde. Stryke's opening speech set the tone for the rest of the play:

The object which the Aesthetic High Art Company, Limited, has in view is the cultivation of The Ideal as the consummate embodiment of The Real, and to proclaim aloud to a dull, material world the worship of the Lily and the Peacock's Feather.

(Exclamations from the rest of the cast – 'Perfect', 'Too Precious', 'Consummate'!) The Queen's own able pen takes up the story:

The piece given was *The Colonel* in three acts, a very clever play, written to quiz and ridicule the foolish aesthetic people who dress in such an absurd manner, with loose garments, large puffed sleeves, great hats, and carrying peacock's feathers, sunflowers and lilies. It was very well acted, and strange to say, most of the actors are gentlemen by birth, who have taken to the stage as a profession. It was the first time I had seen professionals act a regular play since March '61. We got home shortly before twelve, having been very much amused ...

Not only the Queen was amused. The play had already run in London for over six months, and several touring companies were on the road, including the one that performed that evening. Its success was to continue. 'It ran, ran, ran. Over a year!' as Burnand noted with great satisfaction in his memoirs. Unlike *Patience*, however, its fame has not survived, for it lacked both Gilbert's wit and Sullivan's

Left: *My Aesthetic Love* music cover, 1881
Once again peacock feathers, lilies, Japanese fans and Godwin's 'Anglo-Japanese' furniture are satirized. It is intriguing to note that this song was popularized by 'The Great Vance', the *lion comique* of the music halls, who is remembered for his song in praise of Clicquot champagne.

Opposite: *Lady Jane's High Art Dado*
From *The Illustrated Sporting and Dramatic News*, 23 April, 1881
This cartoon first appeared after the first night of *Patience*. For some reason the very word 'dado' was irresistibly funny, an effect which was intensified when it appeared around the substantial figure of the cellist Lady Jane.

music. Indeed much of its success was owed to the sets created with the advice of George Du Maurier, who wrote to Burnand:

> Try & have a room papered with Morris' green Daisy, with a dado six feet high of green-blue serge in folds – and a matting with rugs for floor (Indian red matting if possible), spider-legged black tables & sideboard – black rush-bottomed chairs and arm chairs; blue china plates on the wall with plenty of space between – here and there a blue china vase with an enormous hawthorn or almond blossom sprig ... also on mantelpiece pots with lilies & peacock feathers – plain dull yellow curtains lined with dull blue for windows if wanted. Japanese sixpenny fans now & then on the walls in picturesque unexpectedness.

Although the audience laughed at the extreme Aesthetic style of the furnishings, several critics described them with admiration, notably E.W. Godwin who wrote that:

> the set presented to us as wrong, we find is furnished with artistic and simple things; ... some simple inexpensive Sussex chairs like those sold by Messrs W. Morris & Co., a black coffee table after the well known example originally designed in 1867 by the writer of these notes; a quite simple writing table, matting on the floor, a green and yellow paper, a sunflower frieze, a Japanese treatment of the ceiling and a red sun such as we see in Japanese books, and a hand screen, make up a scheme which if ... forced in sunflowers, is certainly an intriguing room with individuality about it, quiet in tone, and what is most important, harmonious and pleasing.

It is interesting to note that new ideas in Aesthetic furnishing were so generally accepted by 1881 that furniture for the set was purchased in Edinburgh to save the cost of transport from London, and some additional pieces were borrowed from the Prince and Princess of Wales. Queen Victoria's succinct summary of why she was so much amused expresses a view shared by the majority of her subjects, who found the costumes worn by 'foolish aesthetic people' extremely funny, not to mention their ideas about 'the Real' and 'the Ideal'. Indeed, these pretensions have affected all those who have attempted to chronicle the movement. Listen to the voice of the early historian and (qualified) partisan of the movement, Walter Hamilton, who in 1882, a year after Queen Victoria's evening out, wrote the first book on the subject entitled *The Aesthetic Movement in England*. He tempered his admiration for Aestheticism with trenchant criticism of its affectation, writing of paintings seen at the Grosvenor Gallery:

> It is in the portrayal of female beauty that aesthetic art is most peculiar, both in conception as of what constitutes female loveliness, and in the treatment of it. The type most

Lady Jane's High Art Dado.

121

usually found is that of a 'pale distraught lady with matted dark auburn hair falling in masses over her brow, and shading eyes full of lovelorn languor or feverish despair; emaciated cheeks and somewhat heavy jaws; protruding upper lip, the lower lip being indrawn, long crane neck, flat breasts, and long thin nervous hands.

Mrs H.R. Haweis in *The Art of Beauty* (London, 1878) is much kinder in tone:

Those dear and much abused 'Prae-Raphaelite' painters, whom it is still in some circles the fashion to decry, are the plain girl's best friends. They have taken all the neglected ones by the hand. All the ugly flowers, all the ugly buildings, all the ugly faces, they have shown us to have a certain crooked beauty of their own, entirely apart from the oddness which supplies the place of actual beauty sometimes, and is almost as attractive ... The 'Prae Raphaelites' have taught us that that there is no ugliness in fact, except deformity ... Morris, Burne-Jones and others, have made certain types of face once literally hated, actually the fashion. Red hair – once, to say a woman had red hair was social assassination – is the rage. A pallid face with a protruding upper lip is highly esteemed ... now is the time for plain women. Only dress after the Prae-Raphaelite style, and you will be astonished to find that so far from being an 'ugly duck' you are a full-fledged swan!

This practical advice was quite clearly widely followed by a surprisingly large number of women who formed easy targets for the cartoonists, Du Maurier, and Linley Sambourne.

Sometimes things could go sadly wrong. Listen, for example, to 'A chronicler of the time' quoted by Max Beerbohm in his essay on the 1880s, published in the *Yellow Book* in 1892:

There were quaint, beautiful, extraordinary costumes walking about – ultra-aesthetics, artistic aesthetics, aesthetics that made up their mind to be daring, and suddenly gave way in some important point – put a frivolous bonnet on the top of a grave and glowing garment that Albert Dürer might have designed for a mantle. Such descriptions could almost be verbatim instructions for costume designs in *Patience*.

Like Lambert Stryke in *The Colonel*, Bunthorne, the central character of *Patience*, is an amalgam of Wilde's personality with characteristics from other leading Aesthetic figures, Walter Crane's velvet coat and

Opposite: *An Aesthetic lady artist clutching her mahl stick* From *The Illustrated Sporting and Dramatic News*, c. 1880

Above and right: The original programme of *Patience* after it transferred to the Savoy Theatre on 10 October, 1881, and a photograph of the original cast throwing themselves into 'stained glass' attitudes, whilst trying to look 'both angular and flat'.

Whistler's black curls, white lock of hair, moustache, eye glass and the famous Whistler 'Ha, Ha'. Indeed George Grossmith played the role as Whistler. In the character of Grosvenor Rossetti's soulfulness, Swinburne's sensuality and Ruskin's Gothicizing were all parodied. Yet it was Wilde's charismatic personality that the public most closely identified with the piece. In Act I Bunthorne sings:

Though the philistines may jostle, you will rank as an apostle in the high aesthetic band, If you walk down Piccadilly with a poppy or a lily in your mediaeval hand.

Wilde's life can in retrospect be seen as one long jostle with the Philistines. The first night of *Patience* at the Opéra Comique on St George's Day was enjoyed hugely, the patter songs receiving eight encores. Yet rather surprisingly, at the end of April 1881 the impresario and company manager Richard D'Oyly Carte was a worried man. He had welded together the disparate talents of W.S. Gilbert and Arthur Sullivan into the most effective comic partnership of the century and a great theatrical success had just opened under his management. However, he was perturbed for he had read with concern a review of *Patience* in the popular journal, *The Referee*, which noted how many of the jokes had passed over the heads of even the worldly first night London audience. Carte sensed that the theme of the operetta would need explanation for the less sophisticated provincial public.

He issued a helpful circular:

I have the pleasure to announce that my opera company is about to visit your neighbourhood ... The 'movement' in the direction of a more artistic feeling, which had its commencement some time since in the works of Mr Ruskin and his supporters, doubtless did much to render our everyday existence more pleasant and more beautiful. Latterly however, their pure and healthy teaching has given place to the outpourings of a clique of professors of ultra-refinement, who preach the gospel of morbid languor and sickly sensuousness, which is half real and half affected by its high priests for the purpose of gaining social notoriety. Generally speaking the new school is distinguished by an eccentricity of taste tending to an unhealthy admiration for exhaustion, corruption and decay. In satirizing the excesses of these (so-called) aesthetes, the authors of *Patience* have not desired to cast ridicule on the true aesthetic spirit, but only to attack the unmanly oddities which masquerade in its likeness. In doing so, they have succeeded in producing one of the prettiest and most diverting musical pleasantries of the day.

This statement with its slightly uneasy use of such perjorative terms as morbid languor, sickly sensuousness, unhealthy and unmanly, reveals an early awareness of what would now be described as the 'high camp' tendencies latent in many followers of the movement. It clarifies *why* Gilbert satirized Aestheticism, and fortunately we also have Gilbert's own explanation for the initial conception of the piece and its fantastic plot. Gilbert, who breakfasted with Whistler on the first day of the Ruskin libel case, had already dabbled with Aesthetic themes having written *Pygmalion and Galatea* and a parody on Tennyson's *Princess*, later to be reworked as *Princess Ida*. For *Patience* he had originally intended to use clergymen in the plot, entitling the piece *The Rival Curates*, which sounds like a musical version of Trollope's *Barchester Towers*, but:

> I became uneasy at ... dealing so freely with members of the clerical order. ... As I lay awake one night, worrying over the difficulties that I had prepared for myself, the idea suddenly flashed upon me that if I made Bunthorne and Grosvenor a couple of yearning 'aesthetics' and the young ladies their ardent admirers, all anxieties as to the consequences of making them extremely ridiculous would be at once overcome. Elated at the idea, I ran down at once to my library, and in an hour or so I had entirely rearranged the piece upon a secure and satisfactory basis.

We can be fairly sure that Gilbert consulted in his library back numbers of *Punch*. Writing the following year in 1882, the first chronicler of the Aesthetic Movement, Walter Hamilton, was in no doubt that Du Maurier's cartoons had been the direct inspiration for *Patience*. In his book he complains bitterly of the unfairness of all the satires of the Aesthetic Movement but singles out Du Maurier's work for special opprobrium. He wrote:

> the fact is, that Maudle and Company, as portrayed, were not altogether imaginary individuals, but belonged to a comparatively new school, which has done, and is still doing, an immense amount of good towards the advancement of Art in this country and America. That there are persons of Aesthetic tastes who carry them to the borders of absurdity goes without saying; every movement in intellectual, or political, life has its over-enthusiastic apostles, who damage the cause they have at heart; but that there must be some good in the movement is clearly shown by its having earned the abuse of a journal which never has a generous word to say for any one beyond its own immediate and narrow circle.

It was, however, not Du Maurier but Walter Crane whom W.S. Gilbert initially invited to design the decor and costumes for *Patience*, not wanting to be outdone by the success of the sets devised for *The Colonel*. Although Crane actually did some designs for the project, they were never used, for he withdrew from the commission, possibly because he had little enthusiasm for helping to lampoon fellow exhibitors at the Grosvenor Gallery and friends like Burne-Jones. In the event, the costumes were designed by W.S. Gilbert himself and

James Hadley
Aesthetic Teapot, 1882
Glazed porcelain
The base is inscribed,
'Fearful consequences
through the laws of Natural
Selection and Evolution of
living up to one's teapot',
thus neatly satirizing Wilde,
Aestheticism and Darwin's
theories of evolution.

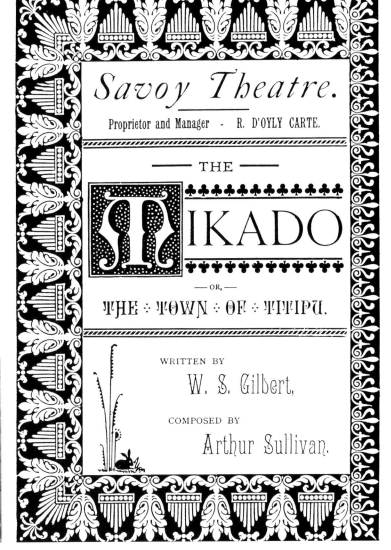

Above left: George Grossmith as Pooh-Bah carrying the samurai sword which fell from Gilbert's wall and inspired him to write *The Mikado*. Only nine months later on 14 March, 1885 the curtain rose at the Savoy Theatre on one of the best-loved comic operettas in the English language.

Above right: Original programme for *The Mikado*, 1885

made up in fashionable Liberty textiles, as advertised in the programme. But when he saw *Patience* Crane thought that some of his ideas had influenced the final effect.

A teapot produced at Worcester is reminiscent of costumes in the piece. One side of the vessel portrays a long-haired, limp-wristed male Aesthete with a sunflower pinned to his chest, while the other depicts a lady with a lily. The base is inscribed 'Fearful consequences through the laws of Natural Selection and Evolution of living up to one's teapot', thus neatly satirizing Darwinism and Aestheticism at a stroke.

In October 1881, *Patience* was moved to the brand new Savoy Theatre, which was custom-built for Gilbert and Sullivan operettas, and equipped for the first time in a public building with the new invention, electric light. The interior decorations were by Collinson and Lock, and although neither in the 'Queen Anne', 'early English' or the so-called 'Aesthetic manner', they would be appreciated, the Management felt, 'by all persons of taste'.

Gilbert and Sullivan
From *The Illustrated Sporting and Dramatic News*, **c. 1867**

In 1902, two years after Wilde's death, the *Encyclopedia Britannica* described his early career at Oxford: and the part he played in what came to be known as the Aesthetic Movement. He adopted what to undergraduates appeared the effeminate pose of casting scorn on manly sports, wearing his hair long, decorating his rooms with peacock's feathers, lilies, sunflowers, blue china, and other *objets d'art*, which he declared his desire to 'live up to', affecting a lackadaisical manner, and professing intense emotions on the subject of 'art for art's sake' – then a new-fangled doctrine which Mr Whistler was bringing into prominence. Wilde made himself the apostle of this new cult, which – although at Oxford his behaviour procured him a ducking in the Cherwell, and a wrecking of his rooms – spread among certain sections of society to such an extent that languishing attitudes, 'too-too' costumes and 'Aestheticism' generally became a recognized pose, and culminated in the production of Gilbert and Sullivan's travesty *Patience* which practically killed by ridicule the absurdities to which it had grown.

We now see that rather than killing by ridicule, *Patience* really put Aestheticism on the map. Its popularity led to Ruskin's favourite adjective 'consummately' becoming a comic catchword. It helped the general public to understand the association of Aesthetic ideas with the emergence of the Queen Anne style. It aroused a new interest in the decorative arts, particularly in the wallpapers and chintzes of Morris & Co which remarkably are the only Aesthetic, indeed the only high Victorian, artifacts which have never ceased to be manufactured nor gone wholly out of fashion right up to the present day.

D'Oyly Carte was even more concerned about the reception that *Patience* met in America where it opened in New York five months later. The idea of sending Wilde to advertise the show and his subsequent tour of America are chronicled in the next chapter. He was not completely unknown there before he arrived, as his coming had already been heralded by Du Maurier's cartoons which had become equally well known in America since they were pirated or appropriated immediately after their appearance in *Punch* by American illustrated papers, notably the *New York Daily Graphic*.

The success of the publicity generated by his tour

can be gauged by the vast numbers of comic cards produced at the time with an Aesthetic theme and also by the publication of original American satirical works of real calibre such as *The Decorative Sisters* by Josephine Pollard. This was a 'Modern Ballad', illustrated by Walter Satterlee, published in New York in 1882, the sad tale of two normal young ladies who become 'intense' and desert a healthy life in the country to: '... gaze upon a lily, so "unutterably utter," With eyes distended wide as if the blossom they'd devour'.

Aestheticism continued to triumph over common sense until well after Oscar Wilde's return from his American tour, and his adoption of the more conventional costume of the dandy. The change was noted on 31 March, 1883 when *Punch* carried a spoof advertisement:

To be sold, the whole of the Stock-in-Trade, Appliances and Inventions of a Successful Aesthete, who is retiring from business. This will include a large stock of faded lilies, dilapidated Sunflowers, and shabby Peacock's Feathers, several long-haired Wigs, a collection of incomprehensible Poems, and a number of impossible Pictures. Also, a valuable Manuscript Work, entitled Instructions to Aesthetes, containing a list of aesthetic catchwords, drawings of aesthetic attitudes, and many choice secrets of the craft. Also, a number of well-used Dadoes, sad-coloured Draperies, blue and white China, and brass fenders ... No reasonable offer refused.

Just as Aestheticism had provided the ideal satirical subject for Gilbert and Sullivan in 1881, so four years later would the cult of Japan. The production of *The Mikado* was the event which really ensured the popularity of Japanese art in England and America by making gentle fun of it. The libretto created the land of Titipu, a satiric mirror of England dressed *'à la japonais'*. Gilbert's own words provide us with the initial moment of inspiration: 'An executioner's sword hanging on the wall of my library – the very sword carried by Mr Grossmith at his entrance in the first act – suggested the broad idea upon which the libretto is based.'

W.S. Gilbert, a stickler for accuracy in his productions, was delighted when, at an exhibition of Japanese goods in Knightsbridge, he found an authentic Japanese geisha girl who could instruct his 'three little maids' in the correct furling and unfurling of their fans to denote wrath, delight or homage, despite the fact that her English was limited to 'sixpence please', the price of a cup of tea in Knightsbridge.

The first lines of the operetta do much to explain the source of popular enthusiasm for things Japanese:
If you want to know who we are

·WISHING·YOU·AN·UTTERLY·CHARMING·TIME·

·VERY·PRECIOUS·WISHES·FOR·YOU·

·MAY·YOU·HAVE·A·QUITE·TOO·HAPPY·TIME·

·WITH·YEARNINGS·FOR·YOUR·INTENSE·JOY·

Opposite: A. J. Ludovici Junior (fl. 1888–90) Four Aesthetic Christmas cards, c. 1880 They caricature what a review of these designs in *Society* on 1 October, 1881 described as 'those aethereal beings who can lunch on a lily, dine on a daffodil, enjoy a Barmicide feast on a sunflower, to whom fans are necessaries of life, and teapots teach high moral lessons'.

Above: Pears Soap advertisement, c. 1885 English advertising in the Victorian era enjoyed humorous topical allusions to passing fads and fashions. This is one of many entertaining soap advertisements issued by Pears who once used Millais's *Bubbles* to further their sales. It shows a pair of children dressed in 'Kate Greenaway' dress arranging a display of 'blue and white'.

We are gentlemen of Japan
On many a vase and jar
On many a screen and fan ...

       The material for the costumes was supplied by Liberty's and 'Liberty's Art Fabrics' were advertised in the programme of the original performance on 14 March, 1885. Liberty's also loyally refused to sell a duplicate set of fabric to an American named Duff, who was rushing to bring out a pirated production of the piece in New York before the official production.

       As Arthur Sullivan remarked of the American judges, who decided against appeals to stop unauthorized performances: 'It seemed to be their opinion that a free and independent American citizen ought not to be robbed of his rights of robbing somebody else'. The piracy of artistic and literary work is a recurrent theme of Anglo-

American relations in the late nineteenth century. Just occasionally it could actually prompt new ideas in the victim. When Walter Crane arrived on his tour of the USA in 1891 he told several reporters that it was a pirated American wallpaper with patterns borrowed and adapted from his children's books which had first led him to design paper hangings in 1875.

Duff's agent went on to Paris, but Richard D'Oyly Carte had purchased every Japanese costume in that city, declaring: 'I don't mind how much money I spend to smash Duff!'. The subsequent successful rush to New York by the official company to open before the pirated version and secure American copyright led, during the winter of 1885–6, to Madison Square Gardens housing a '*Mikado*' village with demonstrations of silk weaving, which prompted the appearance of a *Mikado* room in every New York home of artistic pretensions.

Aestheticism in all its aspects produced ideal themes for mockery from its critics. Many aspects of the life of Bedford Park, 'the Aesthetic Elysium', provided natural themes for parody, notably the fancy dress parties, when ladies dressed 'à la Greenaway' or wore the ubiquitous Japanese kimonos. The most celebrated of such satires was an anonymous poem, *The Ballad of Bedford Park*, published in the *St James's Gazette* on 17 December, 1881. Often reprinted, no book on the Aesthetic Movement is complete without extensive quotation from it. It opens by describing the developer Jonathan T. Carr's quest for a rural site:

'Not too near London, and yet not
What might be called too far.

T'is there a village I'll erect
With Norman Shaw's assistance
Where men may lead a chaste correct
Aesthetical existence ...'

They select Turnham Green as a site:

'Tis here, my Norman tried and true
our houses we'll erect;
I'll be the landlord bold, and you
Shall be the Architect.

'Here trees are green and bricks are red
and clean the face of man;
We'll build our houses here,' he said,
'In style of good Queen Anne'.

And Norman Shaw looked up and saw,
and smiled a cheerful smile.
'This thing I'll do', said he, 'while you
the denizens beguile.'

To work went then these worthy men,
so philanthropic both;
And none who sees the bricks and trees
to sign the lease is loth.

Kate Greenaway
Afternoon Tea
From *Birthday Book for Children*, 1880
A runaway commercial success this birthday book, which first appeared in 1880, sold more than 150,000 copies and earned Kate over £1,100. It was published by Edmund Evans who perfected a technique of colour printing which brought him fame as the printer of children's books not only by Kate Greenaway, but also by Walter Crane and Randolph Caldecott.

'Let's have a stores,' said Jonathan;
said Norman, 'So we will,
For naught can soothe the soul of man
like a reasonable bill.'

'A Church likewise,' J.T. replies
Says Shaw, 'I'll build a Church,
Yet sure I fear the aesthetes here
will leave it in the lurch.'

'Religion' pious Carr rejoined,
'in Moncure Conway's view,
Is not devoid of interest
although it be not true

'Then let us make a house for her,
wherein she may abide,
And those who choose may visit her;
the rest may stay outside'…

With red and blue and sagest green
Were walls and dado dyed,
Friezes of Morris there were seen
And oaken wainscot wide.

Thus was a village builded
For all who are aesthete
Whose precious souls it fill did
With utter joy complete.

For floors were stained and polished
And every hearth was tiled
And Philistines abolished
By Culture's gracious child…

Now he who loves aesthetic cheer
and does not mind the damp
May come and read Rossetti here
By a Japanese-y lamp.

At the stores in Bedford Park its inhabitants could select from a wide range of Christmas cards. The designs show Aestheticism *in excelsis*. W.S. Coleman drew little girls in the nude with titles that speak for themselves: *Girlish Beauties*, *Jocund Youth*, and *Nymphs of the Grove*. Four Christmas cards by A. J. Ludovici are also justly famous, one showing an excited lady Aesthete clutching a teapot, others showing male Aesthetes in poses of affected ecstasy adoring respectively sunflowers and lilies. On another card by A. Gray, a young woman is portrayed as an artist wearing a tight-fitting dress embroidered with sunflowers, holding a palette and brushes. Although it represents painting both her eyes are shut! The text reads 'A most intensely utter Christmas & Ecstatic New Year'. Still another card, also by A. Gray, shows:

A blue and white damozel,

A Japanese damozel,

A China adoring, bric-a-brac storing,

Dresden-and-Sevres damozel:

who is shown kneeling in front of a sunflower frieze, holding a peacock feather and emotionally admiring a blue-and-white dish on the wall. The design on the dish is a crane, caricaturing the signature made famous by Walter Crane.

Other ephemeral visual images which vividly conjure

An eclectic mixture of Aesthetic imagery from children's books and Christmas cards.

Clockwise from top left:
Randoph Caldecott
(1846–86)
Hey Diddle Diddle the Cat and the Fiddle, 1878

An anonymous Christmas card with the ubiquitous Japanese parasol.

Walter Crane
From *The Sleeping Beauty*, 1876
This was one of Crane's most delightful books for children.

Kate Greenaway
Christmas card

William Stephen Coleman
(1829–1904)
Christmas card
Coleman was the Director of Minton's Art Pottery Studios and a successful designer of Christmas cards depicting nubile young nymphettes, surprising messengers of festive greetings.

Anonymous Christmas card featuring a Japanese fan and a sparrow.

up Aesthetic pursuits, are the entertaining sheet music covers by Alfred Concanen (1835–86) with such titles as *Quite Too Utterly Utter*, *The Fine Art Maiden*, and *My Aesthetic Love*, the object of whose affection is a pensive maiden, described in these lines:

She's utterly utter consummate too too!
And feeds on the lily and old china blue,
And with a sunflower she'll sit for an hour,
She's utterly utter consummate too too.

The singer of this song was 'The Great Vance – the Lion Comique of the Halls', whose rival the Great MacDermott achieved fame in 1877 by introducing the word 'jingoism' into the English language. Disraeli, out of office, advocated British participation in the Russo-Turkish war, and MacDermott made every major music hall in London resonate with the belligerent refrain:

We don't want to fight, But, by jingo, if we do
We've got the ships, we've got the men, we've got the money too.

These sentiments, like the poems of Rudyard Kipling, strengthened a general belief in the innate superiority of the British Empire, which played a part in the demise of the Aesthetic age in the 1880s. By 1888 Andrew Lang regretted in his *Ballade of Queen Anne* that although:

F. Hamilton Jackson
(1848–1923)
*St Michael and All Angels,
Bedford Park,* 1881
Colour lithograph,
22.2 x 36 cm
This tranquil garden scene
is distinguished by the large
group of sunflowers, the
little girl carrying a
Japanese parasol, and the
lady reading. The church,
which was designed by
Richard Norman Shaw, to
this day has a sage green
interior.

We buy her chairs
Her china blue
Her red-brick squares
We build anew;
But ah! we rue
When all is said
The tale o'er true
Queen Anne is dead!
Friends, praise the new;
The old is fled:
Vivat FROU-FROU
Queen Anne is dead!

No sooner was the Aesthetic age over and the Queen Anne style at an end than these phenomena came under the clear-sighted scrutiny of the youthful Max Beerbohm who, according to Oscar Wilde, paradoxically 'had the gift of perpetual old age'. In the 1890s Beerbohm moved the role of satire and parody into the centre of the stage. In an essay in the *Yellow Book* he wittily reviewed the events of the 1880s as though they were a remote historical period. In a series of brilliant caricatures he satirized the figures of his own day, both decadent Aesthetes such as Oscar Wilde and 'hearties' like Kipling.

I do wish I could make him [Oscar] less Sybarite, less Epicurean. He said this morning, 'Let me gather the golden fruits of America that I may spend a winter in Italy and a summer in Greece among beautiful things.' Oh dear - if he would spend the money and the time amongst six per cent bonds! I think I told him so, but he thinks I take 'a painful view of life'.

LETTER FROM DION BOUCICAULT, 1882

Napoleon Sarony (1821–96)
Oscar Wilde, 1882
The long photographic session with Napoleon Sarony in New York in January 1882 yielded some twenty different poses, many of which have become very famous, and the group as a whole preserves a vivid record of Oscar Wilde at the age of twenty-seven. He clearly both enjoyed the job of posing and had a keen appreciation of the importance of dress.

As many of the jokes had passed over the head of the worldly first night London audience, D'Oyly Carte suspected that the theme of *Patience* would need explanation for the less sophisticated provincial general public when his touring companies cashed in on its success all over the English-speaking world.

He was particularly concerned about the show's reception in America where it opened on 22 September, 1881 in New York, at the Standard Theatre five months after its London premiere. So close was the liaison between the two theatres that a joint programme was published celebrating the 250th London show and the 100th in New York. There were also two touring companies in England and one in America, where despite all precautions two pirate companies also presented the piece in Chicago.

The idea of a lecture tour of America by the new laureate of Aesthetic values was initially suggested, so Wilde believed, by the great French actress Sarah Bernhardt. The concept was seized on by D'Oyly Carte, who also had business interests in running lecture tours. He saw clearly that the young Oscar Wilde, who was still in his mid-twenties, was a new star worth promoting, and could also help *Patience* to succeed in America. The whole skilfully exploited process can be seen as one of the first major exercises in Public Relations and is thus of particular interest to the media-conscious public of today.

Events began in September 1881 with a cable to Wilde from D'Oyly Carte's New York office offering a tour of fifty venues. This led to negotiations with Colonel W.F. Morse, who managed lecture tours, and by December the tour was arranged. Richard D'Oyly Carte wrote to Helen Lenoir, his business manager in New York in December 1881:

There have been stupid paragraphs in the *Sporting Times* one saying that I was sending Wilde out as a sandwich man for *Patience*, and another one afterwards stating that he was not going, as 'D'Oyly Carte found that he could get sandwich men in America with longer hair for half the money'. Wilde is slightly sensitive, but I don't think appallingly so ... I told him he must not mind my using a little bunkum to push him in America. You must deal with it when he arrives.

Wilde himself was aware of the need for 'a little bunkum' and began to plan what to wear. This proved a problem, for Wilde's initial foray to a furrier from which he emerged wearing 'a befrogged and wonderfully befurred green overcoat' and a Polish cap, was observed by a vigilant Whistler, who screeched in a letter (published in *The World*): 'OSCAR – How dare you! What means this

Above: *Oscar Wilde*, **1883**
This is one of many American caricatures of Oscar Wilde receiving bouquets and coins. The caption reads 'A thing of beauty not a joy for ever'. Wilde himself had a low opinion of such cartoons, writing to Colonel Morse: 'I regard all caricature and satire as absolutely beneath notice'.

Opposite: **Walter Crane**
My Lady's Chamber
From *The House Beautiful*, **1878**
This illustration to Clarence Cook's book provides all the ingredients needed to create a classic eclectic Aesthetic interior: Georgian silver and wall sconces, Japanese fans, blue and white Delft tiles and Chinese porcelain.

unseemly carnival in my Chelsea! Restore these things to Nathans ... [the theatrical costumier]'. Undeterred, Wilde sailed for New York on Christmas Eve, arriving on 2 January, 1882 to a rapturous reception.

Thus began the myth of Wilde's conquest of America for, witty though it is, Max Beerbohm's famous cartoon depicting Wilde lecturing in America is misleading. Entitled *The Name of Dante Gabriel Rossetti is heard for the first time in the United States: Lecturer Mr Oscar Wilde*, it depicts the plump long-haired figure of Wilde clutching a lily, surveying an amazed audience of goggle-eyed Texans, with the inference that Wilde's lectures were the first occasion on which Aesthetic ideals were ever proclaimed, or even heard about, in America. In reality the Aesthetic ideal of the 'pursuit of beauty' was taken most seriously in America, indeed far more so, in many respects, than in England where, as Wilde said in a typical paradox, explaining the Pre-Raphaelites' lack of popularity in England: 'To know nothing about their great men is one of the necessary elements of English education.'

In New York, Daniel Cottier (1838–91) had played a crucial early role in the dissemination of avant-garde taste. Although far less well known than Wilde, he can more justly claim to be the pioneer of Aestheticism in America. A decorator, stained-glass designer and art dealer, Cottier's career in Glasgow, London, Paris and Australia, had brought him into contact with figures as diverse as Ruskin, Madox Brown, Morris and the Parisian dealers Durand, Ruel and Goupil. In 1873 he opened shops in Sydney and New York. The latter was soon the fabric centre for the city, as Clarence Cook wrote in *Scribner's Magazine* in June 1875:

Cottier & Co. have serges in colours which we all recognize in the pictures that Alma-Tadema and Morris, and Burne-Jones and Rossetti paint ... the mistletoe green, the blue-green, the rose amber, the pomegranate-flower, and so forth, and so on, colours which we owe to the English poet-artists, who are oddly lumped together as the Pre-Raphaelites, and who made the new rainbow to confound the scientific decorators who were so sure of what colours would go together, and what colours wouldn't.

Clarence Cook's article in which this eulogy appears, was one of a series entitled 'Beds and Tables, Stools and Candlesticks'. This was reprinted as a book in 1878 with the more effective title of *The House Beautiful* with a frontispiece by Walter Crane showing an Aesthetic lady in a 'Queen Anne' drawing room.

In 1874 Cottier's achievements were praised by the press:

Let a few years pass and we are sure that the lesson Messrs

Cottier are teaching us will have been so learned, that they will be put upon their mettle to keep up with us. For in America, there is a real love of comfort and beauty; we love our homes ... We are all sick of tameness and copying, and only ask to be shown the better way, to walk in it with a will.

Another important early influence on emerging American taste was Charles Locke Eastlake (1836–1906)[1] who as an English journalist in the 1860s published a series of articles on decoration and furniture. Reshaped and provided with illustrations of wallpapers, tiles, furniture and artifacts inspired by mediaeval or 'Early English' sources, the series was published in 1868 as *Hints on Household Taste in Furniture, Upholstery and Other Details*, the earliest and most influential of the many books on the decoration of the home published in England and America in the 1860s and 1870s. First published in London, it went through no less than seven American editions between 1872 and 1886.

In 1895, looking back at his career from his home (named with tongue in cheek Terra Cottage) in Bayswater, Eastlake indulged in one of the stylistic lists the Aesthetes so enjoyed:

Young housekeepers of the present age who sit in picturesque chimney corners, sipping tea out of oriental china, or lounge on seventeenth-century settles, in a parquetry-floored room filled with inlaid cabinets, Cromwell chairs, picturesque sideboards, hanging shelves and bookcases, can form no idea of the heavy and graceless objects with which an English house was filled some twenty years ago – the sprawling sofas, the gouty-legged dining tables, cut-glass chandeliers, lumbering ottomans, funereal buffets, horticultural carpets, and zoological hearth rugs ...

Eastlake was primarily an arbiter of taste, rather than a designer, who also admired Japanese artifacts. His concepts were broadly interpreted by American cabinet-makers such as Isaac Scott in a bookcase of 1875. But just as today when shrewd marketing and subtle advertising have produced a widespread uniformity of 'good taste', so from the 1860s to the 1880s certain manufacturers, particularly in the furniture trade, saw great commercial advantages in jumping on the bandwagon of Aesthetic taste, leading Eastlake to complain:

I find American tradesmen continually advertising what they are pleased to call 'Eastlake' furniture, with the production of which I have had nothing whatever to do, and for the taste of which I should be very sorry to be considered responsible.

Another British writer on design much appreciated in America was Bruce J. Talbert (1838–81), whose short but important career saw him acknowledged as the most influential designer in the

reform Gothic style. A particularly fine example of a piece based on his principles is the cabinet, the design of which is attributed to Frank Furness, and the manufacture by Daniel Pabst of Philadelphia, dating from 1874 to 1877. After training as an architect in Glasgow where he met the pioneer of American Aestheticism, Daniel Cottier, Talbert's highly individual simplified Gothic style can be exemplified by the *Sleeping Beauty* cabinet made by Holland and Sons and exhibited at the Paris Exposition of 1867. A year later he published his *Gothic Forms Applied to Furniture, Metal Work, and Decoration for Domestic Purposes*, a practical demonstration of Charles Locke Eastlake. It too was reprinted in America in 1873 and 1877 respectively. Its text cautioned against the 'repetition of the tracery, buttresses, and crocketing used in stone work' which give 'a monumental character quite undesirable in cabinet work'. Such advice, and even more the illustrations depicting entire rooms in great detail with fabrics, carpets, floors, ceilings and stained glass, had a far-reaching influence on both interior decor and cabinet-making both in England and America. By the 1870s he had progressed stylistically into a skilful exponent of such quintessential Aesthetic themes as the sunflower, designing some famous Sunflower wallpapers for Jeffrey and Company.

The great lift-off for such ideas in America was the Philadelphia Centennial Exhibition of 1876 which was visited by ten million people, and which introduced Japanese ceramics and, via the Woman's Pavilion, English Aesthetic ideas on the furnishing of the 'home beautiful' to America. One of its attractions was Thomas Jeckyll's remarkable Aesthetic iron pavilion by Barnard, Bishop and Barnard in which the sunflower motif was extensively used.

It should also be remembered that the period from the 1860s to the 1880s saw the founding of the great American museums: the Metropolitan in New York, the Philadelphia Museum, the Cincinnati Art Museum, the Detroit Institute and the Corcoran Gallery of Art in Washington. The Museum of Fine Arts at Boston, incorporated in 1870, moved from a pre-Civil War classical Athenaeum to new Gothic premises, near H.H. Richardson's Trinity Church, the finest religious edifice of the American Aesthetic Movement, with its glowing stained glass by Clayton and Bell and Burne-Jones, and the remarkable pioneering opalescent glass by John La Farge.

Designed by Thomas Jeckyll and manufactured by Barnard, Bishop and Barnard
Cast and wrought-iron pavilion for the Centennial Exposition, Philadelphia, c. 1875–6
From the *British Architect and Northern Engineer*, **1 November, 1878**
The subsequent history of this remarkable edifice included a period on exhibition in Paris, before it found a home in a Norwich park, where it was destroyed by enemy action during the Second World War.

139

BOSTON ÆSTHETICISM VERSUS OSCAR WILDE.

John La Farge (1835–1910), who as a young student in Paris had met Gautier and Baudelaire, was one of the most innovative minds in the American Aesthetic Movement. A typical polymath of the period, eminent as landscape artist, collector of Japanese art, and mural painter, he also became a stained-glass designer of great originality. He began to experiment in this medium in 1875, after a visit to England in 1873 where he studied the work of Morris and Company. But La Farge was to take the art of stained glass in different directions from mediaeval revivalism. His windows eschew painted glass, but use opalescent and streaked glass. His mastery of the medium was already apparent in 1877 in his first use of opalescent glass to give tonality to the lilies and sunflowers in the windows of a Newport residence.

Although sunflowers and lilies, and other more central Aesthetic concerns were known in America before Wilde's arrival, it was still an event of great importance. His inaugural lecture was given in the Chickering Hall, New York, on 9 January, 1882, on *The English Renaissance of Art*, although Wilde, a master at adapting himself to the differing demands of varying audiences, elaborated at least four versions of the lecture.

Its main theme was 'Love art for its own sake and then all things that you need will be added to you'. Every aspect of life was related to art: 'Stately and simple architecture for your cities, bright and simple dress for your men and women; those are the conditions of a real artistic movement.' Borrowing both thoughts and turns of phrase from Pater, Wilde described:

men to whom the end of life is action, and men to whom the end of life is thought. As regards the latter, who seek for experience itself and not for the fruits of experience, who must burn always with one of the passions of this fiery-coloured world, who find life interesting not for its secrets but for its situations, for its pulsations and not for its purpose; the passion for beauty engendered by the decorative arts will be to them more satisfying than any political or religious enthusiasm, any enthusiasm for humanity, any ecstasy or sorrow for love. For art comes to one professing primarily to give nothing but the highest quality to one's moments, and for those moments' sake ...

Hewers of wood and drawers of water there must always be among us. Our modern machinery has not much lightened the labour of man after all: but at least let the pitcher that stands by the well be beautiful and surely the labour of the day will be lightened ... For what is decoration but the worker's expression of joy in his work? ... 'I have tried', I remember William Morris saying to me once, 'I have tried to make each of my workers an artist, and when I say an artist I mean a man.'

Like Morris, Wilde saw a direct relationship between socialism and good art, scornfully relating French rococo furniture with the excesses of the monarchy: 'The gaudy, gilt furniture writhing under a sense of its own horror and ugliness, with a nymph smirking at every angle and a dragon mouthing on every claw', a view surely more aimed at pleasing a republican American audience than a deeply-held conviction.

The lecture concluded with a flourish:

You have listened to *Patience* for a hundred nights and have listened to me for only one. You have heard, I think, few of you, of two flowers connected with the Aesthetic Movement in England, and said (I assure you, erroneously) to be the food of some Aesthetic young men. Well, let me tell you the reason we love the lily and the sunflower, in spite of what Mr Gilbert may tell you, is not for any vegetable passion at all. It is because these two lovely flowers are in England the most perfect models of design, the most naturally adapted for decorative art.

> Well! We spend our days looking for the secret of life.
> Well, 'the secret of life is art'.[2]

After his lecture in New York a woman from Boston approached him and said: 'Oh, Mr Wilde, you have been adored in New York; in Boston you'll be worshipped.' But in fact his flamboyance, if acceptable in New York, was regarded with great suspicion in conservative Boston. A cartoon in the New York *Daily Graphic* portrayed a bluestocking Bostonian, haughtily declaring to a suppliant Wilde, offering a bouquet of sunflowers and lilies: 'No, Sir ... we have an Aestheticism of our own'. Such indeed was the case, for Morris wallpapers had been available in Boston since the late 1860s, leading to some rooms in the English style being fitted out by the firm of J.M. Bumstead in 1871. By 1873, the editor of the intellectual magazine, the *Atlantic Monthly*, William Dean Howells, wrote to his friend Henry James: 'We have done some Aesthetic wallpapering, thanks to Wm. Morris whose wallpapers are so much better than his poems.'

Charles Eliot Norton (a Bostonian friend of Ruskin), who founded an American version of the Arts and Crafts Movement, accused Wilde of 'maudlin sensualisms'. Indeed Boston, proud of its cultural elitism, rather scorned Wilde. Its most distinguished literary lion, Henry James, was always to be on his guard against Wilde's flamboyant persona. He had just published *Portrait of a Lady* and *Washington Square*, and after meeting Wilde in Washington, described him in a letter: '"Hosscar" Wilde is a fatuous fool, tenth rate cad, "an unclean beast"'.

But Wilde more than held his own. At Harvard he ridiculed sixty undergraduates who attended one of his lectures, all clad as Bunthornes in knee breeches, bearing sunflowers in appropriate stained-glass attitudes. Tipped off in advance, Wilde, soberly clad in dinner jacket and trousers instead of his usual knee breeches, breathed a fervent prayer, 'Save me from my disciples', offering the students a gift of a sculpture for their gymnasium.

It is tempting to linger on some of the famous events that occurred on that punishing tour. Colonel Morse (like Colonel Parker who shaped the career of Elvis Presley in our own day) devised a series of engagements that led to Wilde crossing and recrossing America with the velocity of a twentieth-century pop star from

Opposite: Decorated by Agnes Pitman and made by the Rookwood Pottery Sunflower Vase, 1885 Glazed and gilded earthenware

Above: Winslow Homer (1836–1910)
Promenade on the Beach, **1880 Oil on canvas, 50.8 x 76.5 cm It is characteristic of an artist of Homer's originality that he should be able to abandon any element of genre painting and add an Aesthetic dimension (witness the Japanese fan) to his lifelong theme of women on the seashore. The work reminds us that although Aesthetics is generally used in connection with the arts, it can also embrace beauty in nature.**

New York to San Francisco, and from McDonald's Opera House, Montgomery, Alabama to Leadville in the Rocky Mountains. There, Wilde had his famous encounter with miners: 'I spoke to them of the early Florentines, and they slept as though no crime had ever stained the ravines of their mountain home.' Because they mined for silver he read them passages from the autobiography of Benvenuto Cellini the great Renaissance metal worker: 'I was reproved by my hearers for not having brought him with me. I explained that he had been dead for some little time which elicited the enquiry, "Who shot him?"'

In a corner of the Casino, Wilde found a pianist sitting at a piano over which was this notice:

"Please don't shoot the pianist; he is doing his best", I was struck with this recognition of the fact that bad art merits the penalty of death, and I felt that in this remote city, where the Aesthetic applications of the revolver were clearly established in the case of music, my apostolic task would be much simplified, as indeed it was.

He described to them one of Whistler's Nocturnes in Blue and Gold: '... they leaped to their feet and in their grand simple style swore that such things should not be. Some of the younger ones

pulled their revolvers out and left hurriedly to see if Jimmy was
prowling about the saloons.'

As his trail of lecture engagements doubled back and
forth across America he found the need for other themes, and worked
up two other basic lectures, one being *Art and the Handicraftsman*; the
other, the more practical *House Decoration*, which when first given in
May 1882, bore the far from snappy title, *Practical Application of the
Principles of Aesthetic Theory to Exterior and Interior House Decoration,
with Observations upon Dress and Personal Ornaments*. In it Wilde,
inspired by the mineral riches he had heard of in his mining
excursions, declared optimistically:

the gold is ready for you in unexhausted treasure, stored up
in the mountain hollow or strewn on the river sand ... search out your
workman. When you want a thing wrought in gold, goblet or shield for the
feast, necklace or wreath for the women, tell him what you most like in
decoration, flower or wreath, bird in flight or hound on the chase, image of
the woman you love or friend you honour. Watch him as he beats out the gold
into those thin plates delicate as the petals of a yellow rose, or draws it into
the wires like tangled sunbeams at dawn. Whoever that workman may be, help
him, cherish him and you will have much lovely work from his hand as will be a
joy for you for all time.

He explored other themes in a lecture that survives in
part in *The Critic as Artist* (1890) which provides a succinct
encapsulation of the central credos of his beliefs, and the change in
valuation of the decorative arts which was a key tenet of Aestheticism:

The art that is frankly decorative is the art to live with. It is,
of all visible arts, the one art that creates in us both mood and temperament.
Mere colour, unspoiled by meaning, and unallied with definite form, can
speak to the soul in a thousand different ways. The harmony that resides in the
delicate proportions of lines and masses becomes mirrored in the mind. The
repetitions of patterns give us rest. The marvels of design stir the imagination.
In the mere loveliness of the materials employed there are latent elements of
culture. Nor is this all. By its deliberate rejection of Nature as the ideal of
beauty, as well as the imitative method of the painter, decorative art not
merely prepares the soul for the reception of true imaginative work, but
develops in it that sense of form which is the basis of creative no less than of
critical achievement.

Wherever he went Wilde's high profile made him an
ideal whipping boy for the press, who accused him of arrogance,
elitism and socialism. Thomas Nast's cartoon *Oscar Wilde as Narcissus*
which echoes the composition of Du Maurier's *Love Agony* is a satire
that usefully represents the criticism levelled at Wilde of 'paganism' by

Louis Comfort Tiffany (1848–1933)
Peacock Mosaic, 1890–1
Cabochon glass and plaster, 132.5 x 163.2 cm
This panel was made for the Henry Osborne Havemeyer house in New York.

an eminent Christian Socialist. But his reception was not always antagonistic, and admiration could unexpectedly take poetic forms. In Louisville, Kentucky, Wilde met the niece of the poet John Keats, who presented him with the autograph manuscript of the poet's *Sonnet on Blue.* He thanked her in these words:

> What you have given me is more golden than gold ... It is a sonnet I have loved always, and indeed who but the supreme and perfect artist could have got from a mere colour a motive so full of marvel ... that godlike boy, the real Adonis of our age.

In Camden, New Jersey, Walt Whitman embraced him with the memorable words: 'I wish well to you, Oscar, and as to the Aesthetes, I can only say that you are young and ardent, and the field is wide, and if you want my advice, go ahead.'

Go ahead, Wilde certainly did, and it succeeded in its initial purpose. His florid praise of the 'gaudy, leonine beauty' of the sunflower and the 'precious loveliness' of the lily which gave 'to the

artist the most entire and perfect joy', had ensured that both *Patience* and Oscar Wilde's name were known across the American continent.

Some of his advice was surprisingly practical. He had pointed out that the commercial spirit upon which American cities were based was no barrier to art, drawing a parallel with the similar spirit which had been responsible for the development of the great cities of Renaissance Italy. His message reached perhaps its most succinct form in a lecture in Philadelphia when he said:

There must be a great mass of handicraft produced before you can hope to effect the masses. And the handicraftsmen must be directed

by the artists; and the artists must be inspired with true designs. It is only through those classes we can work.[3]

The exotic seed of Wilde's vision of a craft Utopia took surprising root in the expanding industrial cities of America. Many artifacts of high quality, from design to execution, were frequently the result of the involvement of many hands. Some remarkable examples of such collaborative productions were provided by the Herter Brothers in New York, and Louis Prang of Boston. Aesthetic design at its most effective can be seen in Tiffany & Co's staggeringly complex *Magnolia* vase of 1893, and the Rookwood Pottery's great sunflower vase of 1885 decorated by Agnes Pitman. This famous pottery in Cincinnati, Ohio, was founded by Maria Longworth Nichols in 1880.

In the 1870s a craze for decorative painting had swept America. It took ceramic form in 1877 in the foundation in New York of the Tile Club, a light-hearted group of twelve artists which met weekly to paint in blue on eight-inch-square ceramic tiles, where the

Opposite: Louis Comfort Tiffany
Seventh Regiment Armoury, 1879–80
Probably the most complete surviving example of the work of Tiffany in New York city is the Veterans Room created in the Armoury of the Seventh Regiment, the epitome of patrician old New York. The decoration was carried out under Tiffany's personal supervision by a team of craftsmen and artists. The chimney-piece is decorated with turquoise mosaics and a relief showing an American eagle crushing injustice and evil in the form of a serpent. The capitals of the miniature columns on either side of the chimney-piece are ingeniously composed of patterned rollers used in the manufacture of wallpaper. On the ceiling above are aluminium stencils reflecting the influence of Japan, while a painted frieze presents scenes showing the history of warfare from the Stone Age to the Civil War. Such an eclectic mixture of design elements makes the Seventh Regiment Armoury one of the most remarkable examples of an Aesthetic interior.

Above: Thomas Wilmer Dewing (1851–1938)
The Days, **1887**
Oil on canvas, 109.7 x 182.9 cm
Dewing practised as a portrait-painter in Albany before studying in Paris for two years from 1876 to 1878. On his return he worked in Boston and New York. It was said that his sole aim was 'to represent beautiful ladies … who seem to possess large fortunes and no inclination for any professional work'.

host for the evening both supplied and retained the tiles in return for hospitality. Some of the most distinguished Aesthetic artists of America took part, including founder members Winslow Homer and Edwin Austin Abbey, William Merritt Chase, Elihu Vedder, Augustus Saint-Gaudens and the architect Stanford White.

They would doubtless have approved of Wilde when he denied that: 'in its primary aspects painting has any more spiritual message for us than a blue tile from the walls of Damascus or a Hitzen vase. It is a beautifully-coloured surface, nothing more, and affects us by no suggestion stolen from philosophy, no pathos pilfered from literature, no feeling filched from a poet, but by its own incommunicable artistic essence.'

The Tile Club's mutual enjoyment of their flirtation with the purely decorative aspects of art gave the group its cohesion, although with increasing fame they turned their attention in other directions, disbanding a decade later. But it is interesting to see in both Winslow Homer's *Promenade on the Beach* (1880) and William Merritt Chase's *At the Seaside* (c. 1892) the motifs of those Aesthetic preoccupations: the Japanese fan and parasol.

One of the most interesting American Aesthetic painters whose work is still far too little known was Thomas Wilmer Dewing (1851–1938). A Bostonian, he studied in Paris before settling in New York in 1880 after marrying the noted flower painter and writer on interior decoration, Maria Richards Oakey, whose needlework designs were much admired by Oscar Wilde. Dewing's work has been likened to that of Burne-Jones, and certainly there is a haunting parallel between *The Days* (1887), inspired by a poem by Ralph Waldo Emerson, and Burne-Jones's *The Golden Stairs* (1880).

After his visits to an artists' colony at Cornish, New Hampshire, in the 1890s Dewing loved to portray women playing musical instruments in lush meadows in a manner reminiscent of the Belgian symbolist Fernand Khnopff. These dream-like images are well represented in the Freer collection in Washington where they form a memorable contrast to the paintings by Whistler.

English Aestheticism was only one of the foreign cultural influences on great American cities such as New York and Chicago in the final quarter of the nineteenth century. In those years society had stratified into three distinct levels. At the bottom were the 'huddled masses yearning to breathe free' arriving off the emigrant boats; the established middle classes of moderate means were perhaps those to whom Aestheticism made its greatest appeal; and at the top, the moneyed ruling elite of railway tycoons and barons of industry and banking. They wanted spectacular results for the money they invested in furnishing their palatial homes and acquired large decorative sculptures and paintings. For these, they looked, not to England and Aestheticism but to Paris and the Ecole des Beaux Arts, the official French academy, for inspiration. Indeed, in the US the term 'beaux-arts' is applied to works created by these French-trained American architects, artists and sculptors.

Their undisputed leader was Augustus Saint-Gaudens (1848–1907), who returned from training in Paris to New York in 1875. Together with John La Farge in 1881–2, he fashioned the entrance hall fireplace of the Cornelius Vanderbilt residence at the corner of Fifth Avenue and Fifty-seventh Street, when that area was being developed with palatial millionaires' homes. Saint-Gaudens's caryatids of Peace and Love support a lintel surmounted by a La Farge mosaic with a Latin inscription which reads in translation: 'The house at its threshold gives evidence of the master's good will. Welcome to the guest who arrives; farewell and helpfulness to him who departs.'

Another palatial New York home was the residence of Henry Osborne Havemeyer, built between 1890 and 1891, notable for being one of the last works of Louis Comfort Tiffany (1848–1933) as

A Cottage Tuxedo Park.
New Jersey.
Bruce Price, Architect.

an interior designer before he embarked on the full-time running of art glass studios. Like his friend La Farge, Tiffany had been trained as a painter in Paris and North Africa, before at the age of thirty-one making the characteristic Aesthetic announcement: 'I have been thinking a great deal about decorative work, and I am going into it as a profession. I believe there is more in it than in painting pictures.'

In the sparsely furnished hall of the Havemeyer house, Tiffany used coloured glass wherever he 'could provide a rational for its sparkle', around the focal part of the room, the Peacock mosaic panel. The total effect was to deeply impress the famous Parisian art dealer Samuel Bing (1838–1905) who founded in 1895 the famous shop known as 'La Maison de L'Art Nouveau' in Paris which was to give its name to the emergent style.

Glass was indeed to be the material which produced some of the finest American work in the Aesthetic style. The remarkable

achievements in the development of opalescent glass pioneered by the work
of John La Farge and Louis Comfort Tiffany took the art of stained glass,
previously largely confined to the form of ecclesiastical glass, in new and
exciting directions. As a journalist in the *Boston Herald* put it: 'The great
Aesthetic wave, which has carried taste and beauty into the adornment of
the modern home, has borne colo[u]red glass upon its crest'.

Another wave of English Aestheticism broke on the
fertile shores of the summer ocean resorts of New England. There,
architects built remarkable variations on the Queen Anne style in the
form of grandiloquent summer cottages for the wealthy at Manchester-
by-the-Sea, Massachusetts, Bar Harbor, Maine, and especially in the
millionaires' haunt of Newport, Rhode Island, with its casino by the
architects McKim, Mead, and White.

The single style of house, timber-framed, hung with
shingles, is one natural to America, so well endowed with woods and
forests. It lends itself readily for use in American Colonial architecture
and the Queen Anne Style, the architectural expression of Aestheticism.
A remarkable group of buildings in this manner was erected at Tuxedo
Park, Orange County, New York. There an Aesthetic colony on the
lines of Bedford Park was established in 1885, in a 7,000-acre wooded
site where the shingle cottages were stained the colour of woods,
russets, greys and dull reds. The spacious site gave room for several
homes to incorporate landscaped Japanese gardens and tea houses.

One distinguished exponent of the Shingle style was
William Ralph Emerson (1833–1917) who designed a large house
eponymously named Shingleside at Swapscott, Massachusetts, and
houses at Mount Desert, and Bar Harbor, Maine. Emerson had visited
and made friends with Walter Crane in London in 1879. When Crane
visited America in 1891 they met again at Emerson's Loring house at
Manchester-by-the-Sea.

Crane's visit to America, nearly a decade after Wilde's,
has fascinating parallels. It was not an official lecture tour because
Crane was accompanying an exhibition of his works, although he did
agree to give a few talks, but like Wilde, for whom he had illustrated
The Happy Prince, Crane was a socialist. The Bostonians gave an initial
tremendous welcome to the 'Lord High Chancellor of the Nursery'
but he soon alarmed the fashionable establishment of the city by
speaking at a meeting in honour of Chicago Anarchists, and a dinner
arranged for him at an exclusive club was suddenly 'postponed'.

A more enjoyable Bostonian experience for Crane was
a meeting with Louis Prang, 'the father of the American Christmas
Card'. He had arrived in New York in 1850, a veteran of the revolutionary

THE·WORKERS·MAY·POLE

[An offering for May-Day 1894 from
Walter Crane]

days of 1848 in Germany, and had subsequently founded in Boston in 1860 the famous publishing company, inventing a system of colour printing from zinc plates. An idealist with boundless confidence in the New World, he is still remembered for the Prang method of education, a system which he devised to awake and develop the creative impulse in the young, as well as his introduction in 1880 of competitions for Christmas card design, a manifestation of his wish to bring good art to the masses. Artists who worked for Prang included Winslow Homer (1836–1910) and Elihu Vedder (1836–1923), winner of the first prize in 1881. Elihu Vedder, who had met Simeon Solomon in Rome is, like him, best remembered for his visionary paintings. Much more unusual are the magnificent cast-iron firebacks of 1882, entitled *The Soul of the Sunflower* and *Faces in the Fire*, which Vedder described as 'filled with a mass of heads ... that lighted by the flames or the flickering light of the dying fire or the glow of the embers ... would seem alive or recall lost or absent friends.'

At the opening of his exhibition at Chicago's Art Institute in Chicago, 500 enthusiastic ladies crowded in to hear Crane's talk, *Design in Relation to Use and Material*, illustrated by rapid chalk sketches. Their applause irritated one citizen who protested against the welcome given to 'Walter Crane, the anarchist, who ought to be locked up'.

It is indeed a curious fact that Wilde, Crane, Edward Carpenter (often described as 'the English Walt Whitman'), and later C.R. Ashbee, who all lectured in America, shared socialist views. But what of the American Whistler, who lectured in England? In his '*Ten o'clock*' lecture delivered in 1885, Whistler satirically denounced the socialist idealism of John Ruskin, William Morris and Oscar Wilde, before turning to his favourite theme, delivering an eloquent plea for the painter to remain autonomous.

The lecture prompted a famous and enjoyable exchange of insults. Reviewing the performance, Wilde noted how Whistler 'spoke for more than an hour on the absolute uselessness of all such lectures'. Whistler was later to respond: 'What has Oscar in common with Art? except that he dines at our tables, and picks from our platters the plums for the puddings he peddles in the provinces. Oscar – the amiable, irresponsible, esurient Oscar – with no more sense of a picture than of the fit of a coat, has the courage of the opinions ... of others!'

Like all great insults, this riposte stung, for in it there was a vestige of truth. Like the avant-garde British artists of our own day, Gilbert and George, the self-styled 'living sculptures', Wilde had become virtually a work of art in his own right, the darling of a certain section of the art public, although regarded by some as a tedious poseur.

'Personally I might go so far as to acknowledge that
I like certain yellows of a tone akin to old satinwood;
that light red or Venetian red brightened by white
and pure, or nearly pure, white itself are favourites
with me. Professionally, I have, of course, to assume
a gloomier style.'

E. W. GODWIN, *MY HOUSE IN LONDON*, 1876

Opposite: E. W. Godwin
(1833–86)
The sheer diversity of
Godwin's interests was
remarkable. A successful
architect, innovative
furniture, wallpaper and
textile designer, practical
man of the theatre with
highly original ideas on
stage, he also made a study
of historic dress and was the
Hon. Secretary of the
Costume Society.

Right: E. W. Godwin
McLean's Fine Art Gallery,
7 Haymarket, London, 1884
Pencil and watercolour,
50.2 x 30.5 cm
One of Godwin's last and
most impressive
architectural designs,
inspired by the gallery he
had designed earlier for the
Fine Art Society in New
Bond Street. The sheer
delicacy of his use of
watercolour is remarkable.

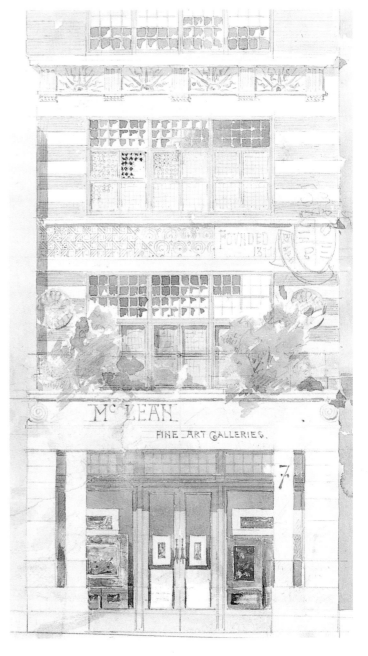

Right above: E. W. Godwin
Congleton Town Hall, Cheshire,
1864
Watercolour, 53 x 33.5 cm
For both Burges and Godwin
the fairytale associations of a
Gothic tower had immense
appeal, and led to the
production of their most
imaginative buildings. At
Congleton Godwin utilized
the awkward narrow site to
maximum effect. Seen today,
the tower dominates the
skyline of Congleton and
provides a powerful symbol
of civic pride.

Right below: E. W. Godwin
Competition design for East
Retford Town Hall,
Nottinghamshire, 1867
Watercolour
The dominant clock tower,
symmetrically centred over
the five traceried windows
which surmount five bays,
clearly reveals the
considerable debt which
Godwin's town hall designs
owe to the Casa del Orologio
at Venice so admired by
Ruskin. However, this design
was not accepted and one by
Bellamy and Pearson was
built instead.

Much is made today by politicians of the traditional
family values of the Victorian age. Both the life and particularly the
death of E.W. Godwin might almost have been designed to refute
this cliché, because for him the *ménage à trois* ... was a way of life.

When Godwin fell mortally ill he was attended by
Whistler's younger brother, Dr William Whistler, and visited every
day by Whistler, who was his wife's lover. Beatrice Godwin was then
living in Paris and Whistler called her back to be with her dying
husband. After Godwin's death Whistler and Beatrice would be
married. Another daily visitor was Lady Archie Campbell, who used
her prominent social position to produce with Godwin some of the
most remarkable open-air theatrical productions ever staged, key
events of the Aesthetic Movement. Whistler contacted the Aesthetic
woman painter Louise Jopling, so that she could break the news of
Godwin's death to the great actress Ellen Terry, his former mistress
and mother of his two children. On hearing the news she cried out:
'There was *no one* like him'.

After Godwin's death, arrangements were made to
fulfil his wish to be buried in a nameless grave in the country, at
Northleigh, near Witney in Oxfordshire. There were only three
mourners, Beatrice Godwin, Lady Archibald Campbell and Whistler.
At a nearby station the coffin was placed upon an open farm waggon,
into which the three mourners clambered. Covering up the coffin they
used it as a table for an al fresco meal eaten as they jolted along
through the country lanes to the unmarked last resting place of a
genius, the corner of a field.

Of all the major figures in the Aesthetic Movement
Godwin remains the most enigmatic. His importance in the evolution
of such varied events as the lectures of Oscar Wilde and the Aesthetic
sensibilities of J.M. Whistler cannot be over-estimated. Yet he remains
curiously elusive, his powerful charisma not having survived his death.
Despite the admiration of his contemporaries his reputation has been
eclipsed, partly because much of his energies in later years was devoted
to the ephemeral art of the theatre.

Edward William Godwin was born at 12, Old Market
Street, Bristol on 26 May, 1833. His father, a builder and antiquarian,
collected 'fragments and crumbling bits from old churches' which held
a mysterious fascination for his son who grew up with the ambition of
becoming an architect. His father, however, though not unsympathetic,
favoured engineering as a career, for Bristol rang with the fame of
Brunel's railways and steamships. 'Engineering,' declared Godwin's
father, 'is more paying than architecture', and so, on leaving school,

E. W. Godwin
The Council Room in
Northampton Town Hall,
1864
This picture shows the
councillors' chairs designed
by Godwin.

young Edward was articled to William Armstrong, City Surveyor, Architect and Civil Engineer, a friend of Brunel. The arrangement was ideal, for Armstrong left the architectural side of the business to the keen young student, a perfect training for Godwin, who practised by making measured drawings of the great church of St Mary Redcliffe, thus gaining valuable direct knowledge of the Gothic style.

In 1854, Godwin opened his own architectural office, designing a school and houses in the Gothic style, before working for three years in Ireland erecting a church in County Donegal and making a series of measured drawings of Celtic crosses. Later in life, he facetiously advised young architects who were offered commissions in Ireland, to refuse them, as 'Ireland was sea-girt, and always damp, and could not help it.'

Back in Bristol he designed an 'Early English' warehouse, restored the south porch of St Mary Redcliffe, and steeped himself in Ruskin's *The Stones of Venice*, then required reading for aspiring Gothic Revival architects. The year 1861 marked Godwin's first major national success, victory in the competition for a design for Northampton Town Hall. His design – in the approved Italian Gothic style – brought congratulatory letters from John Ruskin, and notice in Charles Locke Eastlake's *History of the Gothic Revival* which was published in 1864, the year of the building's completion, and the year in which Godwin won the competition for his other major public building, Congleton Town Hall.[1] Today, Northampton Town Hall remains Godwin's largest surviving building. The furniture that he designed for it already reflects his desire to simplify form and limit decoration to a minimum. Its exterior is distinguished by its polychrome stonework, and the vigorous sculpture which ranges from eight impressive life-sized figures of English kings to relief panels showing local trades, such as shoe-making. Inside, the sculptural treatment possesses a whimsical humour reminiscent of Godwin's friend William Burges, with a series of capitals depicting fables like *The Cock and the Jewels*. The great hall is a richly carved mediaeval-style fantasy, at its most exciting when viewed from one of the small balconies near the roof, which is supported by elaborate iron ribs.

Two years earlier, on 1 November, 1859, in the parish church of Henley-on-Thames, Godwin had married Miss Sarah Yonge, the daughter of the vicar. Years later, Ellen Terry described Sarah as Godwin's 'devoted helpmate', but she died tragically early in 1864. In 1862 he moved with his wife to 21, Portland Square in Bristol. The home that they created became famous for the startling originality of its decor, distinguished by Persian rugs laid on bare, polished boards, walls painted in plain colours, early eighteenth-century furniture and, the most unusual feature, a few Japanese prints.

Godwin's and Whistler's mutual interest in Japanese art led to a lifelong friendship which began in 1863. In the next decade Godwin became one of the foremost figures in the introduction of Japanese influence into European design, creating some brilliantly original textiles, tiles and wallpapers. An excellent musician, Godwin also read widely, studied the history of costume, and began his lifelong love affair with the theatre, paying frequent visits to Bristol's Theatre Royal, and started to write reviews for the local paper, the *Western Daily Press*. This could be a risky occupation, for on one occasion an actor whom he had severely criticized called, and was shown to the room where Godwin, who loved dressing up, was attired in the costume of Henry V. Clad in hose, he could make little resistance when the actor produced a horsewhip! But work as a dramatic critic also brought the compensation of friendship with the Terry sisters, Kate and Ellen, members of the famous theatrical family. Godwin had written admiringly of the historical accuracy of the sets by the designers, the Grieves, for the famous Shakespearean productions of Charles Keane at the Princess Theatre in London, and also praised the performance of a child actress, Ellen Terry, as Puck. The Grieves's designs were always painstakingly researched from historical sources, a practice which Godwin adopted for his own later theatrical work.

In March 1863, the Chute stock company visited the Theatre Royal, Bristol. In the cast was Ellen Terry, then aged fourteen but already a seasoned performer, and her sister Kate, who both became frequent visitors to Godwin's home at Portland Square, Bristol. Chute decided to open the Theatre Royal, Bath, with the *Midsummer Night's Dream* in March 1863, with Ellen playing the role of Titania. She wrote later:

Titania was the first Shakespearean role I had played since I left Charles Keane, but I think even in those early days I was more at home in Shakespeare than anything else. Mr Godwin designed my dress, and we made it at his home in Bristol. He showed me how to damp it and 'wring' it while it was wet, tying up the material as the Orientals do in their 'tie and dye' process, so that when it was dry and untied, it was all crinkled and clinging. This was the first lovely dress that I ever wore, and I learned a good deal from it.

Two years later, when only sixteen and under the influence of the Pattle sisters, Ellen married the forty-year-old artist George Frederick Watts, a brief ill-starred union which ended in their separation after a year and her return to the stage.

E. W. Godwin
The roof of the Great Hall in Northampton Town Hall, 1864

Clockwise from top left:
Japanese 'Mon'-crests, from
Godwin's sketchbook of
c. 1870, copied from a
Japanese print in one of
William Burges's
scrapbooks. All these crests
provided the motifs for
pattern designs, notably the
'Peacock', the 'Peach
blossom', the 'Sparrows' and
the adjacent 'Butterfly'.

This 'Butterfly' Brocade silk
damask, which dates from
about 1874, was woven by
Warner and Son exclusively
for Collinson and Lock.

'Star' wallpaper, 1876

'Bamboo' wallpaper, 1872

In 1865 Godwin moved to London, setting up a
practice at 23 Baker Street, where he gained, in 1867, one of his most
interesting projects, a commission to design and build Dromore Castle
and Glenbeigh Towers in Ireland, an enterprise which occupied him for
much of the next two years. He also began to design furniture, notably a
much-imitated square coffee table of 1867, followed in about 1876 by

157

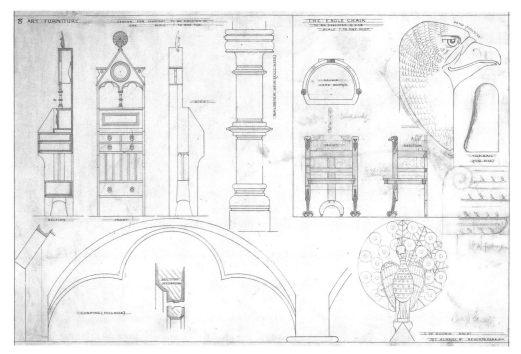

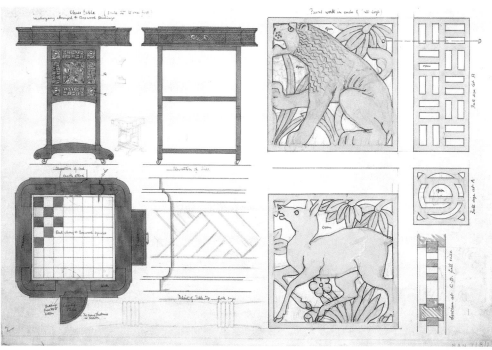

Left above: E. W. Godwin
Designs for a whatnot and
Eagle Chair, 1869

Left below: E. W. Godwin
Design for a chess table for
Dromore Castle of ebony,
mahogany and boxwood
The furniture for Dromore
was built by William Watt in
1869.

a circular eight-legged table and an octagonal eight-legged table. He also worked for the Art Furniture Company, William Watt and Collinson & Lock. With whom in 1872 he signed a design contract of £450 per annum and three guineas a drawing. While working for William Watt he was to produce his celebrated 'Anglo-Japanese' furniture. Less familiar are Godwin's surprising 'Anglo-Greek' and 'Anglo-Egyptian' furniture. But then, as now, the work of top designers was beyond the reach of all but a small minority, so for the mass market, the trade concocted 'art furniture' which corrupted the original designs. The resultant productions were castigated by Godwin a decade later, in the preface to *Art Furniture*, as being 'copied by others in the trade but [they] have unfortunately been travestied even caricatured in the process … I have seen the lines changed, the proportions altered, until that which I regarded as beauty became to me an offence and an eyesore.'

Godwin was extraordinarily versatile both as writer and draughtsman. His written work can be divided into two main phases: the first, as an occasional freelance contributor to *The Building News* and *The Architect* from the late 1860s to the late 1870s; the second, a much closer staff involvement with the Manchester-based *The British Architect* from late 1877 onwards. His first written pieces include notes on his early archaeological interest, reviews of current architectural and art exhibitions, and controversial contributions to the public debates on the decoration of the new Law Courts and St Paul's Cathedral. Conscious of his critical powers and reputation, he adopted at times a highly critical attitude to the work of his contemporaries; his six articles on *Modern Architects and Their Work* in the *Building News* in 1872 leave virtually no individual unscathed.

Godwin's literary style was witty and allusive and his numerous articles would make a fascinating book if republished, giving vivid insights into the taste of the time. He loved to make fun of the more precious adherents of the Aesthetic cause and, in an article entitled *My House 'in' London* of 1876, makes an analogy between the literary and visual tastes of admirers of William Morris's poetry and wallpapers:

Where a household is given more than usual to the cultivation of aesthetics we find the literary yearning is generally in harmony with the dirty green colours used in modern wallpapers, and with those toned – decidedly toned – green and blue serge dresses … which enthusiastic young ladies affect.

Similarly, as a rule, wherever 'the idle singer of an empty day' has found a comfortable resting-place you may be nearly sure to meet dull

Left from top to bottom:
E. W. Godwin
'Greek' chair, c. 1885
Ebonized wood

E. W. Godwin
Octagonal eight-legged
table, c. 1876
Mahogany with brass castors

E. W. Godwin
Coffee table, c. 1867
Ebonized wood
The angled spindles were not
inspired by Japanese, but by
Ancient Egyptian, furniture.

Designed by E. W. Godwin
and probably made by
William Watt
Circular eight-legged table,
c. 1877–8
Ebonized wood

sad greens on walls or floors. When the literary feast consists of Rossetti and Swinburne, taken without salt of course ... this sweet, bewitching, glamourous kind of yellow green art spreads all over the place, and finds expression in the passage hall in the shape of a strip of coconut matting and one sickly green rush-bottom chair.

Later in the article Godwin invents a 'blunt outspoken Doctor of the pure air and fresh water school', who warns of the dangers of green wallpapers: 'The bright green poisons you in an open, direct active manner ... but the dull green ... everyone using it invariably suffers for it physically in some way...' Godwin's sentiments and irony were echoed by Oscar Wilde in his lectures.

His graphic work also falls into two main categories: the sketchbooks and the finished architectural drawings. The latter are distinguished not only for the predictable qualities of clarity and precision, but also for the extreme delicacy of his use of watercolour in the projected realizations of completed projects, a delicacy seen at its most sensitive in his sketches for such varied projects as the Queen Anne design for Kensington Vestry House, and McLean's Fine Art Gallery. The same qualities are apparent in his sketchbooks.[2] Of them Godwin wrote in *The British Architect* on 27 August, 1880, in a series of articles, giving hints *To our Student Readers:*

Careful drawing is an exercise the young architect cannot have too much of: therefore always keep about you a fair sized pocket-book. I always carry one [he then discusses types of sketchbook then available] working with a very fine metallic point, and drawing as delicately and as firmly as I can. One great advantage of this kind of book is that you cannot rub out, and thus you early learn to draw *only when you have something to draw....* Buy the very best drawing materials you can get. Being valuable you will not be so likely to abuse them with wasteful rubbishy usage ... In your pocket book jot down first thoughts for designs, very small and fine; only be sure they are *thoughts* and not mere wanderings or meanderings. You will possibly ask what you are to draw apart from design. *Everything that is beautiful or that fully answers its purpose.* If you come across a dead bird draw every detail of its wing or head or leg as carefully as you would delineate every feature in a thirteenth century door, or seventeenth century staircase ....

But above all things be careful that the shorthand known as outline drawing be not exclusively practised. You will never learn to grasp form if you only draw outline. Much good architecture or building depends almost wholly on its masses and disposition of light and shade: its details – mouldings, carvings, and so on – give it a texture as it were and a special interest to near views of bits and pieces of the work; but the foremost beauty and charm of building as building are always to be found in the measure, the

Above: E. W. Godwin Design for a small display cabinet, c. 1876

Opposite left: E. W. Godwin Design for an Anglo-Japanese cabinet in a room setting, c. 1877

A. J. Cab. (A) Water
Exhibition Cabinet

E. W. Godwin
Cabinet, c. 1877
Satinwood with brass mounts
and a carcass of mahogany
The upper doors are
decorated with four painted
panels (probably by Godwin's
wife, Beatrice) representing
the seasons. The brass-
framed lattice openings on
the lower doors derive from
Hokusai's *Manga*, Vol 5. This
cabinet may have been
intended for the Paris
Exhibition of 1878. It has
been suggested that it
formed part of the
furnishings of Whistler's
White House.

balance, the allotment of its lights and shades .... and therefore you would do well to learn to draw not only in this fine-pointed, fine-lined scientific way, but also with the brush; first of all in broad divisions of light and dark, and then with half shades, and so on, until you can draw a bit of ducal palace something like ... Ruskin.

Godwin shared this enthusiasm for sketching with his friend William Burges, of whom he wrote in a sensitive obituary in *The British Architect*, 1881. 'In his little pocket-books ... the cunning fingers were ever busy noting down the art longings and thoughts of the yet busier brain; and of the many lovely things which he has left behind him, I know of none to compete in interest with those tiny memorandum books, containing as they do his first ideas of nearly everything he subsequently carried out, and of many a dream beside.' These words might with equal justice be used to describe his own sketchbooks.

In 1867 Godwin and Ellen met again, eloping on 10 October, 1868, and beginning a relationship which Ellen Terry later recalled as 'my best times, my happiest times', years devoted to Godwin and their two children Edith (born in 1869) and Gordon Craig (born in 1872). They lived initially at a house built by Godwin in Harpenden, and later at their London home in Taviton Street, a model of Aesthetic taste which provided Godwin with the subject for a series of articles in *The Architect* in 1876. In the drawing room he painted the main woodwork of the room below the dado, selecting: 'a rather dark toned yellow of which yellow ochre is the base, but combined with white, sprinkled with gamboge, Prussian blue and vermilion'. On the walls above this level was a frieze: 'painted in a pale grey green (that green sometimes seen at the stem end of a pineapple leaf when the other end has faded – indeed I may as well as confess that most of the colours in the rooms have been gathered from the pineapple)'.

In February 1874, Ellen Terry returned to the stage in Charles Reade's play *The Wandering Heir* lured by the then vast salary of £40 a week, money which melted in the hands of the talented but improvident couple, some of it presumably on the furnishing of their home in Taviton Street. One of the rooms was vividly described by their friend the actor Sir Johnston Forbes-Robertson:

The floor was covered with straw-coloured matting and there was a dado of the same material. Above the dado were white walls and the hangings were of cretonne with a fine Japanese pattern in delicate grey and blue. The chairs were of wicker with cushions like the hangings and in the centre of the room was a full-sized cast of the Venus de Milo before which was a small pedestal holding a censer from which was curving round the Venus, ribbons of blue smoke ... The whole effect was what students of my time would have called 'awfully jolly'.[3]

Godwin, who did not suffer from false modesty, proudly described the same room in Paterian terms: No description, however, except that which may be conveyed in the form of music, can give an idea of the tenderness and, if I may say so, the ultra-refinement of the delicate tones of colour which form the background to the few but unquestionable gems in this exquisitely *sensitive* room. I say sensitive for a room has a character that may influence for good or bad the many who may enter it, especially the very young.[4]

One cannot help wondering just what the brokers men made of its ultra refinement when they possessed the contents of the house a year later during one of the couple's periods of insolvency... They emptied the rooms save for the life-size cast of the Venus de Milo. In this confusion Ellen Terry was visited by Mrs Bancroft, wife of the distinguished actor manager, who offered her the role of Portia in a new production of *The Merchant of Venice*, and Godwin the contract for designing the sets and costumes, which he based closely on Venetian originals.

Oscar Wilde, then an Oxford undergraduate, attended the first night on 17 April, 1875, and wrote a sonnet to Ellen Terry, describing her dress designed by Godwin:

For in that gorgeous dress of beaten gold,
Which is more golden than the golden sun
No woman Veronese looked upon
Was half so fair as thou whom I behold ...

It was Ellen's first great triumph in a Shakespearean role, and also Godwin's, whose time from this date was to be equally divided between theatrical design and architecture, his designs being acclaimed by the famous actor manager Beerbohm Tree as marking: 'the Renaissance of theatrical art in England'. But the couple's success must have had a Pyrrhic quality for both actress and designer, as their seven-year liaison had ended a month earlier, although they remained on friendly terms, and Godwin continued to design costumes and sets for Ellen, and offer her advice. A charming example of such exchanges is provided by a delightful little note from Godwin in the archives of the Ellen Terry Museum at Tenterden, written during a performance

Above: E. W. Godwin
Designs for a Japanese wall decoration for Dromore Castle, County Limerick, c. 1869
This is the earliest example of Japanese influence in Godwin's interior decorative schemes, and demonstrates his love of eclectic contrast, for the castle, based on a study of the fifteenth- and sixteenth-century remains in Ireland, was Gothic in form. It was built for the Third Earl of Limerick between 1866 and 1873.

Opposite above: E. W. Godwin
A page from a sketchbook containing studies of Roman and Byzantine costume taken from manuscripts in the British Museum. These sketches were used for a production of W. G. Wills's play *Claudian*, which was first performed at the Prince's Theatre on 6 December, 1883.

Ellen Terry as Portia in a new production of *The Merchant of Venice*, 1875. Her costume, which was designed by Godwin, was described by Oscar Wilde as a 'gorgeous dress of beaten gold'.

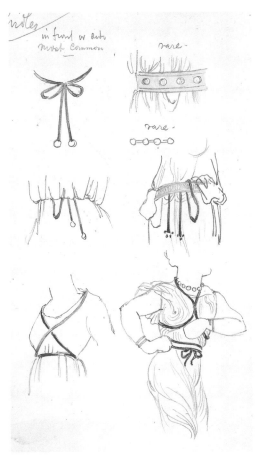

of Tennyson's *The Cup* at the Lyceum in 1880. In it Godwin has drawn figures which show attitudes that are, and are not, archaeologically justified in an actress representing a Greek priestess of the period of the play, as advice to Ellen on how to move in her role.

Godwin's knowledge of Greek costume also proved valuable to his close friend, the writer W.G. Wills, who had given evidence on behalf of Whistler in the Ruskin libel case. Wills's play *Claudian* was produced by Wilson Barrett at the Princess Theatre in December 1883, with Godwin's sets and costumes. Of this production Oscar Wilde wrote in *The Truth of Masks:*

> Mr E.W. Godwin, one of the most artistic spirits of this century in England ... showed us the life of Byzantium in the fourth century, not by a dreary lecture and set of grinning casts, not by a novel which requires a glossary to explain it, but by the visible presentation before us of all the glory of that great town ... showing us by the colour and character of Claudian's dress and the dress of his attendants, the whole nature and life of the man, from what school of philosophy he affected, down to which horses he backed on the turf.

Wilde's admiration of the sets was shared by Wilson Barrett who commissioned Godwin to design a new production of *Hamlet* the following year. Characteristically this led Godwin to visit Elsinore in order to study the correct historical setting, for he was a great advocate of extreme historical realism in theatrical productions, a theme which he expounded in a series of twenty articles published in *The Architect* on 'The Architecture and Costume of Shakespeare's Plays'.

From this date Godwin's main personal preoccupation was theatrical design although he continued to practise as architect, furniture designer, and consultant on interior decor. As an architect he now began more and more to undertake only sympathetic commissions, like that for the house in Tite Street, Chelsea, for Frank Miles, the portrait painter and close friend of Oscar Wilde.

In a lecture to the Architectural Association in March 1879[5], Godwin said, of this design:

> It is for a bachelor, is unpretentious, containing about nine rooms besides a studio. The latter is at the top of the house ... The whole house was designed with balconies and other accessories to meet the taste of a lover of flowers (Miles introduced several new species of flower from Japan) ... I consider it the best thing I ever did. I grant you there are no cornice, no parapet, and no string course; but is architecture a matter of string courses and parapets, and of following out to the letter every detail to which the provisions of the Building Act apply?

Few would disagree with Godwin or with Mark

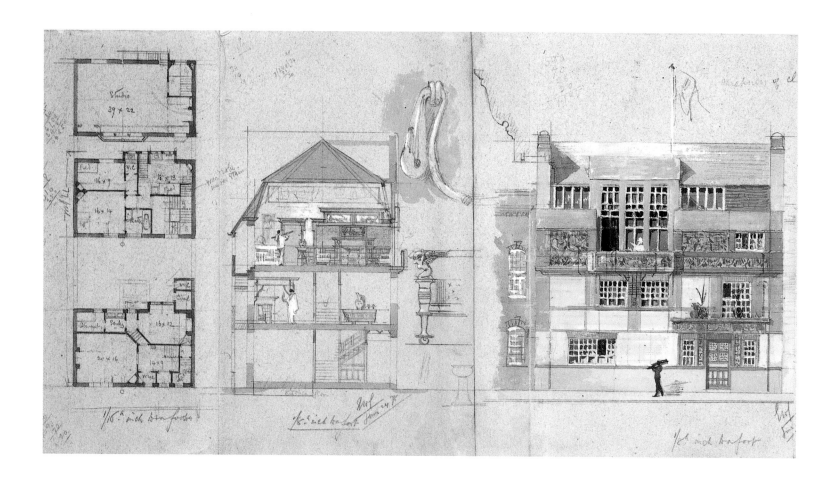

Girouard, who has described this design as being of:

> startling originality ... an abstract composition of interlocking rectangles; ... a composition in colour as well as form, made up of the green of the slates, the alternating red and pale yellow of the brick work, and the many colours of the flowers and foliage.

In 1877 Godwin's friend, Whistler, commissioned him to design and build for him a studio house on a double plot in Tite Street close to the river, since he wished to start an 'atelier' for students, with large and small studios and living accommodation for himself and his mistress.

On 23 October, 1877, Whistler signed an agreement with the Metropolitan Board of Works in which he undertook to submit Godwin's designs to the Board for their approval, although characteristically he started building without obtaining permission. Godwin's stark design carried out in white brick capped by a green roof was extremely controversial, and was rejected, and so on 28 January, 1878, Godwin forwarded further designs for The White House to the Board which were also rejected. Undeterred, Whistler continued to build until the house was almost completed. The Board could in theory have taken back the site since the original agreement had been violated but they decided instead to press Whistler to make various 'ornamental additions' for which Godwin provided the design. In it the parapet has been raised and filled with a panel of sculpture, a statue in an alcove has been inserted between two of the windows, the front door enriched and the main windows given decorative brick surrounds ... The words 'The White House' have been inscribed over the front door, the first recorded appearance of the name.

A year later he collaborated with Whistler on the famous stand at the Paris exhibition of 1878. The stand displayed Godwin's spare, asymmetric 'Anglo Japanese' furniture manufactured by William Watt, the exhibitor. On this occasion Godwin abandoned his favourite medium of ebonized black wood, for the brilliant ginger of light-coloured mahogany, complemented by Whistler's still startling blond yellow and gold abstract designs, reminiscent of the stylized clouds and foliage of Japanese landscape prints. Described by Whistler as a *Harmony in Yellow* it was immediately dubbed 'an agony in yellow' by the critic of the *Magazine of Art*.[6]

After Whistler's bankruptcy in May 1879, on the Sunday before he left the house forever, to go on a working visit to Venice, he held his last reception. Godwin was one of the guests, and it may have been at his suggestion that the artist climbed a ladder and wrote over the Portland stone door the Biblical inscription:

E. W. Godwin
Designs and plans for the front elevation of a house and studio for Frank Miles in Tite Street, Chelsea, London, 1878
Godwin considered this house to be 'the best thing I ever did'. The client, George Francis Miles (1852–91), was a portrait painter who specialized in Aesthetic ladies. His close friendship with Wilde, with whom he briefly shared this house in the summer of 1880, ended tragically when Miles's clergyman father criticized Wilde's lifestyle. Wilde left and Miles subsequently went to pieces and had to be sent to a lunatic asylum near Bristol. He died four years later in 1891.

Right: T. Raffles Davison
(1853–1937)
The façade of the Fine Art
Society
From *The British Architect*,
1881
Ruskin and Whistler, who in
1878 had been involved in
the famous recriminatory
libel action, are amusingly
pictured here in happy
conversation just outside the
Gallery!

Opposite above: Lady Archie
Campbell played Orlando
and Eleanor Calhoun played
Rosalind in this performance
of *As You Like It* in Coombe
Wood, 1884.
Described as 'the epitome of
aestheticism', Lady
Archibald Campbell was
passionately involved with
open-air productions of
Pastoral plays of the
Elizabethan era. In the
Hunterian Museum is
Whistler's *Note in Green and
Brown: Orlando at Coombe* of
Lady Archie, which echoes
another study by Godwin in
a sketchbook in the Victoria
and Albert Museum.

Opposite below:
Performance of *The Faithful
Shepherdess* by John Fletcher
in Coombe Wood, 1885
It is interesting to note in
this glimpse of a Godwin
production the effective use
of orchestrated movement by
the cast, a theatrical device
to be much favoured by
Godwin's son, Gordon Craig.
A drawing in one of
Godwin's sketchbooks
reveals that the impressive
Therm of Pan which the
crowd are saluting, derives
from a tiny classical ivory in
the British Museum.

THE WHITE HOUSE, TITE STREET, CHELSEA
EXCEPT THE LORD BUILD THE HOUSE
THEY LABOUR IN VAIN THAT BUILD IT.
E.W. GODWIN, F.S.A., BUILT THIS ONE.

These were certainly prophetic words, for Harry Quilter, the art critic to whom the house was sold in September, was a most unsuitable owner, whose alterations spoiled the building. It was eventually demolished in the 1960s.

In November, 1877, Godwin began a close association with the Manchester-based magazine *The British Architect* as main leader writer and consultant. He wrote the leading article each week until mid-1879, articles which still bear re-reading as assertions of Aesthetic beliefs. The leader for the first issue of 1878 is a declaration of such aims:

Hitherto we have rarely allowed ourselves to step beyond the professional limits of one art, but for the future we hope to take a wider range, and without slackening our watchfulness in the field of architecture, we shall embrace in our survey the broader ground of painting and sculpture, taking note the while of that art which involves all others, namely the art of the stage ... To reconcile the decorative and constructive, to work for greater harmony and unity of thought in the surroundings of modern life will be [therefore] one of our aims.

Since their first meeting in Oxford in 1875, Godwin and Wilde had become close friends, many of the ideas on interior decoration and dress advocated by Wilde in his lectures being adopted from Godwin's own pronouncements. During the summer of 1884 Wilde leased 16 (now 34) Tite Street. Although it stood in the same street as Whistler's White House and the house for Frank Miles, number 16 was an undistinguished example of mid-Victorian speculative building. But Wilde determined with Godwin's services to make its interior strikingly original – the 'House Beautiful' of his lectures on interior decoration. The completed scheme included a suite of white furniture with chairs in various Grecian styles in the dining room, the removal of all doors except the folding doors in the drawing rooms, and subtle colour schemes throughout the house. These ranged from the white and grey and dull gold of the drawing room which set off a ceiling designed by Whistler with a peacock feather motif. Unfortunately many difficulties were experienced with contractors as Wilde's anguished letters to Godwin reveal: 'I wish you would choose the colours – the red for the drawing room – as the thing is at a standstill. Is it to be vermilion? Is it not? The universe pauses for an answer! Don't keep it waiting!' On the scheme's completion Wilde wrote to Godwin thanking him 'for the beautiful designs for the furniture. Each chair is a sonnet in ivory, and the table is a masterpiece in pearl.'

166

Wilde also described the decor of his home in a letter to W.A.S. Benson, the Arts and Crafts metalworker, in which Wilde criticized the decorative effect of Morris wallpapers, and expressed his preference for Morris textiles:

My eye requires in a room a resting-place of pure colour, and I prefer to keep design for more delicate materials than [wall]papers, for embroidery for instance. Paper in itself is not a lovely material, and the only papers which I ever use now are the Japanese gold ones: they are exceedingly decorative, and no English paper can compete with them, either for beauty or for practical wear. With these and with colour in oil and distemper a lovely house can be made.

Some day if you do us the pleasure of calling I will show you a little room with blue ceiling and frieze (distemper), yellow (oil) walls, and white woodwork and fittings, which is joyous and exquisite, the only piece of design being the Morris blue-and-white curtains, and a white-and-yellow silk coverlet. I hope, and in my lectures always try and bring it about, that people will study the value of pure colour more than they do.

Godwin continued to practise as an architect and was greatly in demand for the design and adaption of commercial art galleries in the Bond Street area. His design for the façade of the Fine Art Society executed in 1881, still functions admirably, the finest of his surviving London buildings. One of the most delicate of all Godwin's architectural drawings, and one of the last that he prepared before his death, was the design for the famous firm of print sellers McLean's. This plan was certainly not carried out above ground-floor level, and it is not clear whether even this was done, although there are certain details in the existing shop front, such as the position of the numbers, which indicate that it may have been. Three other variations for the façade survive, one Gothic in style, but all clearly inspired by the earlier design for the Fine Art Society.

Although such work provided much of Godwin's erratic income, his greatest talent lay in his genius for costume design. This talent was also to be in evidence in another production in 1884 mounted not in the reassuring environment of a theatre but in a Surrey wood, which prompted a memorable description from Max Beerbohm in his witty evocation of the decade of the 1880s in the *Yellow Book*:

Of the purely aesthetic fads of society were also the Pastoral Plays at Coombe Wood, and a very charming fad they must have been. There was one specially great occasion when Shakespeare's play *As You like It* was given. The day was as hot as a June day *can* be, and everyone drove down in open carriages and hansoms, and in the evening returned the same way. It was the very Derby Day of Aestheticism.

The event was the inspired whim of a wealthy titled lady described by Oscar Wilde as 'the Moon Lady, the Grey Lady, the beautiful wraith with her beryl eyes, our Lady Archie'. He referred to Lady Archibald Campbell, the friend and patron of Whistler who sat for several of his finest portraits. A keen advocate of amateur acting, valuing it for 'its freedom of mood', she was opposed to the archaeological tradition of stage design, and pioneered the production of pastoral plays in the open air. In July 1884, with Godwin's help as designer, she put on Shakespeare's *As You Like It* in the grounds of Dr McGragh's hydropathic establishment at Coombe Wood, Norbiton, Kingston-on-Thames, using both professional and amateur performers. The event was a fashionable success, helped by the patronage of the Prince of Wales who doubtless enjoyed the opportunities provided by Godwin's costumes for admiring the attractive legs of Orlando, played by Lady Archie and of Rosalind, played by the American actress Eleanor Calhoun. Whistler also attended performances of the play, painting a charming small oil, *Note in Green and Brown: Orlando at Coombe*, which greatly resembles a sketch in one of Godwin's notebooks.

The following July an even more ambitious production took place at Coombe, the play *The Faithful Shepherdess* by John Fletcher. A note scribbled at a rehearsal by Lady Archie conveys her enthusiasm for unusual effects:

Memo: Satyrs not nearly numerous enough, half a dozen boys ought to be got to play fauns ... One hundred butterflies to bring down on the morning of the day Gardener ... could get them if ordered in time ... Ought not the sheep and shepherds to be brought up for dress rehearsal? Beautiful effect to be got by driving the flock across the stage to the meadow, dogs are trained for this purpose.

This note elicits a reply revealing Godwin for once in an economical mood:

Dear Lady Archie, as there's not the remotest chance of clearing 1/- out of the Coombe plays. Do not I beg you ask me to involve anyone in more debts than already face us yours ever – E.W. Godwin.

His caution can be understood as the cost of the five-night production reached the staggering sum of just over £3,000! The first night was attended by Whistler and Oscar Wilde. Doubtless Whistler, the butterfly of the Aesthetic Movement, appreciated the flight of the real butterflies, and Wilde enjoyed the satyrs!

The next year the venue moved to Wimbledon, the play presented being an adaption of Tennyson's *Becket* renamed *Fair Rosamund*. But in April Godwin began to suffer from an illness which necessitated convalescence in the country, a circumstance

Godwin designed the costumes and set for *Helena in Troas* at Hengler's Cirque in 1886. One of Helen's attendants was Constance Wilde. The author of the play was John Todhunter, a leading figure of the Aesthetic community at Bedford Park, and friend of W. B. Yeats and Florence Farr.

which prompted a delightful 'get well' letter from Oscar Wilde:

Dear Godwino, I am glad you are resting. Nature is a foolish place to look for inspiration in, but a charming one in which to forget one ever had any. Of course we miss you, but the white furniture reminds us of you daily, and we find that a rose leaf can be laid on the ivory table without scratching it – at least a white one can. That is something. We look forward to seeing you robust, and full of vigour. My wife sends her best wishes for your health. Ever yours, Oscar Wilde.

Constance Wilde took part in Godwin's last dramatic venture in May 1886, a tragedy by John Todhunter based on the plays of Sophocles entitled *Helena in Troas* which was produced at Hengler's Cirque, on the site of the London Palladium. Lady Archie, in an article commissioned by Oscar Wilde for the first number of his magazine *Woman's World* described how: 'like figures on a marble frieze, the band of white robed maidens wound through the twilight past the altar of Dionysus, and one by one in slow procession climbed the steps, and passed away, the audience were absolutely stilled in their excitement', while W.B. Yeats admired 'its solemn staging, its rhythmical chorus and ascending incense ... Many people have said to me that the surroundings of Helena made them feel religious. Once get your audience in that mood, and you can do anything with it.' Sadly, however, Godwin was not to get an audience in that mood again, for he fell ill with acute inflammation of the bladder and died on 6 October, 1886. In 1876 he had married Beatrice Phillip, the daughter of a sculptor, with whom he enjoyed a marriage of a very open nature, as Beatrice attached herself more and more to Godwin's friend Whistler, whom she was to marry two years after Godwin's death.

Although Gordon Craig was only three when his parents parted, the life of his father had a profound effect on his own career. In his late twenties in 1901 Craig wrote of Godwin: 'he ... failed so much when he had the gifts to succeed – he is remembered as a failure – and they say "see his son – another failure – like father, like son". This won't do.' In 1910 Craig republished Godwin's articles on the staging of Shakespeare's plays, in his avant-garde magazine *The Mask*, a notable act of filial piety for Craig was himself deeply opposed to archaeological realism in the theatre. But perhaps his most remarkable tribute to the father he never knew, is a haunting wood-cut portrait with which he illustrated an article on the art of E.W. Godwin.

As an anonymous obituary in *The British Architect* pointed out: 'long before any attempt was made to popularize art, he recognized that houses need not be ugly to be comfortable. We are still, alas! in an age of stucco and bastard art, but the little that has

Edward Gordon Craig
(1872–1966)
Idealized portrait of his
father E. W. Godwin
From *The Mask*, October
1910

'been done to beautify our domestic surroundings is mainly due to him'.

The *Dictionary of National Biography's* obituary notice of Godwin strikes a note reminiscent of a cross teacher's school report on a wayward pupil:

... his removal to London proved a mistake from a professional point of view ... he has left no building there really worthy of his capabilities ... he failed to fulfil his early promise ... he found too wide a field for his many talents ...

Such disparaging comments sadly set the tone for subsequent accounts of his life until Dudley Harbron published the pioneering *The Conscious Stone: The Life of Edward William Godwin* in 1949. He still awaits a full-scale biography but until that occurs his finest epitaph is fittingly to be found in the final couplets of a sonnet written by Ellen Terry in her large, generous hand, upon hearing the news of his death:

They tell me he had his faults

I know of one

Dying too soon, he left his best undone.

It's *fang-de-seeaycle* that does it, my dear, and education, and reading French.

JOHN DAVIDSON, *THE WONDERFUL MISSION OF EARL LAVENDER*, 1895

Opposite: T. Privat-Livement (1861–1936)
Absinthe Robette
From *Les Maitres de l'Affiche*, **1896**
Absinthe, a liquor made from wormwood, which possessed a greenish tinge when water was added, was much more than a drink – it became a symbol of decadence. Overindulgence in it was rumoured to send you blind or insane. Banned in the First World War, it is now commemorated by a museum dedicated to the memory of 'le peril verte'.

Lady Bracknell: I'm sure the programme will be delightful, after a few expurgations. French songs I cannot possibly allow. People always seem to think they are improper, and either look shocked, which is vulgar, or laugh, which is worse.

OSCAR WILDE, *THE IMPORTANCE OF BEING EARNEST*, 1895

Right: A. H. Mackmurdo
Century Guild chair, 1881
The twisting organic curves of Mackmurdo's chair, which was designed in 1881 but made by the Century Guild in 1882, were to spark the explosive development of Art Nouveau line seen in the twisting steam of the absinthe poster which it innocently predates.

The term '*fin de siècle*' first emerged in France in the 1880s. It spread with great speed internationally, an indication of the power of the French language and the dominant role of French culture on thoughts aroused by the approaching end of the nineteenth century. In Paris the struggles for supremacy between the accepted art of the salon, Impressionism and Symbolism were striking aspects of the art of those years. These events were mirrored in Britain where the traditions of the Royal Academy were flouted by the followers of the Newlyn school, the vivid Impressionist works painted by Philip Wilson Steer in the 1880s and the low-life themes of the music hall and pub favoured by Walter Richard Sickert. Such works were important in creating the visual mood of the decade. But the era was one in which literature played a dominant role. Poetry, novels and drama vied for attention in the decade of the decadence. One of the most influential books of the time, was the novel by Joris-Karl Huysmans, *A Rebours*, which may be roughly translated as *Against Nature.*

Joris-Karl Huysmans was born in Paris in 1848, the year of revolutions, appropriately for a writer whose work was to revolutionize the frontiers of the art of his time. A junior clerk in the Ministry of the Interior for thirty-two years, he seems a humdrum and unlikely figure to create a novel which produced an incalculable effect on subsequent European literature, and which was to be described by Mario Praz in *The Romantic Agony* as 'the pivot upon which the whole psychology of the Decadent Movement turns; in it all the phenomena of this state of mind are illustrated down to the minutest detail, in the instance of its chief character, Des Esseintes.'

For English readers one of the most memorable chapters in *A Rebours* is the description of how the hero Des Esseintes reads the novels of Charles Dickens to calm his nerves, but they produce exactly the opposite effect. He is seized with a sudden overpowering desire to visit England. His bags are packed, he even sets out upon the fateful mission despite drenching rain, which strikes him as an instalment of English life paid to him on account in Paris. But the mere sight of the English faces at the hotel where travellers gather for the journey is more than enough for Des Esseintes. Looking at them he can almost smell the fog of London, and returns to the reclusive ivory tower of his home, his travel lust sated.

This incident could almost stand as an allegory of the relationship between France and England in the 1880s when the book was first published. Admittedly, Verlaine, Rimbaud and Van Gogh, unlikely though it may seem, did work briefly as school teachers in England. Van Gogh's years in England in the 1870s were greatly to influence his later

Walter Crane
Cover of *Jugend*, **1898**
Walter Crane's design of
1898 for the cover of the
German magazine *Jugend*
(Youth – which was to lend
its name to the German for
Art Nouveau, *Jugendstil*), **is**
another reflection of the
manner in which British and
Continental cultural and
stylistic links flourished in
the heady atmosphere of the
1890s.

career. He admired and collected the powerful realist woodcut portraits of labouring types which appeared in *The Graphic* magazine, and had some contact with the art world of London, which gave him many ideas which would surface later. Ten years later in 1888 he planned a powerful effect to welcome Gauguin to the Yellow House in Arles. He arranged bowls of sunflowers and painted twelve panels depicting the flower, which he described in Whistlerian terms as 'a symphony in blue and yellow'. But on the whole, although France could manage without direct contact with England, again and again progressive English artistic circles looked across the Channel for new ideas and inspiration.

This was particularly true of Oscar Wilde, 'a man who stood in symbolic relation to his age'. He returned constantly to France for creative inspiration. After his American adventures in 1882, Wilde visited Paris in January 1883 on a lengthy working holiday to finish his play *The Duchess of Padua*. In Paris, aged twenty-eight, he took stock of his life, and jettisoned the tight trousers and yellow satin of Aesthetic garb, to don another more long-lasting pose – that of the dandy, a change of gear from the role of Bunthorne to that of Beau Brummel. Of his earlier costume he remarked to his friend Robert Sherard: 'All *that* belonged to the Oscar of the first period. We are now concerned with the Oscar Wilde of the second period, who has nothing in common with the gentleman who wore long hair and carried a sunflower down Piccadilly.'

These words also mark the beginning of the second phase of Aestheticism. In the early 1880s it too shed the affectations satirized by Du Maurier and others to enter upon its transitional role as the precursor of Art Nouveau. This is most notable in the complex yet free-flowing seaweed fronds of the decoration on A.H. Mackmurdo's proto Art Nouveau Century Guild furniture and textile designs. They, like the decorative swans, peacocks and lilies of Walter Crane, were to become a source of inspiration for the European designers.

In Paris with Sherard, Wilde retraced the steps of the poet and dandy Gerard de Nerval, who had paraded the gardens of the Palais Royal with a lobster on a pale blue ribbon, and eventually hanged himself one wintry morning in 1855 with an old apron string he believed to be the Queen of Sheba's garter, while above him his pet raven croaked, '*J'ai soif*'! With Whistler, Wilde climbed a ladder to visit Degas's garret studio in the Rue Fontaine St Georges. Degas had little time for Aestheticism, once remarking: 'Taste – it doesn't exist. An artist makes beautiful things without being aware of it. Aesthetes beat their brows and say to themselves "How can I find a pretty shape for a chamber pot?" Poor creatures, their chamberpots may be works of art but they will immediately induce a retention of urine. They will look at their pots and say to all their friends: "Look at my chamberpot. Isn't it pretty?" No more art. No more art. No more art'.[1]

Even more important contacts for Wilde during his three-month stay were his meetings with poets and writers of the literary decadence, such as Sarah Bernhardt's protégé Maurice Rollinat, hailed as a second Baudelaire whose themes included suicide, madness, live burial, diabolism and putrefaction. In the periodical *Le Chat Noir* Jean Lorrain published stories on the theme of homosexuality, later dedicating one to Wilde. Verlaine also was beginning to publish poems about homosexuality and may have read to Wilde his poem *Langeur* which begins: '*Je suis l'Empire à la fin de la Décadence*'. Stimulated by such contacts Wilde himself wrote both the poem *The Harlot's House* and much of *The Sphinx*. He also met Edmond de Goncourt, the pillar of the French literary establishment, who had written two novels *Manette Salomon* and *La Faustin* which Wilde admired, and from which he would borrow suggestive homosexual and sadistic themes and incorporate them into his own *Picture of Dorian Gray*. The book which was to be the main influence on *Dorian Gray*, J-K.Huysmans's *A Rebours*, was then still being written.

We glimpse its progress in a letter Huysmans wrote while engaged upon it to the poet, Mallarmé, on 27 October, 1882:

I am at present working on a strange story, the subject of which is briefly as follows: the last representative of an illustrious race, appalled by the invasion of American manners and the growth of an aristocracy of wealth, takes refuge in absolute solitude. He is well read, cultivated and refined. In his comfortable retreat he substitutes the pleasures of artifice for the banalities of Nature... For the delectation of his mind and the delight of his eyes, he has decided to seek out evocative works which would transport him from a familiar world, point out the way to new possibilities, and shake up the nervous system by means of erudite fancies, complicated nightmares, suave and sinister visions ... he has one room resembling a monastic cell, another a cabin in a yacht, another a chapel, while elsewhere could be seen a sleigh standing on a white polar bear rug and a gilded tortoise shell set with precious stones like a jewelled ciborium ...

This description is of both the fictional house of the hero Des Esseintes, and the rarely seen home in the Rue Franklin that inspired it. It belonged to the role model for many of the eccentricities of Des Esseintes, M. Robert de Montesquiou-Fezenac, whose portrait Whistler painted in 1894. When the work was exhibited at the Salon de Champs de Mars, the *Magazine of Art* declared it to portray 'the pontiff of aestheticism whom the Faubourg St Germain delights to

George Clairin (1843–1919)
Sarah Bernhardt, 1876
Oil on canvas
Throughout Clairin's adult life he was obsessed by the visual theme of the great actress Sarah Bernhardt. He painted her frequently, both in her home as in this famous example, and on stage. Eventually, if she was unable to model for him herself, she would simply send her clothes to his studio, and he would paint her, with the aid of many sketches, from memory.

honour'. The experience of sitting to Whistler was a memorable one, for the artist strutted about 'like a rare bird; its crest was its forelock, its cries the painter's words'.

Avian imagery again comes to mind in looking at the renowned society portrait painter Giovanni Boldini's (1842–1931) portrayal of M. de Montesquiou-Fezenac, the most celebrated of all depictions of the flamboyant figure. It can be compared with Proust's verbal description '... he had such a way of throwing back his head, gaily and proudly crested with its tuft of golden hair a bit thinned out, and such proud and coquettish suppleness in the movements of his neck – like no other human being – you wondered whether you were watching some wonderful bird walk about in its cage ...'

Huysmans's novel was fatefully only to fall into Wilde's eager hand on his honeymoon visit to Paris in June 1884. The following year Wilde's review of Whistler's '*Ten O'clock*' lecture was to cause a permanent rift between the two great wits of their age. For Wilde, the controversy centred on the fact that he believed that the poet and not the painter was the supreme artist. This theme also occurs in his novel *The Picture of Dorian Gray* in which Wilde plays with the notion that the portrait, capturing youth eternally at its moment of perfection, could also contain the temporal power of literature to capture the story of the degenerate effects of life. He told several stories about the moment in which the concept of the novel came to him.[2] One of the best relates that Charles Ricketts once in 1884 painted Wilde's portrait and having finished, remarked: 'How delightful it would be if you could remain exactly as you are, while the portrait aged and withered in your stead.'

Whatever the truth of this story, the first appearance of *The Picture of Dorian Gray* when it was serialized in 1890, caused a sensation. It was denounced by the London *Daily Chronicle* as 'a tale spawned from the leprous literature of the French Decadents, a poisonous book'. Pater, in his review, with withering irony, commented: 'Clever always, this book seems intended to set forth anything but a homely philosophy of life for the middle class.' Oscar Wilde visualized his hero Dorian Gray as 'Made out of ivory and rose leaves' with 'lips of scarlet' and inspired by *A Rebours:*

It was the strangest book that he had ever read. It seemed to him that in exquisite raiment and to the delicate sound of flutes, the sins of the world were passing in dumb show before him. Things that he had dimly dreamed of were suddenly made real to him. Things of which he had never dreamed were gradually revealed...'For years, Dorian Gray could not free himself from the influence of this book ...' The hero, the wonderful young Parisian, in

Giovanni Boldini
(1842–1931)
Portrait of Robert, Comte de Montesquiou-Fezenac, 1897
Oil on canvas, 200 x 100 cm
The sitter was described as 'the pontiff of aestheticism', and was the model for J-K Huysmans's *Des Esseintes* and Marcel Proust's *Baron de Charlus*. His life, however, was stranger than any novel. A dandy and a poet, he links the symbolism of the decadence with the bold colours of his friend Diaghilev's *Ballet Russe*.

Fernand Khnopff (1858–1921)
Un Masque, **1897**
Ivory, bronze and enamel
While Max Beerbohm was
writing in *The Yellow Book* **of**
'The Truth of Masks', the
Belgian artist Fernand
Khnopff was creating this
enigmatic artifact. *Un Masque*
is a sculpture of the head of
Hermes, probably inspired by
the face of the artist's sister,
Marguerite.

whom the romantic and the scientific temperaments were so strangely blended, became to him a prefiguring type of himself ... it seemed to him to contain the story of his own life, written before he had lived it.

Dorian Gray's reaction to Huysmans' novel *A Rebours* was echoed by a generation of young men. Young writers of the 1890s felt almost a duty to subscribe to such beliefs and to become themselves amateurs of 'strange sensations'. They found inspiration not only in Pater's rallying injunction to youth to seek the life of sensation, but also in the writings of the poet Paul Verlaine, who insisted that the art a poet practised was both its own justification, and its own reward. Verlaine celebrated the '*poetes maudits*' condemned by the society in which they lived to both self-destruction and rebellion, and rhapsodized:

I love this word decadence, all shimmering in purple and gold ... It suggests the subtle thoughts of ultimate civilization, a high literary culture, a soul capable of intense pleasures. It throws off bursts of fire and the sparkle of precious stones. It is redolent of the rouge of courtesans, the games of the circus, the panting of the gladiator, the spring of wild beasts, the consuming in flames of races exhausted by their capacity for sensation, as the tramp of an advancing army sounds.

While Verlaine provided the definition, Wilde's novel was to become virtually a Bible for the Decadents. It inextricably links the concepts of Aestheticism with those of homosexuality in the public mind. There is no ambiguity in the expression of love of the painter Basil Hallward, for his sitter Dorian Gray, a love that had:

nothing in it that was not noble and intellectual. It was not that mere physical admiration of beauty that is born of the senses and that dies when the senses die. It was such love as Michael Angelo *[sic]* had known, and Montaigne, and Winckelmann, and Shakespeare himself.

In this passage we hear for the first time the plea which was to ring out in court five years later in defence of 'the love that dares not speak its name'.

It is difficult today to appreciate the contemporary background to Wilde's declaration and the extent to which homosexual proclivities became overt and public was the 'invention' of the late Victorian era. It came to the fore in the 1880s in the work of writers such as John Addington Symonds, artists such as Simeon Solomon, and the Victorian sexologist Havelock Ellis. The developing homosexual underworld of the 1870s and 1880s was theoretically identified and outlawed by the passage in 1885 of the Labouchère Amendment to the Criminal Law Amendment Act which made all homosexual acts, private or public, illegal. This was the law under which Oscar Wilde was convicted and sentenced to two years' hard labour. It was against this background that Wilde, like Proust, made use of homosexuality as a theme, but only in terms of unhappiness. Wilde was to write two portraits of a man in decay, the novel *The Picture of Dorian Gray* and his own story *De Profundis.*

Wilde and Proust, the two great interpreters of homosexual life, met only twice in the early 1890s, the introduction being effected by the painter Jacques Emile Blanche. Wilde was impressed at Proust's deep knowledge of English literature, especially Ruskin whom he translated, and George Eliot. But Proust's invitation to dinner at the family home in the Boulevard Haussmann turned into a disaster. Wilde who had been expecting an intimate dinner *à deux*, ran away from dining with Proust's parents saying to them with uncharacteristic cruelty: 'How ugly your house is!' This atypical remark was made in 1893 when Wilde was at his most successful and arrogant. It has indeed much more of the ring of Whistler about it, whom Proust idealized. Proust, however, met Whistler only once, but it was, appropriately, a deeply memorable occasion. It took place in the salon of Méry Laurent, a cocotte whose personality contributed a little to the character of Proust's heroine Odette. Predictably Whistler asserted that Ruskin knew nothing about painting; but Proust later wrote triumphantly: 'I made him say a few kind words of Ruskin! And from that occasion I kept his charming grey gloves which I have since lost.' Proust was to use part of Whistler's character as the basis for the fictional Elstir in his *A la Recherche …*

In a letter to Marie Nordlinger, Proust wrote:

Ruskin and Whistler were mistaken about each other because their systems were opposed. But there is one truth, and they both saw it. Even in the action against Ruskin, Whistler said, 'You say I painted this picture in a few hours. But actually I painted it with their experience of my whole life.' But at that very moment Ruskin was writing to Rossetti, 'I prefer the things you do quickly, immediately, your rough sketches, to what you work over. What you work at you spend, say, six months in doing; but what you sketch at one swoop is the expression of years of dreams, of love, and of experience'. On this level the two stars strike the same point with a ray perhaps hostile, but identical.

Despite his enthusiasm for Ruskin, Proust was not an Aesthete of the type of Huysmans, Robert de Montesquiou-Fezenac or Oscar Wilde. His own closest artistic friends were figures such as Jacques Emile Blanche and Paul Helleu, artists too often dismissed as lightweight portrayers of the social scene but who at their best have an

Sarah Bernhardt
Fantastic Inkwell: Self Portrait as a Sphinx, **1880**
Bronze
The great actress was passionately devoted to the fine arts, and was herself a sculptor of great ability. Here she portrays herself as a sphinx, crouched behind the inkwell.

engaging and captivating elegance. Blanche, whose English teacher
was Mallarmé, and was encouraged by Manet and Renoir, was to become
one of the most successful portrait painters of his time, particularly
excelling at the portrayal of women, although his male portraits include
Beardsley, Debussy, Degas, Henry James, Maeterlinck, Ricketts and
Rodin. He was a close friend of Sickert, and also for many years a
resident in Dieppe. Blanche's portrait of Proust, painted in 1892, as a
dapper, white-faced young man with staring black eyes and an orchid in
his button-hole, has become the most familiar image of the writer.
Blanche's contemporary, Paul Helleu, was first introduced to the
fashionable high society of the Faubourg St Germain by his patron
Robert de Montesquiou-Fezenac. Helleu's fastidious taste in dress was
matched by his delight in the sea and yachting, which made him a
prominent figure at the resorts of Trouville and Biarritz. He excelled at
the depiction of fashionable women with elegant coiffures, subjects
which he recorded in many drawings and over 600 exquisite dry points.
A notable example depicts his wife admiring Watteau drawings at the
Louvre, a work which drew the inevitable caustic comment from Degas

Jacques Emile Blanche
Marcel Proust, **c. 1891–2**
Oil on canvas
**For the 1890s this was the
dapper image presented by
Marcel Proust to the
hermetic world of Parisian
high society which he was
later to immortalize.**

that Helleu's work was prone to pastiche – '*Watteau à vapeur*'.

Several English artists identified with Aestheticism also at times enjoyed working in Paris in the early 1890s. Charles Conder, an intimate friend of the poet Ernest Dowson, was indeed more at home in the Rat Mort in Pigalle than in his birthplace, London. He had been brought up in India before arriving in Sydney in 1883 and going to Melbourne in 1886. His remarkable Impressionist work in Australia possesses the highly individual palette and delicacy of vision which distinguished his work throughout his life. From 1890 to 1895 he lived in Paris, where he renewed a friendship with the cartoonist Phil May (1864–1903), whom he had met in Australia and who was sharing a studio with William Rothenstein. Rothenstein drew memorable lithographic records of personalities of the day such as his double portrait of Ricketts and Shannon. In his book *The Parson and the Painter* Phil May's black and white drawings, admired by figures as diverse as Whistler and Leighton, caught vivaciously every nuance of the 'naughty' nineties view of Paris. It contains graphic drawings of the rendezvous immortalized by the poster artist Steinlen, the café *Le Chat Noir* where any behaviour was tolerated as long as it conformed to the precept '*épater le bourgeois*' – of raising two fingers to the middle classes.

Conder and May also used to accompany each other on sketching expeditions to the Moulin Rouge, a location better known through the work of another close friend of Conder, Toulouse-Lautrec. He used Conder as a model in several of his works.

Conder's sensitive landscapes in oil of the French countryside are very different from his unusual watercolours on silk, a support which can produce remarkably subtle results but is extremely fragile. He loved to work at night, and descriptions abound of him taking a roll of silk in one hand, a bottle of absinthe in the other, and disappearing to his studio to paint the fan-shaped compositions of which he was particularly fond. He was not good at selling them, prompting Oscar Wilde to remark: 'Dear Conder! always trying to persuade one to buy a fan for ten guineas for which one would be very happy to pay twenty!'[3] Conder was a dandy, affecting the costume of the 1840s and Murger's *La Vie de Bohème*. From his friend Anquentin who shared his Aesthetic tastes, he acquired a love of Watteau's '*fêtes galantes*' – scenes of flirtation among bosky woods – themes which are reflected in some of his designs for dresses and wall decorations. For the contemporary critic D.S. MacColl: 'Conder reduced nature to the music of colours and evoked perfumed and poetic moods. [He] was to be the main spokesman for art for art's sake and the aestheticism of the "Yellow Nineties".'

From 1895 to 1898 Conder lived chiefly in Dieppe,

Cabaret du Chat Noir — La première des projections d'ombres de 2ᵉ Époque dessinée par Caran d'Ache. (1886)

Le Chat Noir
**From *L'Illustration*, 1888
In the background can be
seen the elaborate circular
setting for the silhouette
shadow plays which were a
great feature of the
entertainment at this
cabaret made famous by
Steinlen's poster, and the
sardonic backchat of its
owner Rodolphe Salis.**

seeing in 1897 much of Aubrey Beardsley. The great illustrator was
then in the last stages of consumption, but still working frantically on
subjects varying from Gautier's *Mademoiselle de Maupin* to the production
of a cover for yet another new magazine to be called *The Peacock*, for
which Beardsley worked only on condition that it contained no work by
Oscar Wilde. Indeed, Dieppe became what might be described as the
capital of English Aestheticism in exile. There congregated from time
to time not only Beardsley and his patron, the lawyer turned publisher
of erotica Leonard Smithers, but also Oscar Wilde and his immediate
circle. Other visitors included figures as various as the poet Ernest
Dowson, and such artists as William Rothenstein, Charles Ricketts,
Charles Shannon, Max Beerbohm, Jacques Emile Blanche, and, of
course, Walter Sickert, whose paintings of Dieppe capture so
memorably the subdued tonality of the port.

Marcel Proust, as a young man in Paris, was very aware
of the potent charm of the poster: 'Every morning I would hasten to
the Moriss Column to see what new plays and words it announced'.
Even Chéret's prodigious powers of invention – he created well over a
thousand posters during his long lifetime – could not satisfy demand
in this new market. Chéret's most famous pupil as poster designer was
Toulouse-Lautrec, whose bold works became well known in England
from two big shows of posters held in 1894 and 1896 at the then famous

Right above: Charles Conder
Souvenir de Murger, 1905
Watercolour on silk,
30 x 39.5 cm
Conder loved the 1830s, as
described by the novelist,
Henri Murger, in *Scènes de la
vie de Bohéme*, and frequently
wore the costumes of that
era. Here he evokes the
period in a watercolour on
silk, which like his fans has
qualities described by
Ricketts as 'delightful in
colour, design and the sense
of wit and romance which
they evoke, the sense of
luxury which they express,
and the love for beautiful
things that pass away, like
laughter and music, the
mirage of noon, the magic
of night, the perfume of
flowers, and youth and life'.

Right below: Pierre Bonnard
(1867–1947)
Le Revue Blanche, 1894
Colour lithograph,
80 x 63 cm
Thadée Natanson, publisher
of *La Revue Blanche*,
champion of the Nabis group
of painters and Bonnard's
lifelong friend and
biographer, commissioned
this poster. It was the first of
more than thirty-five images
Bonnard produced for the
brilliant avant-garde journal
between 1893 and 1903.
The poster depicts Misia,
Thadée's wife, as the central
figure of the glamorous
Parisienne holding a copy
of the magazine.

venue, the Westminster Aquarium, London. The French section was selected and accompanied by Toulouse-Lautrec, who designed a poster for the exhibitions' chief British organizer, the confetti manufacturer Bella. The impact produced by Lautrec's posters is admirably demonstrated by the poster *Reine de Joie*, made for a now forgotten novel, which appeared in a series entitled *La Menagerie Sociale*, and describes the life of a corrupt stockbroker at the Paris Bourse. Its author, Victor Jozé, commissioned Lautrec to capture the grotesque reality of the fat roué, the cocotte, and the tired dandy (modelled on Charles Conder). So powerful was the aversion the poster aroused in the Bourse, that one broker sent out two clerks to obliterate the hated image!

More Aesthetic themes were developed within the covers of the avant-garde Parisian journal *La Revue Blanche* run by the intellectuals Misia and Thadée Natanson, for which Pierre Bonnard (1867–1947) produced one of his most striking posters. Both Bonnard and Edouard Vuillard (1868–1940), who were much admired by Proust, contributed to one of the first exhibitions of Les Nabis group in 1891. Les Nabis – 'the Prophets' – enjoyed the best of both worlds by describing themselves as being both '*Symbolistes et Impressionistes*'. Their work ranged from easel painting to the design of stained glass, book illustration or posters, all tempered with a sensitive and decoratively controlled line which possesses certain affinities with the spirit of Aestheticism and Japanese prints. These aims were described by the theoretician of the group, Albert Aurier, who wrote in 1891: 'Painting can be created only to decorate with thoughts, dreams and ideas the banal walls of human edifices.' Another member of the group, the Dutch artist Dom Willibrad Verkade opined: 'There are no such things as pictures, only decoration.' Such thoughts are reflected in the later 'Intimistes' work of Bonnard and particularly Vuillard, who loved to depict the atmosphere of the shuttered, curtained rooms of the bourgeoisie, lined with densely patterned wallpapers.

It was in the field of decorative arts that English Aesthetic work made its greatest impact on Paris, notably in the shop, the *Maison de L'Art Nouveau*. It was opened by Samuel Bing, offering for sale work by all those with 'a distinct personal perception whose designs were not re-incarnations of the past'. Among the British work on view was the metalwork of W.A.S. Benson, wallpapers and fabrics by Walter Crane, William Morris and Charles Annesley Voysey, and paintings by Frank Brangwyn. The British influence was also shown in works by their Belgian admirer Henri Van der Velde who was accused by a reviewer in the English *Art Journal* in 1897 of copying Walter Crane's work, and rendering his ideas without charm. This may be one of the factors which

Charles Conder
Scene in Seville
Watercolour and gouache on silk, 192 x 203 cm (irregular) As a support, silk is extremely fragile, yet Conder loved to paint in watercolour on silk and produced remarkably subtle effects. As he was usually content to paint on silk fans, this is an example of one of his most ambitious works in this medium.

FIGARO ILLUSTRÉ

The Eiffel Tower
Cover of *Figaro Illustré*, **1900**
The famous iron structure
erected on the south bank of
the Seine for the Paris
Exhibition of 1889, was still
the centre of attention
during the 1900 exhibition.

led Crane later to attack violently what he described as 'that strange decorative disease known as Art Nouveau' with its 'wild and whirligig squirms'.

It would, however, be wrong to suggest that Paris only appealed to intellectual visitors from England. Music hall artistes, particularly dancers, achieved fame in both capital cities. Lautrec designed posters both for British stars appearing in Paris such as May Belfort and for French dance troupes visiting England, such as the troupe of Madame Eglantine.

A century ago, although the Channel tunnel was already the subject for jokes by Linley Sambourne in *Punch*, Paris was for the first time within relatively easy striking distance for a wide cross-section of society. Charles Keene's last drawing for *Punch* of 1890 depicted a working class Cockney in Paris entitled '*Arry on the Boulevards*, while Charles Coburn celebrated the delights of the French capital and the

'ARRY ON THE BOULEVARDS.

Charles Keene (1823–91)
'Arry on the Boulevards
From *Punch*, **c. 1890**
**Keene's drawings were
admired by artists as varied
as Menzel and Degas. In
this, his last contribution to**
Punch, **he prophetically
chronicles an aspect of the
1890s, when for the first time
travel between Paris and
London became easily
possible for all social classes,
and many music-hall stars
made a career on both sides
of the Channel.**

south of France with the '*The Man who Broke the Bank at Monte Carlo*'.

The two great exhibitions of 1889 and 1900 held in Paris changed the landscape of the city. The Grand Palais, the Petit Palais and the Alexandre III Bridge were all designed for the exhibition of 1900 and are still part of the city's cultural life. Even more a symbol of the city is the Eiffel Tower, the centrepiece of the exhibition of 1889, admired by no less than 32 million people from all over Europe who flooded into Paris in 1889.

If you couldn't get to Paris, however, Paris could be brought to you, and the Blackpool Tower was built between 1891 and

Cliché Chrétien.

LA PARISIENNE

PAR M. MOREAU-VAUTHIER

Statue surmontant la Porte Monumentale de la Place de la Concorde

Opposite: Augustin-Jean
Moreau-Vauthier
La Parisienne, 1900
The sculpture, over six
metres in height, which
surmounted the Porte Binet,
a monumental entrance on
the Place de la Concorde to
the Paris Exhibition of 1900.
The figure displayed a smart
robe designed by Madame
Pacquin.

Right above: Madame
Pacquin
Tannhäuser, 1899
This rose silk robe with its
delicate floral beadwork
seems rococo, rather than
Wagnerian in its inspiration,
but an admiration for both
Wagner's opera of 1845,
Swinburne's poem *Laus
Veneris* of 1866, Burne-Jones
and Beardsley's pictorial
visualizations explain the
ongoing potency, charm and
appeal of the theme.

Right below: Madame
Pacquin
Sappho, 1899
This evening wrap, with its
use of the ubiquitous yellow
and black of the 1890s,
reflects with its layered
textures, cascading ruffles,
and sparkling spangles a
fashionable style closely
allied to the work of
Beardsley who had died the
previous year.

1894 in direct emulation of the Eiffel Tower, although admittedly only 500 and not 984 feet high. A similar structure was also erected in Prague, but the one at Wembley only got as far as the first stage before the scheme ran out of money.

Parisians themselves admittedly had their reservations about the Eiffel Tower. Some visited the restaurant on the first floor because it was the only place in Paris where you could not see the structure, others like Edmond de Goncourt and Zola dined there because the view provided a realization: 'of the greatness, the extent, the Babylonian immensity of Paris ...'

The great exhibitions were not to the taste of Henry James who wrote to Edward Warren:

This extraordinary Paris with its new – I mean more and more multiplied – manifestations of luxurious and extravagant extension, grandeur and general chronic *expositionism* ... it strikes me as a monstrous massive flower of national decadence, the biggest temple ever built to material joys and the lust of the eyes, and drawing to it thereby all the forces of the nation as a substitute for others – I mean other than Parisian – achievement. It is a strange phenomenon – with a deal of beauty still in its great expansive symmetries and perspectives – and *such* a beauty of light.

In this remarkable passage Henry James captures the strange visual alchemy of Paris, the city of light, and also defines its status, which it still retains, as the major temple for 'the lust of the eyes', an artistic centre of the world where both the fine arts and high fashion flourish.

With the establishment of her fashion house in Paris in 1891, Madame Pacquin offered the first important female challenge to the supremacy of Worth and Doucet – the two great male designers then dominating French *haute couture*. Her success was immediate and immense with dresses given such evocative titles as 'Sappho' – an evening wrap in typically *fin-de-siècle* black and yellow – and 'Tannhäuser', a rose silk robe of potent sensuality. In 1900 she was appointed president of the section dedicated to fashionable dress at the *Exposition Universelle*, and it was a classic robe of her design that was displayed on the colossal sculpture *La Parisienne* by Moreau-Vauthier which surmounted the Porte Binet. This monumental entrance gateway to the exhibition built on the Place de la Concorde, was created to deal with crowds of 60,000 an hour approaching the turnstiles. Over six metres high, the figure of *La Parisienne* was designed to be seen from a low viewpoint, which also dictated the strained pose and bold handling of detail. The choice of a fashionable woman as the symbol of Paris reflected how the status of women had changed in the 1800s.

Lazy, laughing languid Jenny

Fond of a kiss and fond of a guinea

Whose head upon my knee tonight

Rests for a while, as if grown light…

Why, Jenny, you're asleep at last!-

Asleep, poor Jenny, hard and fast,-

So young and soft and tired; so fair,

With chin thus nestled in your hair,

Mouth quiet, eyelids almost blue

As if some sky of dreams shone through

Dante Gabriel Rossetti
Fair Rosamund: Study, **1861**
Coloured chalks,
32 x 25.5 cm
A study of Rossetti's
mistress, Fanny Cornforth,
made as she was posing for
the oil painting of 1861,
which depicted the story of
Fair Rosamund, the mistress
of Henry II, whose secret
retreat in the centre of a
maze at Woodstock, near
Oxford, was discovered by
Henry's wife Queen
Eleanor. This deeply
sensuous drawing is one of
the most beautiful of all
Rossetti's drawings of
Fanny.

… Let her sleep.

But will it wake her if I heap

These cushions thus beneath her head

Where my knee was? No, – there's your bed

My Jenny, while you dream. And there

I lay among your golden hair

Perhaps the subject of your dreams,

These golden coins.

DANTE GABRIEL ROSSETTI, *JENNY*, C. 1860–70

Rossetti's poem, *Jenny*, describes the emotions of a man looking at the sleeping prostitute whom he has met at a dance hall. It was one of the unpublished poems which he buried in the coffin of his wife, Elizabeth Siddal, when overcome with grief at her death in February 1862. Seven years and a relationship with Jane Morris later, he wished to retrieve the poems in order to publish them. After the exhumation of the manuscript in October 1869 he wrote to Ford Madox Brown: 'there is a great hole right through all the leaves of *Jenny*, which was the thing I wanted most. A good deal is lost; but I have no doubt the things as they are will enable me, with a little rewriting and a good memory and the rough copies I have, to re-establish the whole in a perfect state.'

The poem is one of the earliest and most memorable explorations of potent romantic subjects including sensuality, languor, sleep and death. The symbolic identification of these states with the portrayal of women was to provide the Aesthetic Movement with some of its most rewarding themes.

The late nineteenth century saw the dawning of a new era for women, a process which an intense Aesthete of the period might well have likened to the dramatic emergence of a butterfly from its cocoon. The colours and forms of emergent varieties of 'butterflies' took varying forms, ranging from the quiet protective greens and browns of the Medieval-cum-Renaissance dress of the Aesthetic lady influenced by the paintings of the Pre-Raphaelites, to the fawns and terracotta-coloured soft clinging draperies affected by the Greek side of the Movement.

These forms of dress freed the wearer to some extent from the restrictions of the ordinary female fashions of the day. But the desire for change did not stop there. In 1887 a meeting of the Rational Dress Society was held at Westminster Town Hall chaired by Mrs Oscar Wilde. Its principal speaker was Lady Harberton, clad in 'Tarbush trousers of black satin merveilleuse with a sash round the hips, and a black velvet jacket trimmed with jet passementerie, caught together at the waist with a buckle over a full waistcoat of white satin and lace.' She emphasized important points in her speech by cracking a riding whip. The main thrust of her remarks was a sensible plea that woman should:

have an equal right with men to use the limbs that God gave them … petticoats are exhausting, unhealthy, dirty and dangerous. The trouser is not only more comfortable, healthy and clean, but also more decent as less liable to derangement. The modern idea of decency, which exposes the whole of the upper part of a woman's body for the mere sake of display when she is in

Opposite above: John William Waterhouse (1849–1917) *The Lady of Shallot*, 1888 Oil on canvas, 149 x 196 cm Waterhouse began his career by closely emulating the work of Alma-Tadema and Leighton, but he soon added Pre-Raphaelite intensity and poetry to their classical traditions, especially in his female figures with their wistful evocative sensuality. Tennyson's *Lady of Shallot* describes how, half sick of shadows, she looks on life not through a mirror, but directly, and then in a boat floats down river and watchers 'heard her singing her last song'.

Opposite below: Sir John Everett Millais (1829–1896) *Ophelia*, 1851–2 Oil on canvas, 75.6 x 100.8 cm This famous painting, whose subject is from *Hamlet* Act IV, scene VII, is Pre-Raphaelitism at its most intense. It was Edgar Allan Poe who wrote: 'The death of a beautiful woman is without doubt the most poetic subject in the world'. Millais's *Ophelia* was among the first of a whole morgue full of drowned women, both by the Northern symbolists, Toorop and Delville, and by the French painters, Aman-Jean, Lévy-Dhurmer and De Feure, who created what Phillipe Jullian memorably described as 'Ophelias of the Seine'.

meditation. Notable works were produced by Gustave Moreau, Eugène Carrière, and the Belgian Fernand Khnopff. Khnopff was a great admirer of Burne-Jones, and Belgian correspondent to the *Studio* magazine. He first visited England in 1891 when he made a bronze inspired by the *Head of Hypnos* of 350 BC in the British Museum. Hypnos, a god who symbolized sleep, appears in his painting of the same year, *I Lock the Door upon Myself*. Another great Symbolist painter influenced by a visit to a museum was the Frenchman Odilon Redon, whose painting *Closed Eyes* of 1890, reflects his meditation before 'the closed eyes' of the *Slave* of Michelangelo in the Louvre ...'He sleeps, and the worried dream that crosses the brow of this marble lifts our dreams into a pensive and moving world'.

Indeed, the depiction of sleep became one of the most potent themes of Aesthetic art. On the whole, women are more often portrayed asleep than men. It is rewarding and satisfying for an artist to depict a sleeping figure as the model can hold a sleeping pose and keep completely still, but this is clearly an over-simplistic reason for the attraction of the subject. In sleep, problems of the relationships between men and women are postponed, so that the sleeping person for the viewer becomes an object of admiration or worship and physical involvement is sublimated. Eroticism is, of course, present in the relaxed poses of the models, but it is tempered by the respect felt by those awake at the sight of those asleep, a reluctance to intrude into the privacy of the sleeper's dreams.

Most leading artistic exponents of the Aesthetic style found the theme inspiring, particularly notable examples being Albert Moore's *Midsummer* of 1887 and Lord Leighton's *Flaming June* (c. 1895), which possess a remarkable affinity both of subject and intensity of colour. Frederick Sandys, Sir Edward Poynter, J.M. Strudwick, Alma-Tadema, Sir William Reynolds-Stephens and the photographer Lady Hawarden also produced variations on the theme, but Leighton, Moore and Burne-Jones used the motif of the sleeping woman repeatedly as the principal subject of their most important paintings. Indeed, Albert Moore used the theme of sleep throughout the whole of his career in a conscious attempt to eliminate expressive human emotions as in *Dreamers* and *Beads*. The distancing from the real world provided by the theme, was particularly suited to their temperaments. All three men kept the world at arm's length; the deeply unworldly Burne-Jones, the reclusive life-long bachelor Albert

Moore, and the establishment icon Lord Leighton, whose vast palatial studio home contained only one extremely small single bedroom, despite being satirized by Henry James in *The Private Life* as someone so social that he ceased to exist when no one was around him.

        Cultures all round the world have a version of the Sleeping Beauty story, and new variants constantly arise. A decadent variant was Bram Stoker's classic horror story *Dracula* with its sinuous figures of the 'living dead' whose beautiful purity is turned to voluptuous wantoness as they suck the blood of their sleeping victims. This tale has been constantly retold as play or film ever since it was created in 1897. But the older, darker elements of the story of the Sleeping Beauty inherited from the European tradition have been forgotten. They relate to the way in which the Princess is tricked into a deep sleep until she is ready for sexual awakening by the Prince whose struggle through the thickets is a test both of his courage and the rite of passage to manhood. The finest pictorial treatment of this theme was produced between 1870 and 1890 by Burne-Jones in his series of paintings *The Legend of the Briar Rose*, one of the most memorable of all the achievements of the Aesthetic Movement. They derive from Tennyson's *Day Dream*, although they had their origin in a set of tiles which Burne-Jones designed in the early 1860s illustrating Perrault's *Sleeping Beauty*. Burne-Jones would also have known Walter Crane's *The Sleeping Beauty in the Wood* of 1876, one of the most delightful of all his picture books for children. When completed in 1890 the series comprised four paintings: *The Prince entering the Briar Wood*, *The Garden Court* showing a group of servant girls asleep at their work, *The King and his Courtiers Asleep*, and *The Princess and her Maidens Asleep*. Burne-Jones' deep-seated desire to shun the arena of human contact is revealingly demonstrated by the way he avoids painting the most obvious moment of the story, the climax, when the Prince wakes the Princess with a kiss. He was content to leave the Prince caught forever in the overgrown tangle of brambles at the edge of the wood, symbolizing perhaps the overwhelming power of naturalist ornament, which in the 1890s was to take the new sinuous organic forms of Art Nouveau. The paintings were first shown to enthusiastic crowds in London's West End at Agnew's in 1890, and the following year in the East End at Toynbee Hall, Whitechapel. In the same year, 1890, St Petersburg saw the first performance of Marius Petipa's ballet *The Sleeping Beauty* with music especially commissioned by Tschaikovsky, surely the most famous of all evocations of this story.

        An eerie echo of the Briar Rose series was produced a few years later by the little known but important artist Edward Robert

Opposite above: Albert Moore
Dreamers, **1882**
Oil on canvas, 68 x 118.1 cm
One of the most elaborate and carefully composed of all Moore's many paintings representing his favourite theme of dreaming and sleeping women. Moore's entire career was an Aesthetic paradox, a conscious attempt to eliminate human emotion from his paintings.

Opposite centre: Sir Edward Burne-Jones
The Legend of the Briar Rose: The Garden Court, **1871–90**
Oil on canvas, 120.9 x 226.8 cm
While Burne-Jones was working on the installation of the series *The Briar Rose* at Buscot, his friend William Morris who lived a mile or two away across the meadows at Kelmscott Manor, would walk over to discuss the work's progress with his friend. To accompany the paintings Morris wrote some verses describing how: 'The fateful slumber floats and flows About the tangle of the rose'

Opposite below: Sir Edward Burne-Jones
The Legend of the Briar Rose: The Princess and her Maidens Asleep, **1871–90**
Oil on canvas, 120.9 x 226.8cm
The series, one of the finest of all Aesthetic works of art, concludes with this painting of the sleeping princess who was described by Morris thus: 'There lies the hoarded love, the key To all the treasures that shall be; Come fated hand the gift to take And smite this sleeping world awake.'

Hughes. His *Oh, What's in that Hollow?* of 1895 illustrates Christina Rossetti's poem *Amor Mundi* in which two wayward lovers encounter a warning of their fate, a corpse covered by briars and dog roses. Hughes's most well-known much later painting was significantly entitled *Night with her Train of Stars and her Great Gift of Sleep* (1915).

Death, sleep, dreams, and the romantic tragedy of the early death of a royal prince were to be woven together by the greatest sculptor of the Aesthetic Movement, Alfred Gilbert, in one of the finest of all late Aesthetic works. This was the tomb of the Duke of Clarence in the Albert Memorial Chapel at Windsor Castle, conceived in 1892 but not completed until 1928. Gilbert, born the same year as Oscar Wilde, shared with him a charismatic yet flawed personality and a fantastic imagination, revealed in this description of him at work:

Gilbert ... enjoyed most doing minute and intricate work. With commissions awaiting completion, he would spend days weaving copper wire, lead and tin-foil paper or the lids of sardine tins into fantastic rings and chains, or designing handleless spoons that could have no other purpose than to amuse his restless mind and fingers and to be presented to friends.

Other and better-known early works include the beautiful Jubilee memorial to Queen Victoria at Winchester of 1887, described by Rodin 'as the finest thing of its kind in modern times' and London's most loved memorial *Eros* (1886–93). These works are very familiar in comparison with the Duke's Tomb. In the Tomb around the sleeping Duke arises a grill entwining the figures of the Virgin, angels and twelve saints, notably St Elizabeth of Hungary, St George and St Michael. As writer Richard Dorment has pointed out, Gilbert never uses natural forms, but 'it is not too much to see the grill as a thicket enveloping the sleeping Prince who, like the Briar Rose, will one day waken'.

The Duke's Tomb is unusual for, on the whole, men count for little or nothing in the inspiration or language of Symbolism, but the sleeping and the veiled woman play dominant roles. Hallucinations, the sleep of death, perversity and a furious sensuality are all mirrored again and again in works by the Symbolists, but few subjects possessed more appeal on both sides of the Channel than Salomé. Many poets, painters and dancers in the dying years of the nineteenth century dwelt upon her veiled sensuality, one of the key themes of the age. Salomé, as the symbol of Decadence, was also the subject of poems by Symons and Mallarmé, and haunts the works of Yeats, as well as many lesser poets.

The direct inspiration for Wilde's play was Mallarmé's

Alfred Gilbert (1854–1934)
The Virgin, 1892
When Gilbert was commissioned to design a tomb for the Duke of Clarence in 1892, the result was one of the largest and most elaborate of all royal burial places. A statue of the young prince lies asleep, surrounded by a dense grill punctuated by twelve polychromed figures of the Virgin and Saints supported by panels of pirouetting angels. Of the Virgin, one of the most striking figures, Gilbert said: 'I have represented her as standing in the midst of a wild rose bush, circling her feet, it forms a natural crown of thorns, which, sprouting, send their shoots upwards around the figure, in their turn giving off roses to within reach of her clasped hands, when a white lily rises to her touch.'

Gustave Moreau (1826–1898)

Salomé Dansant, 1874–6

Oil on canvas, 145 x 140 cm The Biblical story of Salomé had a mysterious and erotic appeal for painters, writers and dancers in the late nineteenth century. One of Moreau's favourite books was Flaubert's *Salambo* of 1862, and his interpretation of Salomé was in part based on the description in it of the Carthaginian Princess. A further inspiration was Baudelaire's Sonnet XXVII in *Les Fleurs du Mal*: '*Avec ses vêtements ondoyantes et nacrés Même quand elle marche on croirait elle danse.*' (With her flowing mother-of-pearl robes One would think she was dancing even when she walks …)

Moreau also probably read Mallarmé's and Theodore de Banville's treatments of the theme. In the Salon of 1876 Moreau exhibited *Salomé Dansant*, a theme on which he played many variations in this example. The richly robed dancer, holding a lotus in her right hand, performs for Herod who is seated before a statue of Diana of Ephesus, the fertility goddess, in an elaborate architectural setting. This inspired Huysmans's famous description in *A Rebours* of Salomé as 'the symbolic deity of indestructible lust'.

Herodiade, the most famous unfinished poem since Coleridge's *Kubla Khan*. A lengthy quotation from Mallarmé's poem is made by Huysmans in his novel, as well as memorable descriptions of two paintings of Salomé by Gustave Moreau which echo the exotic language of Flaubert's *Salambo*.

Huysmans's hero Des Esseintes sees Salomé not just as the dancing girl of the New Testament, for 'she had become in some way, the symbolic deity of indestructible lust, the Goddess of immortal Hystera, the accursed beauty exalted above all other beauties … the monstrous Beast …'

One night, in 1891, Wilde told the Salomé story to a group of young French writers, and returned to his hotel in the Boulevard des Capucines. A blank notebook was on a table and it occurred to him that he might as well write down the story which he had just been improvising. After writing a long time he looked at his watch and thought: 'I can't go on like this.' He went out to the Grand

Café on the corner, called the leader of the gypsy orchestra to his table, and said, 'I am writing a play about a woman dancing with her bare feet in the blood of a man she has craved for and slain, I want you to play something in harmony with my thoughts'. They 'played such wild and terrible music that those who were there stopped talking and looked at each other with blanched faces. Then I went back and finished *Salomé*.'

This amusing story is only marred by the fact that the final revision was undertaken in the more prosaic setting of Torquay. On one occasion Wilde discussed the possible staging of *Salomé* with the young stage designer W. Graham Robertson:

'I should like,' said Wilde, throwing off the notion, I believe, at random, 'I should like everyone on stage to be in yellow'.

It was a good idea and I saw its possibilities at once – every costume of some shade of yellow from clearest lemon to deep orange, with here and there just a hint of black – yes, you must have that – and all upon a pale ivory terrace against a great empty sky of deepest violet.

'A violet sky,' repeated Oscar Wilde slowly. 'Yes – I never thought of that. Certainly a violet sky and then, in place of an orchestra, braziers of perfume.

Think – the scented clouds rising and partly veiling the stage from time to time – a new perfume for each emotion!'

'Ye-es,' said I, doubtfully, 'but you couldn't air the stage between each emotion, and the perfumes would get mixed and smell perfectly beastly and – no, I don't think I care for the perfume idea, but the yellow scheme is splendid.'

Sadly, this olfactory and emotional sensation was to remain unrealized. The play, once completed, was refused a licence for performance in England by the Lord Chamberlain, as it represented a Biblical subject, despite Wilde's threat that if this happened he would become a French citizen, a prospect which provoked a number of humorous cartoons of Wilde as a *legionnaire* or old soldier. Before the censor's decision Wilde had rehearsed the role with Sarah Bernhardt who was approaching fifty, but enigmatically answered, 'Never you mind!', when asked for her plans about the dance.

An enjoyment of both Parisian pleasures and the more earthy delights of the music hall was characteristic of many key figures of the English literary Decadence, notably Arthur Symons (1865–1945), the son of a Welsh Methodist minister, whose first volume of verse *Days and Nights* was praised by Pater. A frequent visitor to France and a friend of Mallarmé and Verlaine, Symons became the leading British authority on contemporary French

Left: Aubrey Beardsley
The Stomach Dance
Illustration for *Salomé*, 1894
The story of Salomé continued to exert its potent spell on the 1890s. *The Stomach Dance* is one of Beardsley's most erotic illustrations for Wilde's play. Yet Wilde, who wrote his play in French, disliked both Beardsley's illustrations, and the maladroit translation by Douglas.

Opposite: Walter Richard Sickert (1860–1942)
Miss Minnie Cunningham, 1892
Oil on canvas, 76.5 x 63.8 cm
Dance and dancers held a powerful fascination for the aesthetes of the 1890s. Minnie Cunningham was a 'serio-comic' dancer, aged thirty-nine, when Sickert painted this memorable portrait at the suggestion of the poet Arthur Symons. She is probably shown performing a song she herself had written entitled 'The Art of Making Love', for the sub-title of this painting, when it was first exhibited at the New English Art Club in 1892, was a line taken from it: 'I'm an old hand at love, though I'm young in years'. Both Symons and Sickert admired her expressive control of her body, the powerful irony of her song, and the visual *double entendres* produced by her childish frock, which Sickert paints as a brilliant, erotic red.

W. Sickert.

Symbolist and Decadent writers. In 1896 he became editor of *The Savoy*.

One of Symons's great enthusiasms was for the dance, both for the ballet and for music hall dancers whom he described as 'Maenads of the Decadence', admiring the way in which 'the dancer, with her gesture, all pure symbol, evokes from her mere beautiful motion, idea, sensation, all that one need ever know of event'.[1] Symons believed that music hall performers deserved critical appraisal as a serious art form, and wrote a lengthy review of the act of the serio-comic singer and dancer Minnie Cunningham, describing it as 'an invention of absolute originality' and versifying her Primrose Dance at the Tivoli Music Hall:

Skirts like the amber petals of a flower,

A primrose dancing for delight ...

A mazy dancing of the swallow ...

So, in the smoke-polluted place,

Where bird or flower might never be,

With glimmering feet, with flower-like face,

She dances at the Tivoli.

With his friend, the young painter Walter Sickert, also the friend of Whistler and Degas, Symons went to see Cunningham perform. Sickert's earlier painting of the singer Katie Lawrence performing at the music hall Gatti's had caused a storm of criticism. But undeterred Sickert painted a magnificent portrayal of Minnie Cunningham's frail, wraith-like body, clad in a bright scarlet diaphanous gown and hat, a colour which suggests the subtle *double-entendres* of her song, 'The Art of Making Love'.

In Paris, Symons was also impressed by the 'free' dancing of Jane Avril, a favourite pictorial subject for Toulouse-Lautrec, who featured her on posters on several occasions. For her Symons wrote his best dance poem *La Melinite: Moulin Rouge*. But he also applauded the most original dancer of her time, Loïe Fuller (1862–1928), whose impact on the visual and literary arts of the 1890s was profound. Not only Symons, but poets as diverse as Stephen Mallarmé and W.B Yeats, wrote works inspired by her, and visual interpretations of her performances were legion. Toulouse-Lautrec produced a set of fifty lithographs, all individually hand-coloured and sprinkled with gold and silver dust, to show the changing lights she employed. Jules Chéret, the great poster designer, produced for her a poster printed in four colours of her famous Fire dance performed on a sheet of glass illuminated from below, a dance described by Mallarmé

Opposite above: Loïe Fuller (1862–1928)
Roger Marx, a great admirer of the dancer, described her Lily dance in a passage which vividly captures the abstract qualities which made her so unique a performer: 'as soon as the flight spirals up more rapidly and raises the hem of the gauze...the arabesque of the lines simulates, amidst the flare of the corolla, a gigantic lily; around the pistil symbolized by the body of the dancer herself, the open petals revolve, rise and compose a moving flower; the identification is prolonged, favoured by a thousand expansions and contractions'.

Opposite below: Jules Chéret (1836–1932)
La Danse du Feu, c. 1890
Cheret designed this poster for the Folies-Bergère in four differing colourways, in an attempt to capture the spectacle so vividly described by Yeats as: 'An agony of flame that cannot singe a sleeve'.

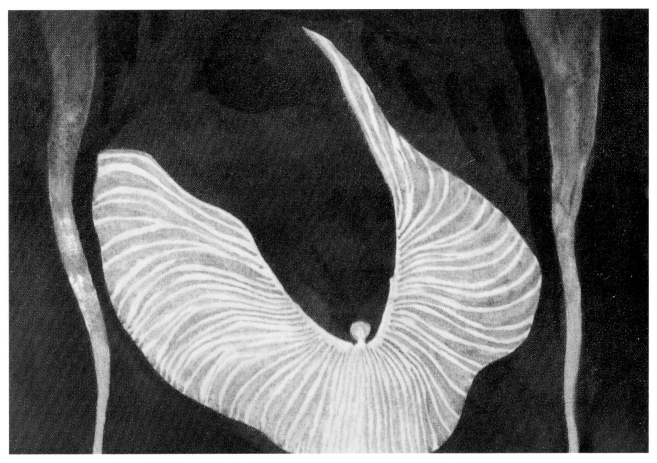

as 'a spectacle defying all definition, radiant, homogeneous'. Yeats wrote of the dance memorably as:

An agony of flame that cannot singe a sleeve.

A page of one of Whistler's sketchbooks vibrates with drawings inspired by her Butterfly dance; and remarkable paintings, prints and drawings recording her work were created by the Austrian Koloman Moser, the German T.T. Heine, and the American Will Bradley; the latter's being a remarkable swirling abstract composition punctuated abruptly by the dancers' feet. Her impact on the decorative arts was equally striking, her dances inspired bronzes by Raoul Larche and Pierre Roche; glass by Emile Gallé; lamps appropriately employing the new invention of electric light which she used to such effect; scarves and even stoves. No dancer at any time since has achieved greater fame, but today, although the artifacts which she inspired are keenly collected by connoisseurs of the Art Nouveau style, Fuller's theories on the dance and performances are relatively little remembered.

Originally a comic actress in the USA and London, she once improvised a costume for a hypnotic scene, using a light Indian

dress sent to her by an English army officer. She wrote of its effect on stage:

> My robe was so long that I was continually stepping upon it, and mechanically I held it up with both hands and raised my arms aloft, all the while that I continued to flit around the stage like a winged spirit.

> There was a sudden exclamation from the house: 'It's a butterfly! A butterfly!'

> I turned on my steps, running from one end of the stage to the other, and a second exclamation followed: 'It's an orchid!'[2]

Light and colour were from the first of paramount importance in the evolution of her dance theories as was her robust physique, an essential element of her innovative success. She achieved the extraordinary elevation of the fabrics mounted on sticks which she used, by bending backwards from the waist and lifting her batons at the climax of her dances completely above her head in a technique not dissimilar to that employed in manipulating a rod puppet. This demanded great physical strength and also gave her a bad back.

Isadora Duncan described how bravely Loïe Fuller vanquished this painful back once on stage[3]:

> the suffering patient ... turned before our very eyes to many-coloured shining orchids, to a wavering, flowering sea-flower, and at length to a spiral-like lily, all the magic of Merlin, the sorcery of light, colour, flowing form. What an extraordinary genius! ... She transformed herself into a thousand colourful images before the eyes of her audience.

Significantly, it was her abstract dance variations which provided Loïe Fuller with her greatest triumphs. Her more dramatic roles met with a mixed response. When she ventured on a performance entitled *La Tragédie de Salomé* at the Comédie Parisienne, in 1895, one critic described her as 'sweating and with make-up ... a laundress misusing her paddles ... with the grace of an English boxer and the physique of Oscar Wilde ... a Salomé for Yankee drunkards'. Less brutal critics considered this production as a praiseworthy attempt to produce a drama in light and colour.

While Loïe Fuller came to symbolize the dance internationally, Ellen Terry in England and Sarah Bernhardt in France, the two greatest actresses of their day, also both stood in a symbolic relationship to their countries. The charismatic personality of 'la divine' Sarah Bernhardt represented the great national heroine of Joan of Arc, and ranged across the spectrum of great female roles from the classicism of *Médée* to the poignancy of Dumas's great romantic heroine *La Dame aux Camelias.*

Many of her roles were immortalized by the work of

Right: Alphonse Mucha
Poster of Sarah Bernhardt,
1896

Far right: Photograph of
Sarah Bernhardt as
Mélisande in
La Princesse Lointain, 1896
Edmund Rostand, author of
Cyrano De Bergerac, whose
house near Biarritz is a major
Aesthetic monument, wrote
a poetic drama in 1895 for
Sarah Bernhardt called *La
Princesse Lointain*. For it
Mucha sketched a poster
which was never executed.
But the following year, for
the celebration of Sarah
Bernhardt Day on 9
December, 1896, Mucha
used the head and shoulders
for this poster design.

the great poster artists of the day. Eugène Grasset's early work was
profoundly influenced by the Gothic Revival architect Viollet-le-Duc
who restored the town of Carcassone in the Pyrenees to its original
condition of a completely walled mediaeval town. Grasset worked with
great flair in an artistic discipline with similar problems to the poster –
that of the design for stained glass. But as a poster designer Grasset
met with more mixed fortunes. In 1893, he interpreted Bernhardt as
the Maid of Orleans, treating the subject with respectful dignity.
Bernhardt was herself a sculptor of great ability, and knew artistically
just what she wanted. The solemnity of Grasset's image did not meet
with her unqualified approval, for she wanted a more graphic
interpretation of her stage role, and demanded alterations which

Grasset carried out with great reluctance. At the time his work was extremely Aesthetic, although later it gained horrifying power when recording such decadent themes as drug addiction.

Grasset was to produce no further posters for the great actress but his loss, however, was to be the gain of Alphonse Mucha, the brilliant young Czech designer. Mucha came to the attention of the world on New Year's Eve 1894, when groups of people gathered around his poster which advertised Sarah Bernhardt in a new play, Sardou's *Gismonda*. It was highly original both in format and technique, suggesting a mosaic or fresco, and so rich in tones that it was thought at least eight stones had been used to achieve the sonorous colour effect. It was signed Mucha. Who was this artist, and how had the poster come to be produced?

Born in Moravia in 1860, Mucha led a wandering life in central Europe and Italy before training in Munich and Paris, where he made a wide circle of friends, including figures as disparate as August Strindberg, Whistler (who greatly admired Mucha's powers as a draughtsman), the composer Frederick Delius, and French artists ranging from Pierre Bonnard to Paul Gauguin. Several funny stories and entertaining photographs survive of the parties held at Mucha's atelier including one of Gauguin trouserless playing the harmonium. On Christmas Day 1894, the proprietor of a lithographic works offered Mucha the chance of producing, within a week, a poster for the great actress's new play. Mucha, who had never seen her act, went to the evening rehearsal. Mucha's rough drawings and oil sketch were translated on to the stone with immense success, and led to further commissions from Bernhardt for a series of plays including *La Dame aux Camelias, Lorenzaccio* and *Médée*.

Mucha also designed posters for Bernhardt for purely publicity purposes. Mucha took a photograph of the great actress in 1896 with the tiara worn in a play entitled *La Princesse Lontain,* and evolved from it a poster which emphasizes the luxurious lilies and elaborate corsage, adding the favoured Art Nouveau device, a positive torrent of sinuous and luxuriant hair.

From that moment Art Nouveau and the 'Mucha style' became almost synonymous, and his fame spread throughout the world. His advertisement, slightly reminiscent of the Romanesque figures in the Ravenna mosaics, for the great champagne house of Möet and Chandon, shows the model's head haloed by the letter 'O', a favourite device of the artist. It was said that short-sighted old peasants mistook a similar poster advertising beer for a representation

John Singer Sargent
Ellen Terry as Lady Macbeth, 1889
Oil on canvas, 221 x 114.5 cm
W. Graham Robertson recalled in *Time Was*: 'As Lady Macbeth her appearance was magnificent: long plaits of deep red hair fell from under a purple veil over a robe of green upon which iridescent wings of beetles glittered like emeralds, and a great wine coloured cloak, gold embroidered, swept from her shoulders. The effect was barbaric and exactly right, though whence the wife of an ancient Scottish chieftan obtained so many oriental beetles wings was not explained. I remember Oscar Wilde remarking "... Lady Macbeth seems an economical housekeeper and evidently patronises local industries for her husband's clothes... but she takes care to do her own shopping in Byzantium"'.

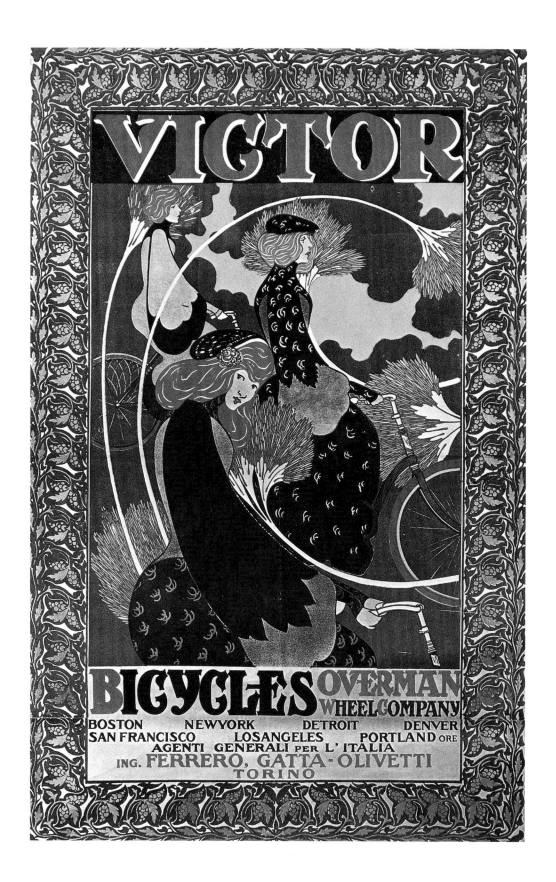

of Mary, and had been surprised worshipping the poster!

The most spectacular of all Aesthetic dramatic figures was surely Ellen Terry. The great actress was seen at her most striking in the role of Lady Macbeth, painted by John Singer Sargent in 1889. The dress she wears was designed by Mrs Comyns Carr, who describes the dress's creation:

I was anxious to make this particular dress as much like soft chain armour as I could, and yet have something that would give the appearance of the scales of a serpent ... the fine yarn ... [came from] Bohemia – a soft green silk and blue tinsel ... It was sewn all over with real green beetles' wings, and a narrow border in Celtic designs, worked out in rubies and diamonds hemmed all the edges.[4]

Ellen Terry was also, like Sarah Bernhardt as Joan of Arc, to star in another role with symbolic overtones, that of Queen Guinevere, the heroine of the Arthurian cycle which so inspired such diverse talents as Tennyson, Burne-Jones and Beardsley. In 1894 Irving commissioned a play on the subject of *King Arthur* from W.G.Wills, the playwright who had given evidence for Whistler in the Ruskin libel case, but not liking the result, he turned to the managing director of the Lyceum Theatre, J. Comyns Carr, brother of the founder of Bedford Park, to write another. This he not only did, but he also persuaded Burne-Jones to design costumes, armour, furniture and settings. At first Burne-Jones revelled in seeing his settings carried out on a large scale by scene painters, and the set, according to Mrs Comyns Carr who wrote a fascinating account of carrying out the costumes, created 'a real sensation'. But later, disillusion set in for Burne-Jones who wrote to his friend Mary Gaskell:

The armour is good – they have taken pains with it – made in Paris & well understood – I wish we were not barbarians here. The dresses were well enough if the actors had known how to wear them – one scene I made very pretty – of the wood in Maytime – that has gone to nothing – fir trees which I hate instead of beeches and birches which I love – why – ? – never mind ...

Merlin I designed carefully – they have set aside my designs and made him filthy and horrible – like a witch in Macbeth – from his voice I suspect him of being one of the witches – I hate the stage, don't tell – but I do – don't tell but I do

Opposite and right: Will H. Bradley (1868–1962)
Victor Bicycles
Bar-Lock Typewriter
These two advertisements for the great liberating activities for women of cycling and typing economically use virtually the same design. Bradley first used the design for Victor Bicycles. The identical ladies have their hands first on bicycle handles, then a typewriter, but the ornate frame remains

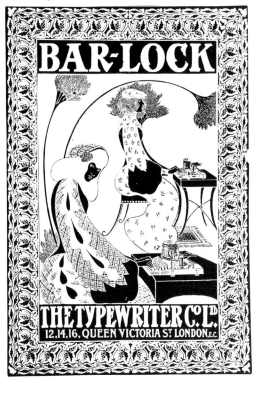

but don't tell ...

King Arthur was played by Henry Irving, Guinevere by Ellen Terry and Sir Lancelot by Johnston Forbes-Robertson. The incidental music was by Sir Arthur Sullivan, who was so inspired by the production that he asked Comyns Carr to adapt it into a libretto for an opera, although the idea came to nothing. *King Arthur* opened at the Lyceum on 12 January, 1895, and after a hundred performances was taken to America. Unfortunately all the scenery was destroyed in a warehouse fire after their return.

Five years before Irving and Ellen Terry enacted the roles of the Arthurian cycle, Henrik Ibsen's *A Doll's House* (1879) was first performed in London in 1889. The heroine Norah's performance of the tarantella and her action in slamming the front door on husband and children can be seen as a parallel to Salomé's Dance of the Seven Veils, since in both cases women assert their independence both sexually and as individuals. Ibsen's *Hedda Gabler* (1890) and *Ghosts* (1881) both followed London productions in 1891 dealing with the unpalatable themes of venereal disease, alcoholism, and suicide, which *Punch* dubbed as the horror of 'Ibsenity'.

Ibsen's heroines and their cry for independence became associated in the popular mind with the emergent claims of women for equality, both at the polling booth, in the medical profession and at universities. Two new machines were also to become identified with the liberation of women: the bicycle which brought with it freedom of movement, of association and dress, and the typewriter which made available a far wider choice of employment.

Inevitably such breaks with the accepted social order, like the 'rational dress' of divided knickerbockers affected by women cyclists, aroused in chauvinist males derisive laughter and parodies. A characteristic example is a poster for a satirical play of the period called *The New Woman*, by Sydney Grundy. It is interesting to note that the emancipated young lady is shown having inadvertently lit her cigarette at the wrong end, perhaps when overexcited by the novels she has been reading called *Naked but Unashamed* and *Man the Betrayer*.

The 'New Woman' was the feminine antithesis to the masculine 'Decadent' role. Many more timid souls feared that the two genders were becoming far too close for comfort, a surmise confirmed by an article by Max Beerbohm in the first number of the *Yellow Book* entitled *A Defence of Cosmetics* in which he claimed that a fusion of the two sexes was 'one of the chief planks in the decadent platform'.

Beerbohm's carefully adjusted sexual mask almost slips to reveal alarm at the spectre of the New Woman at a lunch given by

William Reynolds-Stephens (1862-1943)
Summer, **1891**
Oil on canvas, 152 x 305 cm
Sir William Reynolds-Stephens was talented as a painter, sculptor and interior designer. A student of the Royal Academy, he was commissioned by Sir William Vivian to design the interior for the drawing room of his house at 85, Queen's Gate and painted *Summer* **as an integral part of the design, to be triumphantly displayed over the fireplace. The architectural frame gives it the appearance of being part of the setting.**

the editor of the *Yellow Book* for an actress Elizabeth Robins, famed for her portrayal of the heroines of Ibsen. It was attended by Beardsley and Beerbohm, the latter describing the event in a letter to novelist Ada Leverson, known by Wilde as the Sphinx:

We fed by the light of candles, with nice thick green curtains between us and the day … Robins … is fearfully Ibsenish and talks of souls that are involved in a nerve turmoil and are seeking a common platform. This is *literally* what she said. Her very words. I kept peeping under the table to see if she really wore a skirt. The letter concludes by warning of the attacks of a so-called New Woman, a well dressed female lunatic of homicidal tendencies then terrorizing Kensington.

Like Wilde, Beerbohm might well have reflected, 'in so vulnerable an age we all need masks'. The new twentieth century would see the gradual emancipation of women, first in Ibsen's Norway in 1912. With equality the old symbolic roles changed. The Sleeping Woman awoke to new challenges.

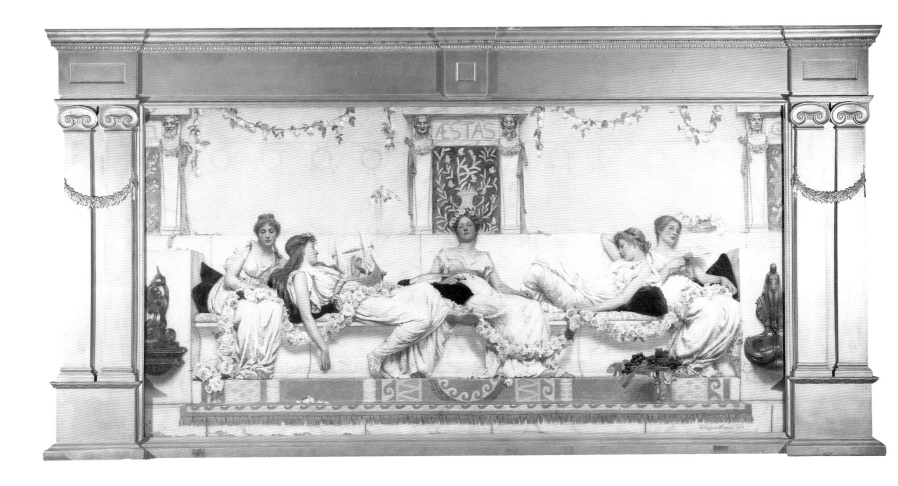

Some Persons of "the Nineties"
little imagining, despite their Proper
Pride and Ornamental Aspect,
how much they will interest
Mr. Holbrook Jackson and Mr. Osbert Burdett,

Max
1925

Oh Wilde, Verlaine, and Baudelaire, their lips were wet with wine;

Oh poseur, pimp, and libertine! Oh cynic, sot, and swine!

Oh votaries of velvet vice ... Oh gods of light divine!

ROBERT W. SERVICE, *COLLECTED WORKS*, 1960

Opposite: Sir Max Beerbohm (1872–1956)
'Some persons of "the Nineties" little imagining, despite their Proper Pride and Ornamental Aspect, how much they will interest Mr Holbrook Jackson and Mr Osbert Burdett', 1925
The books referred to are Holbrook Jackson's *The Eighteen Nineties* **(1913) and Osbert Burdett's** *The Beardsley Period* **(1925). From left to right,** *back row*: **Richard Le Gallienne (1866–1947), poet; Sickert (1860–1942), artist; George Moore (1852–1933); John Davidson (1857–1909), poet; Oscar Wilde (1854–1900); William Butler Yeats (1865–1939),** *front row*: **Arthur Symons (1865–1945), poet and critic; Henry Harland (1861–1905), novelist; Charles Conder (1868–1909), artist; William Rothenstein (1872–1945), artist; Max Beerbohm (1872–1956); Aubrey Beardsley (1872–1898). Just at the top on the right Yeats seems to be talking to the shadowy figure of Enoch Soames, the main character in Beerbohm's brilliant satire of the Aesthetes and decadents of the 1890s.**

Right: Aubrey Beardsley Unused cover design for *The Yellow Book*, **1890s**
The image stands here as a symbol of the 1890s passion for the book beautiful.

The Aesthetic Movement of the 1870s and 1880s gave birth in the 1890s to three very different yet closely related artistic phenomena, the Arts and Crafts Movement, Art Nouveau, and the literary 'Decadence'. Richard Le Gallienne, a young 'decadent' poet, looking back at the 1890s in later life, recalled that: 'The amount of creative revolutionary energy packed into that decade is almost bewildering in its variety', and that: *'épater la bourgeoisie* – shocking the middle classes – was a gospel of the period'. His reminiscences were entitled *The Romantic '90s*, a title he justified in language couched in a familiar, if somewhat faded, echo of Pater:

I have called the '90s 'romantic', not merely because it was romantic to have lived in them, or because they included so many romantic figures, but because their representative writers and artists emphasized the modern determination to escape from the deadening thralldom of materialism and outworn conventions and to live life significantly – keenly and beautifully, personally and, if need be, daringly; to win from it its fullest satisfaction, its deepest and richest and most exhilarating experiences.

Another strange re-interpretation of Pater's famous injunction was provided by Henry James, whose reaction to the Aesthetic credo, and Pater's contribution in particular, was characteristically both muted and ambivalent. In a letter in 1894 to Edmund Gosse he wrote:

Well, faint, pale, embarrassed, exquisite Pater! He reminds me, in the disturbed night of our actual literature, of one of those lucent matchboxes you place, on going to bed, near the candle, to show you, in the darkness, where you can strike a match – he shines in the uneasy gloom – vaguely, and he has a phosphorescence, not a flame. But I quite agree with you that he is not of the little day, but of the longer time.[1]

Henry James is here almost echoing Gilbertian paradox in transforming Pater's famous advice 'to burn always with a hard, gemlike flame' into a recommendation 'to shine faintly with a phosphorescent glow'.

But the climate of taste was changing. A period was over. A new period had begun. The Aesthetic Movement, yesterday's fashion, gave way to the Decadent Movement, not only in literature but the arts. What exactly was meant by the term decadence? It was defined by Arthur Symons, as an urge 'to fix the last fine shade, the quintessence of things, to fix it fleetingly; to be a disembodied voice, and yet the voice of a human soul, that is the ideal of decadence'.

Such ideas, as we have seen, had first gained prominence in France where Paul Verlaine, Arthur Rimbaud, and Stéphane Mallarmé had developed the idea of literary 'decadence'. Meanwhile, England characteristically agonized over the problem of

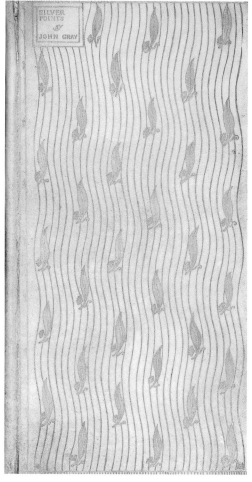

who would succeed to the empty chair of the Poet Laureate left vacant by the death of Alfred Lord Tennyson in 1892. Browning had died in 1889, both Morris and Swinburne were considered to be too controversial, and the honour passed in 1896, amidst widespread mockery, to the waspish nonentity Alfred Austin.

Paradoxically, although Austin's appointment devalued the Laureateship, an outstanding crop of minor poets had emerged. They were all bent on being celebrated as '*poets maudit*' in the Gallic manner. Amateurs of 'strange sensations' and curious passions, determined to *épater la bourgeoisie*, they with like-minded prose writers and artists were the principle legatees of Aestheticism.

Foremost among the ranks of the artists were the great illustrators Charles Ricketts and his life-long companion Charles Shannon. They became 'almost official artists' to Oscar Wilde, who dubbed them 'Orchid' and 'Marigold'. Their house (which had belonged to Whistler) in a Chelsea cul-de-sac called The Vale was praised by Oscar Wilde as 'the one house in London where you will never be bored'.[2]

They jointly designed and decorated Wilde's *House of Pomegranates* in 1891. A critical review in *The Speaker* enabled Wilde to defend the appearance of the book with the retort: '... there are only two people in the world whom it is absolutely necessary that the cover should please. One is Mr Ricketts, who designed it, the other is myself whose book it binds. We both admire it immensely!'

Many of Wilde's other major works, in their first printed form, made their appearance in bindings by Ricketts. In 1893 he also designed one of the finest bindings ever devised for a slim volume of verse. Entitled *Silverpoints*, it was written by John Gray, a young friend of Wilde, generally thought to be the model for *The Portrait of Dorian Gray*. Wilde paid for the costs of the publication of the edition of only 275 copies. Its tall, narrow format and green cloth cover, subtly strewn with gilt leaves, was widely admired and imitated. Recalling the taste for such exquisite little volumes during the period, the novelist Ada Leverson (nicknamed the Sphinx by Wilde), wrote:

There was more margin, margin in every sense of the word was in demand, and I remember looking at the poems of John Gray (then considered the incomparable poet of the age), when I saw the tiniest rivulet of text meandering through the very largest meadow of margin, I suggested to Oscar Wilde that he should go a step further than these minor poets, that he should publish a book *all* margin; full of beautiful unwritten thoughts, and have this blank volume bound in some Nile-green skin powdered with gilt nenuphars and smoothed with hard ivory, decorated with gold by Ricketts and printed on Japanese paper, each volume must be a collector's piece, a limited 'first' (and last) edition: 'very rare'.[3] He approved, responding:

> It shall be dedicated to you, and the unwritten text illustrated by Aubrey Beardsley. There must be five hundred signed copies for particular friends, six for the general public, and one for America.

Sadly, Ada Leverson's fantasy was to go unrealized.

The cult of the 'book beautiful' which Ada Leverson so amusingly describes in the above passage, owed much to the subtle visual approach to typography developed by Whistler in the exquisite layout of *The Gentle Art of Making Enemies,* published in 1890. In it he put together a random collection of personal insults, letters to newspapers, criticisms by his victims with his own stinging replies, attacks, aphorisms, and the full text of his '*Ten O'clock*' lecture. In the wide margins his butterfly signature dances delicately and provocatively develops a wickedly barbed sting.

It is easy to find such productions over-precious, but, at their best, such books became amongst the most remarkable achievements of the marriage of Aestheticism and the Arts and Crafts Movement, not only in Ricketts's and Shannon's Vale Press, but most famously in William Morris's Kelmscott Press. A.H. Mackmurdo remembered, with justifiable pride, showing Morris in 1888:

> a number of the *Hobby Horse*, the magazine of the Century Guild which I had established – and telling him of the difficulties one had to overcome in getting a page of printed text that was a pleasure to look at. What art there was in proportioning its mass; in setting this text with nicely proportioned margins upon the page, in the spacing of letters and lines; in the choice of ink, of paper, and above all of available type ...! [This] fired Morris with enthusiasm. He instantly saw what could be done. 'Here is a new craft to conquer and to perfect. A new English type needs to be founded.' He then and there resolved to master the situation by setting up a press of his own.

The publication of the *Century Guild Hobby Horse,* the first art journal in the late 1880s, as well as playing an important part in influencing William Morris's decision to found the Kelmscott Press, also heralded the birth of a whole series of illustrated periodicals in the 1880s and 1890s.

The most important of these was undoubtedly *The Studio,* launched by Charles Holmes in 1893 with a eulogy on the remarkable new artist Aubrey Beardsley, followed in the next number by an article bringing into prominence the work of C.F.A. Voysey, one of the most important Arts and Crafts architects and designers. No journal prior to *The Studio* had been so consistently concerned with the emergence of new ideas. This made it an ideal platform for the promulgation of both Art Nouveau style, and Arts and Crafts ideology,

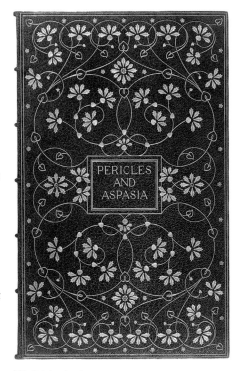

T.J. Cobden Sanderson (1840–1922)
Cover for *Pericles and Aspasia,* **1904**
It was Cobden-Sanderson, bookbinder and printer, who first fatefully united the words 'Arts' and 'Crafts'. He took up book binding late in life at the age of forty-three on the suggestion of Jane Morris. Cobden-Sanderson went on to produce some of the most beautiful bindings ever made at the Doves bindery. In 1904 he wrote *The Ideal Book.*

Far left above: Walter Crane
A Floral Fantasy in an old English Garden
The idea for *A Floral Fantasy* originated in the summer of 1898 when Walter Crane rented an Elizabethan farmhouse in Kent with trimmed lawns and hedges and neat flowerbeds.

Far left below: Eugène Grasset
La Grande Dame
Cover for *Revue de l'Elégance des Arts*, 1895
Grasset came to occupy the same position in France as Walter Crane did in England. He developed a highly personal style, a blend of mediaeval tendrils and foliage, together with flowers and stalks in an Art Nouveau rhythm arranged *à la Japonais*. It is amusing to note that even for the January issue of a magazine, Grasset used his favourite motif of the sunflower with Aesthetic, if unseasonable, success.

Left: Théo Van Rysselberghe (1862–1926)
Le Quatrième Salon Annuel de la Libre Esthétique, 1897
Just as in France, so in Belgium, Anglophilia was widely prevalent in the late nineteenth century. Brussels and London were brought closely together by the artist Fernand Khnopff who wrote eighteen articles for *The Studio* magazine. Théo Van Rysselberghe, who created this poster for a fine book fair, also illustrated an edition of poems by the Belgian poet Emile Verhaeren. This book was hailed in a *Studio* article 'as evidence of English ideals set forth in the idiom of a country that has for centuries remained in friendly relations with our own'.

both in well-illustrated articles and in its keenly contested monthly competitions which continued the Aesthetic tradition of amateurism. Its rapid international success can be gauged by its impact on such different readers as Diaghilev in St Petersburg, the painter Aoki Shigeru in Tokyo, and the young Picasso in Barcelona, fired by an article in *The Studio*, who set out to see Burne-Jones's work in Birmingham, but somehow never got further than Paris. Diaghilev's magazine *Mir Ikkuskva (The World of Art)* (1898), the Austrian *Ver Sacrum* (1898), the German *Pan* (1895), and *Dekorative Kunst* (1897), and a host of other publications in Europe and America were founded in emulation of *The Studio's* example. Emboldened by its remarkable early success, Holmes was able to embark on another cherished project, the publication of a series of distinguished books on aspects of the arts known as *The Studio Special Numbers*.

    In 1898 C.R. Ashbee acquired from Morris's trustees the stock and plant of the Kelmscott Press, using Morris's two Albion

presses in the productions of the Essex House
Press. Other notable aspects of the private
press movement include the Eragny Press of
Lucien Pissarro, the bindings of Cobden
Sanderson at the Doves Bindery, the work of
the Guild of Women Binders and 'the
exquisitely dainty bookbindings that bear the
name of Jessie M. King'.[4]

Pater's 'hard, gemlike flame'
had blazed up in the 1890s to establish the
predominant colour of the decade – yellow. On
his first visit to Ricketts's and Shannon's home,
Wilde had dutifully admired the distempered
yellow walls hung with Hokusai prints:

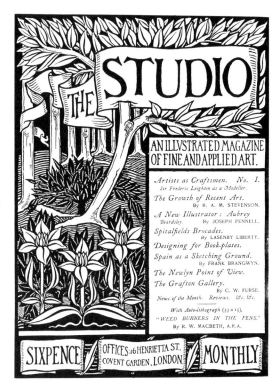

What a charming old house you
have, and what delightful Japanese prints – Yes the
Japanese understand conciseness and compact
design … How did you discover the Vale? I like the
name – And you have yellow walls, so have I –
Yellow is the colour of joy …[5]

Richard Le Gallienne in a perceptive, if slightly bilious,
piece entitled 'The Boom in Yellow' had charted the colour change:

… the green of the aesthete does not suggest innocence. There
will always be wearers of the green carnation, but the popular vogue which
green has enjoyed for the last ten or fifteen years is passing … in our so called
aesthetic renaissance the sunflower went before the green carnation – which is
indeed, the badge of but a small schism of aesthetes … A few yellow
chrysanthemums will make a small room look twice its size, and when the sun
comes out upon a yellow wall-paper the whole room seems suddenly to
expand, to open like a flower … Bill posters are beginning to discover the
attractive qualities of the colour. Who can ever forget meeting for the first
time upon a hoarding Mr Dudley Hardy's wonderful Yellow Girl, the pretty
advance guard of *Today?* … Let us dream of this: a maid with yellow hair, clad
in a yellow gown, seated in a yellow room, at the window a yellow sunset, in
the grate a yellow fire, at her side a yellow lamplight, on her knee a Yellow
Book.

But there was a price to pay for all this butter! When
The Yellow Book first appeared in April 1894, its publisher, John Lane,
deplored the 'universal howl' that went up in protest of Beardsley's
cover and title page designs. *The Times* called it 'a combination of
English rowdyism and French lubricity'. The leading American journal
The Critic, in a review entitled *A Yellow Impertinence*, called *The Yellow*

Book 'the Oscar Wilde of periodicals', even though Oscar, miffed at being shunned as a contributor, wrote to Alfred Douglas on the appearance of the first number: 'It is dull and loathsome: a great failure – I am so glad.' And elsewhere he rejoiced at its 'not being yellow at all'.

Despite Wilde's petulance, and largely as a result of Beardsley's powerful cover designs, the journal enjoyed a *succès de scandale*. Ever since it has come to represent the quintessence of 'The Nineties' in the popular imagination. Its sinister reputation (which it has retained to this day) is almost entirely due to Beardsley's contributions which were regarded with some trepidation by such closet homosexuals as the fastidious figure of Henry James, even before Wilde's arrest. On being solicited for a contribution for the first issue of the quarterly in 1894 by Henry Harland, James submitted a story *The Death of the Lion*, after receiving assurances that Beardsley would neither illustrate the story nor would his work even appear in the same issue.

Another regular contributor to the journal whose work proved highly controversial was the young Max Beerbohm, said by Oscar Wilde to have been born with the gift of perpetual old age. An essay which Beerbohm contributed to the first volume of *The Yellow Book* entitled *A Defence of Cosmetics* caused great public outrage, the *Westminster Gazette* finding Beerbohm's pose as a dandified ironic critic deeply offensive. Beerbohm later explained:

What in the whole volume seems to have provoked the most ungovernable fury is, I am sorry to say, an essay about Cosmetics that I myself wrote. Of this it was impossible for anyone to speak calmly. The mob lost its head, and, so far as anyone in literature can be lynched, I was ... [it was] urged 'that a short Act of Parliament should be passed to make this kind of thing illegal' ... my essay 'the rankest and most nauseous thing in all literature' ... 'was a bomb thrown by a cowardly decadent' ... If I had only signed myself D. Cadent or Parrar Docks ...

Irony, as Beerbohm was often to find, is a double-edged weapon. It depends upon an informed audience for its proper

Left above: **Aubrey Beardsley Cover of** *The Yellow Book*, **Volume 1, April 1894**
The Yellow Book was conceived on New Year's Day 1894 by Beardsley and Henry Harland, the novelist, at Harland's house in the Cromwell Road. It was published by Elkin Matthews and John Lane, London, and Copeland and Day, Boston (Mass, USA). Beardsley was its art editor and all his cover designs were printed in black on yellow cloth boards. Beardsley was dismissed from his post at the time of the Wilde scandal.

Left below: **Aubrey Beardsley Cover of** *The Savoy*, **No. 1, January 1896**
Beardsley enlivens this Claudian composition by showing the putto as if about to urinate upon a copy of *The Yellow Book*, a savage reference to his summary ejection from his post on that magazine eight months earlier.

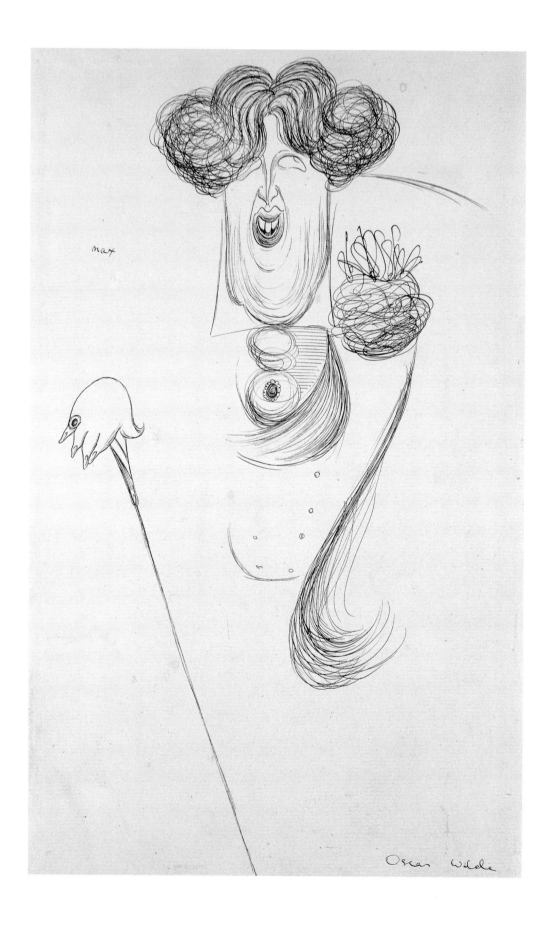

appreciation. An 'in' joke is essentially elitist, and liable to create anger or blank incomprehension in those excluded members of the public who take statements literally and are baffled by humour they cannot share …

As a draughtsman Beerbohm's creative methods were fascinating. Using as a mental point of departure the profile figures made familiar by Ape and Spy in *Vanity Fair*, he evolved a faux-naïf likeness of remarkable power. In a private character notebook he would first write down a penetrating analytical verbal portrait, before making the finished drawing alone at night in the privacy of his room.

The notes which he wrote before drawing the caricature of Oscar Wilde published in *Pick-Me-Up* on 22 September, 1894, are particularly revealing as is the finished work used against Wilde after his arrest. Beerbohm wrote:

luxury – gold-tipped matches – hair curled – Assyrian – wax statue – huge rings – fat white hands – not soignée – malmaison – catlike tread – heavy shoulders – enormous dowager – or schoolboy-way of laughing with hands over mouth – stroking chin – looking up sideways – jollity overdone – But real vitality – Effeminate, but vitality of twenty men. Magnetism – authority – Deeper than repute or wit – Hypnotic.

Years later, writing of this caricature, Beerbohm regretted that 'when it was published, I hardly realized what a cruel thing it was: I only realized that after Oscar's tragedy and downfall.'

Beardsley's contributions ceased abruptly after Volume Four, when Wilde on his arrest, on 5 April, 1895, was reported to be carrying 'a yellow book' (actually a copy of the recently published novel *Aphrodite* by Pierre Louÿs). *Punch* jeered at 'Mr Danby Weirdsley', while in the magazine *The World*, during Wilde's trial, appeared an ingenious satire on *The Yellow Book* written in the style of Lewis Carroll's *Jabberwocky*:

Beware the Yallerbock, my son!
The aims that rile, the art that racks,
Beware the Aub-Aub Bird, and shun
The stumious Beerbomax!

Beardsley and Arthur Symons left *The Yellow Book*, and in the following year started *The Savoy*, conceived primarily as a vehicle for Beardsley. *The Yellow Book* itself was to survive for two more years until January 1897.

A typical literary contributor to *The Yellow Book* was the poet and Aesthete Lionel Johnson, described by Yeats, his closest friend, as 'almost a dwarf but beautifully made, his features cut in ivory'. His essay *Tobacco Clouds* makes very curious reading today:

Cloud upon cloud: and, if I were to think that an image of life can lie in wreathing, blue tobacco smoke, pleasant were the life so fancied. Its fair changes in air, its gentle motions, its quiet dying out and away at last, should symbolise more than perfect idleness ... Cloud upon cloud ...

It is that death, out and away upon the air, which charms me: charms more than the ... blown red rose, full of dew at morning, upon the grass at sunset. The cloud's end, their death in air ... the image of a reasonable life is there, hanging among tobacco clouds. The blue smoke curls and glides away, with blue pagodas, and snowy almond bloom, and cherry flowers, circling and gleaming in it, like a narcotic vision. Oh! magic of tobacco!

Smoke, steam and fog, of one kind or another, drifts through the art, literature and life of the 1890s. 'What I like most about London is the fog', said Claude Monet, for 'without the fog, London would not be a beautiful city.' Bram Stoker's *Dracula* manages literally to turn himself into a baleful 'pillar of cloud by day, and of fire by night'. Privat-Livemont uses the steamy potent aroma of the product to form the name of l'Absinthe Robette, the drink which all Decadents affected. But it was particularly tobacco smoke which was perfectly adapted to the flowing sinuosities of the Art Nouveau style. It drifts and swirls through the 1890s, praised by Aesthetes and hearties alike – it twines and twists across posters for 'Smoking Concerts' by Burkan. Both Chéret and Mucha designed effective posters combining beautiful long-haired models with smouldering cigarettes. From their smoke emerged the name Job – the Biblical allusion perhaps implying that via tobacco one might find more effective comfort than his friends brought to the afflicted Old Testament figure.

For the Decadents of the nineties the act of smoking became almost a duty, an aspect of the activity best, as always, summed up by Oscar Wilde. Lady Bracknell in *The Importance of Being Earnest* asks John Worthing, in an examination of his eligibility as a prospective husband for her daughter Gwendoline:

Do you smoke?

Worthing: Well, yes, I must admit I smoke.

Lady Bracknell: I am glad to hear it. A man should always have an occupation of some kind. There are far too many idle men in London as it is.

The Picture of Dorian Gray also abounds in smoky metaphors, both in descriptions of gold-tipped cigarettes and the swirling fogs through which Dorian Gray sets out, saying: 'A new hedonism – that is what our century wants' while 'from some chimney opposite a thin wreath of smoke was rising. It curled, a violet ribband, through the nacre coloured air'.

Opposite: I Burkan
(fl. 1890–1900)
*Smoking Concert at the
Swallow*, c. 1895
Lithograph, 113.4 x 73 cm
Nothing is known about the
designer of this fine poster,
which appropriately uses
trailing clouds of heavy
tobacco smoke as the
dominant motif to advertise
a 'Smoking Concert'.
At such events in the 1890s
smoking was not only
permitted but encouraged as
a background to popular
songs.

Right: Alfons Mucha
Job, 1898
Mucha did several striking
posters for the downmarket
product Job cigarette papers
for rolling one's own. This
example is closely derived
from a Sybil in
Michelangelo's Sistine
Chapel, right down to the
big toe.

Oscar Wilde and Alfred
Douglas, c. 1893
The notorious pair enjoying
a cigarette while being
photographed at an Oxford
photographic studio.

At the first night of *Lady Windermere's Fan* Wilde came
forward from the wings to cries of 'Author!' wearing a green carnation,
with a cigarette in his mauve gloved hand. Both he and Lord Alfred
Douglas smoke cigarettes in the famous photograph of them together
at Oxford in 1893. Again and again the smoke of innumerable
cigarettes forms a miasma through which the salient features of Wilde's
career can be perceived in changing forms.

In spite of the injunction in *The Importance of Being
Earnest* that 'it is a very ungentlemanly thing to read a private cigarette
box', these slender gold or silver plated cases, designed to hold ten or
twenty cigarettes occupy a mechanistic role in the Wilde tragedy, not
dissimilar to that of the handkerchief in *Othello* or the fan in *Lady
Windermere's Fan*.

Listen to the cut and thrust of the brilliant cross-
examination of Wilde by Edward Carson in the libel suit, 'performing
his task' as Wilde noted, 'with the added bitterness of an old friend'.

Carson: You made handsome presents to all these young fellows?

Wilde: Pardon me, I differ. I gave two or three of them a cigarette case. Boys of that class smoke a good deal of cigarettes. I have a weakness for presenting my acquaintances with cigarette cases.

Carson: Why did you burn incense in your rooms?

Wilde: Because I liked it.

With such admissions, the inference of the great cliché that: 'There's no smoke without fire' followed, with its inevitable consequences.

The events of Wilde's last five years progress with tragic inevitability. When we re-read the story we watch helplessly as his love affair with Lord Alfred Douglas is succeeded by the idiotic folly of suing Lord Queensbury for libel, his own trials, disgrace, imprisonment and later his death in Paris. His famous speech from the dock upon the theme of 'the love that dare not speak its name' possesses within a homosexual context something of the resonance of Martin Luther's declaration of faith when called upon to retract his writings in 1521 before the Diet of Worms: *'Hier stehe ich, ich kann nicht anders'* – 'Here I stand, I can do nothing else.' To read the catalogue of the Wilde bankruptcy sale, the destruction of the 'House Beautiful' by the Philistines, is a moving experience. Whistler's works were sold for a few pounds, Simeon Solomon's *Love Among the Schoolboys* and *Amor Sacramentum* went for a few shillings, and Keats's autograph sonnet and a collection of blue and white china went for nothing.

In the 1880s, even at its most affected, Aestheticism had only aroused feelings of amused irritation from its critics. But now, Wilde's flagrantly overt advocacy of the intimate connections between the 'slim gilt souls' of true Aesthetes and 'the love that dare not speak its name' aroused disgust. Philistinism flourished, and 'revulsion' and 'unhealthiness' became epithets often used to describe both Art Nouveau artifacts and the 'decadent' literature of the *fin de siècle*.

It was Aubrey Beardsley's work which summed up all the tendencies of the Decadent Movement which contemporaries found both frightening and ridiculous. His faultless, matchless, deathless line had a power to shock only equalled by the bizarre fantasy of his prose style. Sadly, the full text of his book *The Story of Venus and Tannhäuser* written in 1894 was not to be published in his lifetime, and is still far too little known. The legend had a particular fascination for the second half of the nineteenth century. It was employed by Wagner in his opera, which Beardsley loved; by Swinburne in his poem *Laus Veneris* which inspired Burne-Jones's painting; and by William Morris in his poem *The Hill of Venus.* Beardsley's brilliantly perverse parody of

the story makes us realize the truth of Arthur Symons's observation: 'I think Beardsley would rather have been a great writer than a great artist...' The first three chapters, with a new title *Under the Hill*[6], appeared with several Beardsley illustrations in the first number of *The Savoy* in January, 1896, a fourth chapter following in the April issue.

These pages provide graphic testimony that the Aesthetic style, so closely linked with literature, really found its most complete expression in illustration, the visual bride of prose and poetry. Aubrey Beardsley's whole career demonstrates his complete mastery of the discipline from his initials for Malory's *Morte D'Arthur* to the rococo extravaganzas of Alexander Pope's *The Rape of the Lock*. It was these drawings which led Whistler to make his pronouncement 'Aubrey, I have made a mistake. You are a great artist.'

The frenetic energy imparted to those dying of tuberculosis gave Beardsley the strength to move from Dieppe to the south of France. From there he wrote the tragic last letter to his publisher, Leonard Smithers:

> Menton
>
> Jesus is our Lord and Judge
>
> I implore you to destroy all copies of Lysistrata and bad

drawings ...

> By all that is holy all obscene drawings.
>
> Aubrey Beardsley – In my death agony.

It was 1898 and he was twenty-five.

Beardsley converted to the Roman Catholic faith on 31 March, 1897, an action which was to be followed by other leading figures of the Decadence. Among them were Oscar Wilde in 1900 on his deathbed, Lord Alfred Douglas, Huysmans himself, Ernest Dowson, John Gray, who became a priest, Lionel Johnson, and the two women, Katherine Bradley (1846–1913) and her niece Edith Cooper (1862–1914) whose joint work (twenty-seven tragedies and eight volumes of verse) was published under the pseudonym 'Michael Field'. In 1907 they both became Catholics, later dying of cancer a year apart.

The familiar and tragic stories of the trials of Oscar Wilde in 1895, and the death of Beardsley in 1898, mark the end of the main stream of the Aesthetic Movement. Wilde's conviction and imprisonment had far-reaching repercussions, for they mark the victory of Philistinism in a far more decisive sense than the Whistler/Ruskin affair nearly two decades earlier. Yet aspects of the Aesthetic credo continued to flourish in England in the Arts and Crafts Movement, particularly in jewellery design in its use of subtle

shades of grey pearls and moonstones, green garnets and yellow sapphires.

C.R. Ashbee surely behaved Aesthetically, both when he designed a peacock brooch, and when he wrote of semiprecious stone's 'intrinsic beauty ... without regard to commercial value', and waxed lyrical on 'the fiery ruby with the passionate blue sapphire; the pale amethyst with twinkling crystal; the dreamy moonstone on its bed of dark grey silver ... the fairy carbuncle ... the green prismatic olivine ... and the glorious opal.'

In Scotland, Aesthetic values shaped Charles Rennie Mackintosh's fastidious and highly individual blend of Art Nouveau and proto-modernism. The rooms he designed in 1897 for Miss Cranstone's Buchanan Street Tearooms in Glasgow echo very clearly the peacock doors in Whistler's famous room created twenty years earlier. On the continent Aesthetic influences were felt as far afield as Brussels and Paris in the Symbolist movement, and in Austria in the work of Gustav Klimt at the Vienna Secession.

Somewhat surprisingly the Aesthete who was most powerfully to carry on and re-interpret Aesthetic ideals in the changed world of the new twentieth century, was the slight figure of Max Beerbohm. For him Aesthetic themes and personalities never palled, but provided entertaining exercise for his satiric pencil. *The Poet's Corner* of 1904 includes a portrait of Verlaine as a schoolmaster, and the wonderful depiction of Dante Gabriel Rossetti in his back garden.

He drew no less than nineteen portraits of Henry James and wrote remarkable parodies in the style of James. When asked about his next book, James pointed to Max Beerbohm, his parodist, and replied: 'Ask that young man. He knows me better than I know myself.'[7]

In 1922 appeared *Rossetti and his Circle*, still by far the best introduction to the Pre-Raphaelite Movement, which also contains the memorable images of Whistler and Carlyle in *Blue China*, and *Oscar Wilde lecturing in America*. Less familiar, but equally worthwhile, are the many splendid drawings in the Ashmolean Museum, Oxford, notably *At the Pines* depicting Swinburne and his mentor Watts-Dunton in old age, and *Aspects of Wilde* a visual accompaniment to his written portrait, *A Peep into the Past*, of December 1893.

Dubbed by Bernard Shaw, the 'Incomparable Max', Beerbohm's oblique, exquisite wit is currently out of fashion in an age which distrusts urbanity, although it will surely continue to convey its insider view of the Aesthetic and Decadent periods to future

Opposite above: Max Beerbohm
Dante Gabriel Rossetti, in his back garden
From *The Poet's Corner*, 1904
This was Beerbohm's first retrospective look at the Pre-Raphaelites and remains one of his most effective cartoons. From left to right in the background are: the poet Algernon Charles Swinburne; his chaperon Theodore Watts-Dunton; George Meredith the novelist; Hall Caine, Rossetti's friend the sensational novelist. In front of the wall Whistler's white forelock is pulled by Swinburne while Burne-Jones gives the kangaroo, one of Rossetti's exotic pets, a flower to smell. Morris declaims poetry while on the right Holman Hunt and Ruskin look on in disapproval. Meanwhile Rossetti gets down to drawing an exotic model.

Opposite below: Aubrey Beardsley
The Death of Pierrot
From *The Savoy*, No 6, October, 1896
A text printed with this illustration reads: 'as the dawn broke, Pierrot fell into his last sleep. Then upon tip-toe, silently up the stair, noiselessly into the room, came the comedians Arlecchino, Pantaleone, Il Dottore, and Columbina, who with much love carried away upon their shoulders, the white frocked clown of Bergamo; whither we know not'. Haunted by approaching death, like so many men of the 1890s, Beardsley identifies himself with the figure of Pierrot in the *Commedia dell'Arte*.

generations. But the work of his art editor on *The Yellow Book*, Aubrey Beardsley, has never lost its appeal, nor its power to shock.

The lasting triumph of the Aesthetic ideals emerges from its clear-cut advocacy of the supremacy of the role of the artist as innovator and arbiter of style. Indeed echoes of Aesthetic arguments can be heard in twentieth-century criticism of works as diverse as the paintings of Jackson Pollock (new pots of paint in the public's face?), and the abstractions of Mark Rothko, sometimes so reminiscent of Whistler's magical and mysterious Nocturnes. The supremacy of the artist's own personal vision in which Whistler believed so intensely is also surely echoed in the manifestos and statements which accompany works as varied as Carl André's *Bricks* and the annual arguments over the Turner Prize ...

Yet, when all is said, it is most fitting to leave this appraisal of Aesthetic style with some lines from a minor but haunting poet, one of those described by W.B.Yeats in his autobiography as 'the tragic generation'. Ernest Dowson (1867–1900), whose semi-autobiographical novel *A Comedy of Masques* gives a vivid account of artistic life in the 1890s, shared Verlaine's taste for absinthe and experimented with taking the drug hashish. Both his parents committed suicide in 1894 and for the remainder of his life he lived in Paris, returning destitute and ill to die in England of tuberculosis. His unrequited passion for the daughter of a Soho restaurateur led to the creation of his most memorable poem *Cytherae*, one line of which gave its title to one of the most famous films of all times:

> I have forgot much, Cynara! gone with the wind,
> Flung roses, roses riotously with the throng,
> Dancing, to put thy pale lost lilies out of mind;
> But I was desolate and sick of an old passion,
> Yea, all the time, because the dance was long:
> I have been faithful to thee, Cynara! in my fashion ...

The golden sunflowers, languid lilies, peacock feathers and green carnations of Aestheticism had established the mood in which Yeats could pluck:

> The silver apples of the moon,
> The golden apples of the sun ...and magically describe how:
> ... I, being poor, have only my dreams;
> I have spread my dreams under your feet;
> Tread softly because you tread on my dreams.

That mood and those dreams, like other aspects of Aesthetic style, still retain the power to entrance ...

'I will never outlive the century. The English People would not stand for it'

declared Oscar Wilde in October 1900 shortly before his death. The tenets of Aestheticism, like Wilde, did not survive long in the new century, although some of its precepts were echoed by the Bloomsbury Group in their early years. They were influenced by G.E. Moore's *Principia Ethica* (1903) which has a familiar ring, proclaiming: 'By far the most valuable things ... are ... the pleasures of human intercourse and the enjoyment of beautiful objects...' But what were these objects, and how far could agreement be reached on how to enjoy them? How different, for example, was the Aesthetic ornamental use of the sunflower, virtually the movement's logo, compared with Van Gogh's vivid celebration of the flower. Van Gogh was one of the painters dubbed as Post-Impressionist by Roger Fry (1866–1934) and shown by him together with such controversial artists as Cézanne, Gauguin and Seurat at two exhibitions held at the Grafton Galleries in 1910 and 1912. The chorus of outrage which greeted these artists enabled Fry to say proudly: 'There has been nothing like this outbreak of militant Philistinism since Whistler's day.'

These exhibitions were affirmations of Fry's new gospel, his re-writing of Aesthetic principles. 'In my youth,' he wrote in *Retrospect*, 'all speculations on aesthetic had revolved with wearisome persistence around the question of the nature of beauty. Like our predecessors we sought for the criteria of the beautiful whether in art or nature. And always this search led to a tangle of contradictions ...' Fry found his solution by bringing up to date the doctrine of Art for Art's sake and identifying art with pure or significant form, writing in the Preface of the 1912 catalogue: 'They [the Post Impressionists] do not seek to imitate form, but to create form; not to imitate life, but to find an equivalent for life'.

Yet, though deeply conscious that he belonged to a new age, Roger Fry wrote brilliantly on certain Aesthetic concerns, posthumously describing Beardsley in 1904 in an unforgettable analogy as 'the Fra Angelico of Satanism'. But not all manifestations of the Aesthetic Movement gained Fry's approbation. In 1919, Fry looked back to the 1880s, with distaste. Writing in *The Athenaeum* he recalled how at the time:

the Ottoman and Whatnot still lingered ... I can remember the sham Chippendale and the sham old oak which replaced them. I can remember a still worse horror – a genuine modern style which as yet has no name, a period of black polished wood with spidery lines of conventional flowers incised in the wood and then gilt. These things must have belonged to the eighties – I think they went with the bustle … But … our successors will be able to create … amusing and wonderful interiors out of the black wood cabinets and 'aesthetic' crewel-work of the eighties … We have at this moment no inkling of the kind of lies they will invent about the eighties to amuse themselves … our collector is likely enough to ask us to admire his objects, not for their social emanations, but for their intrinsic aesthetic merit, which, to tell the truth, is far more problematical. Certain it is that the use of material at this period seems to be less discriminating, and the sense of quality feebler, than at any previous period of the world's history, at all events since Roman times.

Despite Fry's dislike of the 'Ottoman and the Whatnot' his critical work owed a specific debt to the formal values of Aestheticism. The attention directed by the Aesthetic Movement to the early Italian school (How Botticellian! How Fra Angelico!) was also important to the art historian Bernard Berenson. His book *Florentine Painters of the Renaissance* (1896), which introduced the term 'tactile values', emerges as one of the most important of all the innumerable lists of cultural subjects which the Aesthetes so enjoyed compiling. Are there also perhaps echoes of such lists in some of Virginia Woolf's magical descriptions in her novel *Orlando*?

Just as Fry predicted, 'amusing and wonderful interiors' have been created using works of art of 'problematical' value from the 1880s. Indeed much of the long-term influence of the Aesthetic style can be seen in the field of interior decoration. As an activity it has often been parodied in such works as Sir John Betjeman's *Ghastly Good Taste* and Osbert Lancaster's *Home, Sweet Home*. It nevertheless performs an important function reflected today in such magazines as *The World of Interiors, House and Garden*, and *Ideal Homes*. The writers in such journals inherit the roles not only of Wilde and Godwin but of the many anonymous journalists who advised in fitting out the 'House Beautiful' in Aesthetic periodicals from the 1860s to the 1890s.

In 1973 Sir John Betjeman wrote an introduction to an anthology on the 1890s:

Draw the Curtains, kindle a joss-stick in a dark corner, settle down on a sofa by the fire, light an Egyptian cigarette, and sip a brandy and soda, as you think yourself back to the world which ended in prison and disgrace for Wilde, suicide for Crackenthorpe and John Davidson, premature death for Beardsley, Dowson and Lionel Johnson, religion for some, drink and drugs for others, temporary or permanent oblivion for many more.

Our attitude to the *fin-de-siècle* quality so amusingly

described by Betjeman is rather different today. We approach the conclusion not just of a century, but a millennium, with a sense of trepidation that has been called 'Endism'.

Our perceptions of the 1890s are heightened by a surprising sense of familiarity and recognition of intriguing parallels and discrepancies. Both the decades of the 1890s and 1990s have in common a shared concern with the effects of sexually transmitted diseases upon society, respectively syphilis and Aids.

The problems of inherited syphilis inspired such plays as Ibsen's *Ghosts* (produced in London in 1891) and Eugene Brieux's *Damaged Goods*. In France the madness caused by the disease in its final stages, indeed the illness itself, became part of the legend of the *poète maudit*. The infection was carried defiantly, almost like a decoration, a red badge of courage, by such great writers as Baudelaire, the Goncourt brothers, Flaubert, Maupassant and Daudet. In England, syphilis played its part in the Wilde tragedy, for on acquiring the disease in 1878 a remorseful Wilde contemplated joining the Roman Catholic Church, but instead of arriving at the Brompton Oratory for instruction sent a box of lilies instead. The subject became entwined with the arts, politics and daily life, just as Aids does today.

In *The Great Scourge and How to End it* Christabel Pankhurst, the suffragette leader, produced a new battlecry for the twentieth century – 'Votes for women and chastity for men!' During the same year, 1913, effective cures for the disease began at last to be found, as eventually there will surely come a cure for Aids.

In conclusion, we can reflect that today, although it is still remembered, the ephemeral *Yellow Book* with all its 'new' hopes and hectic aspirations, has long since passed away. Yet the first truly popular newspaper, the *Daily Mail*, established by Alfred Harmsworth, Lord Northcliffe, two years later in 1896, still flourishes. Sensationalism has triumphed over Aestheticism.

All the more reason to revalue Aestheticism's aims, which, although they have their comic aspects, are not entirely ridiculous, nor irrelevant, to our dilemmas at the close of the twentieth century.

Aubrey Beardsley
Queen Victoria as a Degas Ballet Dancer
In February 1893 Beardsley worked for a short time for the Pall Mall Budget and visited the Mint to inspect plaster casts for the new coinage. The experience inspired him to make a series of caricature designs for new coins, which included Queen Victoria as a Degas Ballet Dancer. This illustration was never published as being too risqué but makes a fitting end to this survey of the Aesthetic Movement from the dado to the decadence.

NOTES

CHAPTER ONE
1   T. Gautier. *Mademoiselle de Maupin*, 1835.
2   W. E. Gladstone. *Contemporary Review*, October 1874.
3   *Art Journal*, 1887, pp 187-8.
4   Lady Mount Temple. *Memorials*, 1890.
5   Daphne du Maurier (editor). *The Young George du Maurier*, 1951.
6   Mrs Panton. *Suburban Residences and How to Circumvent Them*, 1896.
7   Raffles Davison. *Art Journal*, 1892, p. 329.

CHAPTER TWO
1   Claude Monet. *Les Peintres Impressionistes*, 1878.
2   *En écoutant Cézanne, Degas et Renoir*, 1938.
3   It is interesting to note that in England the custom of putting fans into fireplaces in suburban homes in summer survived until recent years.

CHAPTER THREE
1   E.R. and J. Pennell. *The Whistler Journal*, 1921.
2   Peter Ferriday. 'The Peacock Room' from *Architectural Review* CXXV, 1959, p. 412. The fullest account of the creation of the room.
3   Pennell, op.cit.
4   Ferriday, op.cit.
5   Letter from Whistler to Mrs Leyland, December 1876.
6   The Vasari story, which is actually by Baldinucci but is in any event untrue, relates how Caravaggio was paid for his last work in pennies and, weighed down by them, collapsed in the hot sun and died.
7   Letter from Whistler to Mrs Leyland.
8   Letter from Whistler to F.R. Leyland, November 1872.
9   *Notes on Some Pictures of 1868.*
10   Walter Pater. 'The School of Giorgione' from *The Fortnightly Review*, October 1877.
11   *American Architect and Building News*, 27 July, 1878.

CHAPTER FOUR
1   *Time Was. The Reminiscences of W. Graham Robertson*, 1931.
2   George Augustus Sala. *Paris Herself Again*, 1880.

CHAPTER SIX
1   I. Cooper-Willis (editor). *Vernon Lee's Letters*, 1937.
2   *Punch*, Vol. 81, 1881.
3   Letter from Wilde to Frank Burnand, 28 July, 1880.

CHAPTER SEVEN
1   He was the nephew of the famous Director of the National Gallery with virtually the same name, Sir Charles Locke Eastlake (1793–1865). To add to the confusion both men held at different times the same post, that of Keeper of the National Gallery.
2   Oscar Wilde. *Essays and Lectures*, 6th edition, 1928.
3   'Art and Decoration' from *Oscar Wilde Discovers America* (1882) by Lloyd Lewis and Henry Justin Smith, republished in 1936. It is surprisingly difficult to obtain the texts of Wilde's lectures, which do not feature in the many collected editions of his works.

CHAPTER EIGHT
1   Congleton Town Hall.
2   They were given to the Victoria and Albert Museum by Edward Godwin, the son of E.W. Godwin and Beatrice Phillips. Before giving them to the museum, he carefully removed any mention in them of his father's liaison with Ellen Terry and of their children, Edith and Gordon Craig. But even in their censored state they form both a treasury of design and a unique record of the visual concerns of an extremely busy man with a passion for observation and notation.
3   J. Forbes Robertson. *A Player under Three Reigns*, 1926.
4   *Architect*, 5 August, 1876.
5   See also *Building News*, 7 March, 1879.
6   *Magazine of Art* I, 1878.

CHAPTER NINE
1   Daniel Halevy. *My Friend Degas*, 1966.
2   See Richard Ellmann. *Oscar Wilde*, 1987.
3   Sir John Rothenstein. *The Life and Death of Conder*.

CHAPTER TEN
1   Arthur Symons. *The World as Ballet*.
2   Loïe Fuller. *Fifteen Years of a Dancer's Life*.
3   Isadora Duncan. *My Life*.

CHAPTER ELEVEN
1   Leon Edel (editor). *Henry James: Letters*. Vol. 3, 1974-80.
2   William Rothenstein. *Men and Memories*. Vol. 1.
3   From the Preface to *Letters to the Sphinx from Oscar Wilde*, 1930.
4   *The Studio*, 1899.
5   Charles Ricketts. *Recollections of Oscar Wilde*, 1932.
6   Decades later it was to have a profound influence upon the style of that brittle genius, Ronald Firbank, in his novels, *The Eccentricities of Cardinal Pirelli*, *Prancing Nigger* and *Valmouth*.
7   'The Mote in the Middle Distance' in *A Christmas Garland*, 1912.

SELECTED BIBLIOGRAPHY
Note: place of publication is London, unless otherwise stated.

Adburgham, Alison. *Liberty's: A Biography of a Shop*. George Allen & Unwin Ltd, 1975.
Alcock, Sir Rutherford. *The Capital of the Tycoon*. 2 vols. 1863.
Alford, Lady Marion. *Needlework as Art*. 1886.
Aslin, Elizabeth. *The Aesthetic Movement: Prelude to Art Nouveau*. Elek Books Limited, 1981.
Aslin, Elizabeth. *E. W. Godwin: Furniture and Interior Decoration*. John Murray (Publishers) Ltd, 1986.
Baily, Leslie. *The Gilbert and Sullivan Book*. Spring Books.
Baker, Lady. *The Bedroom and the Boudoir*. 1878.
Baldry, A.L. *Albert Moore: His Life and Work*. 1894.
Beardsley, Aubrey. *The Letters of Aubrey Beardsley*. Edited by Maas, Duncan and Good. 1971.
Beckson, Karl. *Aesthetes and Decadents of the 1890s*. New York: Vintage Books, 1966.
Beerbohm, Sir Max. *Rossetti and his Circle*. William Heinemann, 1922.
Carr, Mrs J. Comyns. *Reminiscences*. 1920.
Cole, Malcolm. *Whitelands College: May Queen Festival 1881–1981*. Whitelands College, 1981.
Cole, Malcolm. *Whitelands College: The History*. Whitelands College, 1982.
Cole, Malcolm. *Whitelands College: The Chapel*. Whitelands College, 1985.
Conway, Moncure Daniel. *Travels in South Kensington*. 1882.
Cook, Clarence. *The House Beautiful*. New York, 1878.
Cooper, N. *The Opulent Eye: Late Victorian and Edwardian taste in Interior Design*. 1976.
Crane, Lucy. *Art and the Formation of Taste*. 1882.
Crane, Walter. *An Artist's Reminiscences*. 1907.
Crane, Walter. *William Morris to Whistler*. 1911.
Dresser, Dr Christopher. *Japan, its architecture, art and art manufactures*. 1882.
Du Maurier, Daphne. *The Young George Du Maurier*. Peter Davies, 1951.
Eastlake, C. L. *Hints on Household Taste*. 1867.
Ellmann, Richard. *Oscar Wilde*. Hamish Hamilton, 1987.
Ferriday, Peter. 'The Peacock Room' from *Architectural Review* CXXV, 1959, pp 407–414.
Fletcher, Ian. *Romantic Mythologies*. Routledge and Kegan Paul, 1967.
Fletcher, Ian. *Walter Pater*. Longmans, Green & Co., 1959.
Franklin, Colin. *The Private Presses*. Studio Vista, 1969.
Fry, Roger. *Vision and Design*. 1920.
Gaunt, William. *The Pre-Raphaelite Tragedy*. Jonathan Cape, 1942.
Gaunt, William. *The Aesthetic Adventure*. Jonathan Cape, 1945.
Gaunt, William. *Victorian Olympus*. Jonathan Cape, 1949.
Girouard, M. *Sweetness and Light: The 'Queen Anne' Movement 1860–1900*. Oxford: Clarendon Press, 1977.
Grossmith, George and Weedon. *The Diary of a Nobody*. First published as a serial in *Punch* in 1888. First published as a book in 1892.
Hamilton, Walter. *The Aesthetic Movement in England*. 1882.
Harbron, Dudley. *The Conscious Stone: The Life of Edward William Godwin*. 1949.
Harrison, Martin and Waters, Bill. *Burne-Jones*. Barrie & Jenkins, 1973.
Haweis, Mrs H. R. *The Art of Beauty*. 1878.
Haweis, Mrs H. R. *The Art of Decoration*. 1881.
Haweis, Mrs H. R. *Beautiful Houses*. 1882.
Hillier, Bevis. *Posters*. Weidenfeld and Nicholson, 1969.
Hitchens, Robert. *The Green Carnation*. 1894.
Hutt, Julia and Alexander, Hélene. *OGI: A History of the Japanese Fan*. Dauphin Publishing Ltd, 1992.
Huysmans, J-K. *Against Nature*. 1884. Translated by Robert Baldick. Harmondsworth: Penguin, 1959.
Jackson, Holbrook W. *The 1890s*. 1912.
James, Henry. *Letters*. Edited by Leon Edel, 4 vols. Cambridge, Mass., 1974–80.
James, Henry. *Notebooks of Henry James*. Edited by F. O. Matthiesen and K. B. Murdoch. New York and Oxford: 1947.
Kermode, Frank. *The Romantic Image*. 1957.
Lasdun, Susan. *Victorians at Home*. Weidenfeld and Nicholson, 1981.
La Gallienne, Richard. *The Romantic '90s*. New York: 1925.
Levey, Michael. *The Case of Walter Pater*. Thames & Hudson, 1978.
Lewis, L. and Smith, H. J. *Oscar Wilde Discovers America, 1882*. New York: 1936.

Merril, Linda. *A Pot of Paint: Aesthetics on Trial in Whistler v. Ruskin*. Washington and London: Smithsonian Institute, 1992.
Michener, James A. *The Hokusai Sketch-Books. Selections from the Manga*. Vermont: Charles E. Tuttle Company, 1958.
Milner, John. *Symbolists and Decadents*. Studio Vista, 1971.
Milner, John. *The Studios of Paris*. New Haven: Yale University Press, 1988.
Mount-Temple, Lady. *'M. T.' Memorials*. 1890.
Ormonde, Leonee. *George Du Maurier*. Routledge and Kegan Paul, 1969.
Pennell, Elizabeth and Joseph. *The Life of James McNeill Whistler*. 2 vols. London and Philadelphia: 1908.
Peters, Robert L. *The Crowns of Apollo*. Detroit: 1965.
Pevsner, Sir Nikolaus. *Studies in Art, Architecture and Design*. Vol II *Victorian and After*. 1968.
Penny, Nicholas. *Ruskin's Drawings in the Ashmolean Museum*. Oxford: Ashmolean Museum, 1988.
Peters, Robert L. *The Crowns of Apollo*. Wayne State University Press, 1965.
Quennell, Peter (editor). *Marcel Proust, 1871–1922: A Centenary Volume*. Weidenfeld and Nicholson, 1971.
Reade, Brian. *Aubrey Beardsley*. Woodbridge, Suffolk: Antique Collectors' Club.
Reade, Brian. *Sexual Heretics*. Routledge and Kegan Paul, 1970.
Ricketts, Charles. *Recollections of Oscar Wilde*. Nonesuch Press, 1932.
Riewald, J. G. *Beerbohm's Literary Caricatures*. Allen Lane, 1977.
Robertson, W. Graham. *Time Was*. Hamish Hamilton, 1931.
Rothenstein, Sir William. *Men and Memories*. 1931.
Saint, Andrew. *Richard Norman Shaw*. New Haven: Yale University Press, 1977.
Sansom, William. *Proust*. Thames and Hudson, 1973.
Sutton, Denys. *Nocturne: The Art of James McNeill Whistler*. Country Life Ltd, 1963.
Spencer, Isobel. *Walter Crane*. Studio Vista, 1975.
Spencer, Robin. *The Aesthetic Movement*. Studio Vista, 1972.
Swinburne. *Poems and Ballads*. 1866.
Taylor, Ina. *The Art of Kate Greenaway*. Webb & Bower, 1991.
Whistler, J. M. *The Gentle Art of Making Enemies*. 1890. Reprinted New York: 1967.
The Letters of Oscar Wilde. Edited by Rupert Hart-Davis. Rupert Hart-Davis Ltd, 1962.
More Letters of Oscar Wilde. Edited by Rupert Hart-Davis. John Murray, 1985.
Yamada, Chisaburoh F. (editor). *Dialogue in Art: Japan and the West*. A. Zwemmer Ltd, 1976.
Young, Andrew McLaren, Margaret Macdonald, Robin Spencer and Hamish Miles. *The Paintings of James McNeill Whistler*. 2 vols. New Haven and London: Yale University Press, 1980.

EXHIBITION CATALOGUES

In recent years much of the most rewarding research into the Aesthetic period has been published in the catalogues of exhibitions.
Bury, Shirley, Barbara Morris and others. *Liberty's: 1875–1975*. Victoria and Albert Museum, 1975.
Christian, John. *The Last Romantics*. Lund Humphries in association with the Barbican Art Gallery, 1989.
Dorment, Richard and MacDonald, Margaret F. *James McNeill Whistler*. Tate Gallery Publications, 1994.
Green, Richard. *Albert Moore and his Contemporaries*. Laing Art Gallery, Newcastle upon Tyne, 1972.
Komanecky, Michael and Butera, Virginia Fabbri, *The Folding Image: Screens by Western Artists*. Yale University Art Gallery, New Haven, 1984.
Reade, Brian. *Art Nouveau and Alphonse Mucha*. Victoria and Albert Museum, H.M.S.O., 1963.
Reade, Brian. *Aubrey Beardsley*. Victoria and Albert Museum, H.M.S.O., 1966.
Sato, Tomoko and Watanabe, Toshio. *Japan and Britain: An Aesthetic Dialogue 1850–1930*. Lund Humphries in association with Barbican Art Gallery and the Setagaya Art Museum, 1991.
Spencer, Robin. *The Aesthetic Movement and Cult of Japan*. Fine Art Society, 1972.
Thomson, Richard. *Toulouse Lautrec*. South Bank Centre, 1991.
Various authors. *In Pursuit of Beauty: Americans and the Aesthetic Movement*. Metropolitan Museum of Art, New York, 1986.
Various authors. *Victorian High Renaissance*. Minneapolis Institute of Arts, 1978.

PLACES OF INTEREST

Birmingham City Museum and Art Gallery
Chamberlain Square, Birmingham
One of the most important Pre-Raphaelite collections in the world. The
Burne-Jones collections in his home town are of particular interest, notably
'The Holy Grail' tapestry sequence.

Bristol City Museum and Art Gallery
Queen's Road, Bristol
Notable particularly for its collection of E. W. Godwin furniture, the gallery
also possesses paintings by Gustave Moreau and Odilon Redon.

Carlisle Museum and Art Gallery
Castle Street, Carlisle
A little-known collection of Pre-Raphaelite works with sketches of Burne-
Jones at work by George Howard (Lord Carlisle).

Castle Ashby
Northamptonshire
Although a conference centre and not open to the public, it is worth
recording the Chinese bedroom of 1870 at Castle Ashby, which is one of
E. W. Godwin's most remarkable decorative schemes.

Cheltenham Museum and Art Gallery
Clarence Street, Cheltenham
The superb collections of Arts and Crafts furniture by the Cotswold school
and the work of C. R. Ashbee and C. F. A. Voysey are of great interest.

Cragside House
Rothbury, Northumberland
A splendid Victorian masterpiece designed by Norman Shaw, and built
between 1864 and 1895. The interior of the house reflects both his taste
and that of its original owner Sir William (later the first Lord) Armstrong.
Fine collections of the work of Evelyn and William De Morgan.

The Faringdon Collection
Buscot, Berkshire
Includes Burne-Jones's great series of paintings entitled *The Briar Rose*. A
visit can be combined with one to Kelmscott Manor, William Morris's
home, which is only a mile or two away.

Haworth Art Gallery
Manchester Road, Accrington, Lancashire
The largest single collection in Europe of about 130 pieces of Tiffany
'Favrile' hand-made glass, presented in 1933 by Joseph Briggs, an
Accringtonian who emigrated to America and became Design Director for
Louis Comfort Tiffany.

Cecil Higgins Art Gallery and Museum
Castle Close, Bedford
An extensive collection of the work of William Burges brought together in
a room decorated in his style, with important works from the key Handley
Read collection of Victorian art, and the Hull Grundy collection of
jewellery.

Hunterian Art Gallery
Hillhead Street, Glasgow
In 1935 and 1958 Miss Rosalind Birnie Philip (1873–1958) bequeathed the
estate of her brother-in-law, James McNeill Whistler, to Glasgow
University. This included some 80 oil paintings, 120 pastels, several hundred
prints and drawings and the contents of the artist's studio at his death.
Recently the gallery has also acquired the Godwin/Whistler 'Butterfly'
cabinet. The Hunterian also has many other attractions outside the scope of
this book.

Kelmscott Manor
Near Lechlade, Gloucestershire
Morris's much-loved Cotswold home near the Thames. Recently
imaginatively restored.

Leighton House
Holland Park Road, London W14

Designed by George Aitchison, the house is the personal creation of
Frederic, Lord Leighton. The splendid Arab Hall housed in its day the
most fashionable parties in London. It is a remarkable reconstruction, lined
with Islamic tiles from Rhodes, Damascus, Cairo and elsewhere, and a
mosaic frieze of peacocks by Walter Crane in brown, blue, silver and gold.
In the Great Studio above and throughout the house major works by
Leighton and his contemporaries can be seen both from the permanent
collection and on loan.

Lady Lever Collection
Port Sunlight, Merseyside
At the centre of the garden village of Port Sunlight, the Lady Lever Art
Gallery records the taste of one man, Viscount Leverhulme, successful
millionaire soap manufacturer. Amongst its treasures are Lord Leighton's
largest canvas, *The Daphnephoria* (1876) and *The Garden of the Hesperides*
(1892), and several important Pre-Raphaelite paintings including Holman
Hunt's *The Scapegoat*. A number of Victorian subject paintings used for soap
advertisements are worth seeing, notably an amusing depiction by Louise
Jopling of two ladies washing up blue and white porcelain.

The Metropolitan Museum of Art
New York
The American Wing houses one of the most remarkable collections of
American Aesthetic artifacts. American ceramics came into their own in the
years after the Centennial, with the craving for what a contemporary
described as 'civilising, refining and elevating' works of art. Amongst many
major items it is only possible here to mention the representation of the
work of artist-potters such as the Rookwood Potter of Cincinnati, the
Grueby Faience Company of Boston, the Tiffany loggia, wisteria window,
Peacock Window and 'Magnolia' vase.

Middlesex University, The Silver Studio Collection
Bounds Green Road, London N11
The Silver Studio, directed by Arthur Silver (1852–96) and later by his son,
aimed to bring 'together a body of men to establish a studio which would be
capable of supplying designs for the whole field of fabrics and other
materials used in the decoration of the home'. In all the collection
comprises about 20,000 designs, 2,000 wallpapers, 4,000 textile samples and
other items ranging from the circle of William Morris and Walter Crane to
the brilliant Art Nouveau designer Harry Napper.

William Morris Gallery and Brangwyn Gift
Walthamstow, London E17
The boyhood home of William Morris houses a wide-ranging collection of
items associated with his life and work. There is furniture, stained glass,
wallpapers, carpets, embroideries and textiles (including the unique
Woodpecker tapestry), a complete set of books printed at the Kelmscott Press,
and many letters and photographs. Another feature of great importance is
the extensive collection of textiles, furniture and metalwork by A. H.
Mackmurdo and the Century Guild, including Selwyn Image and Herbert
Horne. There are also extensive collections of stained-glass designs by
Christopher Whall, ceramics by De Morgan, the Martin Brothers and
Frank Brangwyn, who with Mackmurdo was instrumental in setting up the
gallery.

Olana
Upper New York State
Situated high on a hill overlooking the Hudson, with the most majestic
views. Olana was the home of Frederick Church, the landscape painter of
the Hudson River school. The house vies with Linley Sambourne's home in
London for the accolade of being the most complete surviving example of
eclectic Aesthetic tastes.

The Richmond Fellowship
Addison Avenue, London W14
Open by written application. Designed by Halsey Ricardo. This building,
the home of Sir Ernest Debenham, the patron of the Arts and Crafts
movement, houses the greatest collection of De Morgan tiles in the world.

Ruskin Museum
Coniston, Cumbria
A collection of works by Ruskin and his circle. The museum is placed near
to Brantwood, Ruskin's home from 1872 until 1900.

Linley Sambourne House
Stafford Terrace, London W8
One of the most remarkable surviving Aesthetic interiors, this is the
perfectly preserved home of Edward Linley Sambourne, a leading cartoonist
on *Punch*.

Smithsonian Institution
Freer Gallery of Art, Washington DC
Apart from the Peacock Room, now enhanced with blue and white
porcelain on its shelves, the Freer houses the largest collection of Whistler's
work in the world, fine Oriental collections of paintings and porcelain, and
several fine examples of the work of Thomas Wilmer Dewing.

Standen
Near East Grinstead, West Sussex
Standen was designed in 1894 by Philip Webb, and is full of light, air and
colour with original Morris textiles and wallpapers, William De Morgan
pottery and furniture and paintings of the period.

Ellen Terry's House
Smallhythe, Kent
The great actress Ellen Terry's last home, which houses the only collection,
in a suitable domestic setting, of the highly individual furniture of E. W.
Godwin.

Victoria and Albert Museum
South Kensington, London SW7
In the vast collections of the Victoria and Albert Museum, the Victorian
Refreshment Room decorations have a particular Aesthetic interest. First in
date was the Green Dining Room, Morris and Company's second major
decorative commission. It is adjacent to the Gamble Room, the work of
Alfred Stevens's associate Godfrey Sykes, and the Poynter Room (also
known as the Grill Room or Dutch kitchen). The Poynter Room is tiled
with a series depicting the months, and decorative panels of peacocks, and is
one of the most sumptuous Aesthetic interiors in London.

In the Henry Cole Wing can be seen the Ionides Collection, which
includes Rossetti's *Day Dream* and Burne-Jones's *The Mill*. The collection as
an entity is a remarkable survival, the most complete evocation of a
discriminating Aesthete's collection.

The Watts Gallery
Down Lane, Compton, near Guildford, Surrey
A unique collection of the paintings and sculpture of George Frederick
Watts.

Wightwick Manor
Near Wolverhampton, West Midlands
One of the most complete interiors furnished by Morris and Company, with
a small but rewarding collection of Pre-Raphaelite paintings and drawings.

Windsor Castle
Windsor, Berkshire
Sir Alfred Gilbert's masterpiece, the Tomb of the Duke of Clarence lies just
north of St George's Chapel. It is advisable to visit it *before* going to the
castle since it frequently shuts early.

ACKNOWLEDGEMENTS

l = left; r = right; c = centre; t = top; b = bottom
BAL = Bridgeman Art Library

Peter Aprahamian 76(c); Arcaid/Mark Fiennes 24(l), 25(t); Victor Arwas 205; Ashmolean Museum, University of Oxford 13(r), 15(r), 88, Courtesy Mrs Eva Reichmann 212, 220; Author's collection 68(t), 70, 118(t), 182(t), 184(t), photography Ian Jones 54, 129, 130, 132(tr, bl, bc, br); The Master and Fellows of Balliol College, Oxford 11(l); BAL/British Library 101 (tr); BAL/Courtesy of The Fine Art Society 25(bc); BAL/Fitzwilliam Museum, University of Cambridge 101(tl); BAL/Giraudon, Musée d'Orsay 181; BAL/Giraudon, Musée de Petit Palais 177; BAL/Guildhall Art Gallery, Corporation of London 34; BAL/Oriental Museum, University of Durham 30(b); BAL/Plaket Museum, Essen 71(l); BAL/Private collection 23(tl), 30(t), 33(l), 75, 132(tl), 199, 203(b); BAL/Roy Miles Gallery 84; BAL/Russell Cotes Art Gallery and Museum, Bournemouth 195(t); BAL/Courtesy of the Board of Trustees of the Victoria and Albert Museum 46, 58(b), 93; Richard Berenholtz 146; Copyright Bibliothèque Royale Albert Ier, Cabinet des Estampes, Brussels 179; Birmingham Museums and Art Gallery 9, 17(b), 92, 197(t); Mr Bishop 74; *British Architect and Northern Engineer* 139; British Architectural Library, RIBA, London 78(r), 158; Copyright British Museum 39, 214(b); Bryn Mawr College Library, The Maser Collection/photography Karl Dimler 4, 59(b); *Building* 149; Gerald Carr 24(r); The Trustees of the Cecil Higgins Art Gallery, Bedford 190; Martin Charles 12, 13(tl, bl); Christie's, New York 204(l); Cincinatti Historical Society 142; Copyright The Art Institute of Chicago 63(ct); Copyright *Country Life* Picture Library 155; Copyright The Detroit Institute of Arts, Bequest of Henry Glover Stevens in memory of Ellen P. Stevens and Mary M. Stevens 90, Gift of Dexter M. Ferry, Jr. 101(bl); Dyson Perrins Museum, Worcester 124; Edifice, London 86, 148; E.T. Archive 23(tr), Greenaway Collection, Keats House 77(r); The Faringdon Collection Trust 197(c, b); Fine Art Photographic Library 35(l); Courtesy of The Fine Art Society, London 32, 33(r), 45(b), 159(ct, b), 166; Fogg Art Museum, Harvard University at Cambridge, MA 8, Grenville L. Winthrop Bequest 200(tl), 219(b); Courtesy of The Freer Gallery of Art, Smithsonian Institute, Washington, D.C. 43, 48, 53, 56, 56-7, 57, 62, 63(b); Copyright The Frick Collection, New York 50; Dennis Frome 17(t); Gabinetto Fotografico Soprintendenza B.A.S., Florence 11(r), David Giles 23(cr); Giraudon - Lauros 178, Musée de la Ville de Paris, Musée Carnavalet 183; Glasgow Art Gallery & Museum, Kelvingrove 97; *Grammar of Ornament* 14, 15(l), 16(l, r); Hallmark Cards Inc., Kansas City 150; High Museum of Art, Atlanta, Virginia Carroll Crawford Collection 38(t); Angelo Hornak 226, 227; Hugh Lane Municipal Gallery of Modern Art, Dublin 66; Copyright Hunterian Art Gallery, University of Glasgow 64; *Illustrated Sporting and Dramatic News* 121; *Keramic Art of Japan* 49; Hans van Lemmen 23(cl); Library of Congress, Washington D.C. 99(b), 134; The Maas Gallery, London 76; Copyright Manchester City Art Galleries 80; Mansell Collection, London 76(b), 136; The Martin Brothers Potters/Richard Dennis 25(br); Mary Evans Picture Library 112, 126, 224; The Metropolitan Museum of Art, Bequest of Susan Dwight Bliss, 1967 105, Friends of the American Wing Fund (1985) 138(t), Gift of Kenneth O. Smith (1969) 38(b); University of Michigan School of Art and College of Architecture and Urban Planning, on loan to the University of Michigan Museum of Art (1986) 145; Musées des Arts Décoratifs, Paris 40; Museo de Arte de Ponce/The Luis A. Ferré Foundation, Inc. 73, 195(bl); By courtesy of Museum of Fine Arts, Boston, 1951 Purchase Fund 41, Anonymous gift in memory of Charlotte Beebe Wilburs 52, Emily L. Ainsley Fund 99(t), Helen and Alice Colburn Fund 180; Museum of Fine Arts, Springfield, MA, Gift of the Misses Emily and Elizabeth Mills in memory of their parents, Mr and Mrs Isaac Mills 143; Museum of London 78(l); By courtesy of the Trustees of the National Gallery, London 42(b); National Gallery of Art, Washington, Rosenwald Collection 110; Board of Trustees of the National Museums and Galleries on Merseyside/Lady Lever Art Gallery 79; By courtesy of the National Portrait Gallery, London 19(t), 95, 106(t); *Daily Graphic* 140; Norfolk Museums Service, Bridewell Museum, Norwich 35(r); By courtesy of Northampton Borough Council 156; Philadelphia Museum of Art, the John G. Johnson Collection 45(t); Copyright The Pierpont Morgan Library 91; Princeton University Library 47; Private collection 7; Public Record Office, London 157(br); *Punch* 114(c,b), 116(t, b); The Raymond Mander and Joe Mitchenson Theatre Collection 123(b); Copyright RCHME 51(c,b); Copyright Photo R.M.N./Musée d'Orsay, Paris 194; The Royal Photographic Society, Bath 81(b); The SandyVal Graphics Ltd. Collection 208; The Savoy 182(b); By courtesy of Sotheby's 55; Stapleton Collection, London 22, 51(t), 102(t), 114(t), 117, 120, 122, 128, 133, 137, 154, 161(l), 209, 213, 217(tl, bl), 229(t); Tate Gallery, London 29, 63(t, cb), 82, 89, 101(br), 108, 109, 193, 207; Theatre Museum, Victoria & Albert Museum, London 123(t), 125, 167; Courtesy of the Board of Trustees of the Victoria and Albert Museum 18, 19(b), 20, 21, 23(b) 26, 27, 28, 31, 37, 68(b), 81(t, c), 87, 138(b), 153, 154(b), 157(tl, tr, bl), 159(t, cb), 160, 161(b), 162, 163(t), 164, 168-9, 171, 172, 184(b), 185, 187, 189, 206(l), 216, 217(r), 222, 223, 232, (endpapers); Wadsworth Atheneum, Hartford, Gift from the estates of Louise Cheney and Anne W. Cheney 3, 147; Whitelands College, London 106(c, b); Whitford Fine Art, London 195(b), 211; The William Morris Gallery, Walthamstow, London 61, 94, 173; By permission of the Dean and Canons of Windsor 198.

AUTHOR'S ACKNOWLEDGEMENTS

Every reasonable effort has been made to acknowledge the ownership of all copyright holders. Any omissions and errors that may have occurred are inadvertent, and will be corrected in subsequent editions.

In 1942 the great interpreter of nineteenth-century art, William Gaunt, published *The Pre-Raphaelite Tragedy*, followed by his classic studies of the artistic movements of the late Victorian age, *The Aesthetic Adventure* (1945) and *Victorian Olympus* (1949), which first separated the Aesthetic goat (Whistler) from the Olympian sheep (G.F. Watts). Like every subsequent writer on these themes, I am deeply indebted to Gaunt's work.

I would like to thank the staff of Chiswick Reference Library and the Library and Print Room of the Victoria and Albert Museum. Here I have received help and advice from Stephen Calloway, Ron Parkinson and Michael Snodin. Cathie Hail of the Theatre Museum shared with me her knowledge of Gilbert, Sullivan and F.C. Burnand's *The Colonel*. I would also like to thank Amanda Jane Doran, Richard Dennis, Rupert Maas, Peyton Skipwith and Robyn Mackenzie of Melbourne, Australia. The lectures, books and catalogues of Mrs Shirley Bury, Bevis Hillier, Mrs Barbara Morris, Robin Spencer, Geoffrey Squire and Mrs Virginia Surtees have all been particularly helpful.

My son, Patrick Lambourne, strove manfully to enable me, although computer-illiterate, to deliver the text in presentable condition.

At Phaidon Press Roger Sears, Jacky Jackson, Anna Kobryn, Elizabeth Rowe and Derek Wright have in different ways coped with my Aesthetic whims.

My greatest debt of gratitude is, however, to former colleagues and friends now deceased: Elizabeth Aslin, Charles and Lavinia Handley-Read, James Laver, George Nash and Brian Reade who first awoke my interest in different aspects of the theme of Aestheticism.

Lionel Lambourne